Church and State Education
in Revolutionary Mexico City

Church and State Education
in Revolutionary Mexico City

Patience A. Schell

The University of Arizona Press   Tucson

The University of Arizona Press

© 2003 The Arizona Board of Regents

First printing

All rights reserved

♾ This book is printed on acid-free, archival-quality paper.

Manufactured in the United States of America

08 07 06 05 04 03   6 5 4 3 2 1

Library of Congress Cataloging-in-Publication Data

Schell, Patience A. (Patience Alexandra), 1970–

Church and state education in revolutionary Mexico City / Patience A. Schell.

p. cm.

Includes bibliographical references and index.

ISBN 0-8165-2198-0 (Cloth : alk. paper)

1. Catholic Church — Education — Social aspects — Mexico — Mexico City — History.
2. Church and education — Mexico — Mexico City — History. 3. Education — Mexico —
Mexico City — History. 4. Mexico City (Mexico) — Church history. I. Title.

LC505.M62 M67 2003

371.071′27253 — dc21

2003005509

British Library Cataloguing-in-Publication Data

A catalogue record for this book is available from the British Library.

To Arturo, with love

and to the memory of Lorraine Darling Wills

Contents

List of Figures   ix

List of Maps   xi

List of Tables   xiii

Acknowledgments   xv

Introduction   xix

List of Abbreviations Used in the Text   xxvii

1 **Church Politics and Educating Mexicans**
   A Background   3

2 **Primary Education** Programs and Pedagogy   21

3 **Vocational Education** Training Hearts and Hands   43

4 **Urban Missionaries** Teachers, Priests, and Volunteers in
   Classrooms   65

5 **Daily Life in Primary Schools** Moralization in an Immoral
   City   85

6 **Adults in the Classroom** Making Their Own
   Revolution   115

7 **Community Education in Public Spaces** Revolutionary
   Entertainment and Catholic Unions   148

8 **Church-State Tensions Turn into Conflict** From Catholic
   Social Action to the Cristiada   174

Epilogue: "On the Subject of Politics, Morality,
and Bras"   196

Notes   203
Selected Bibliography   229
Figure Credits   247
Index   249

Figures

2.1 Hernán Cortés as a Catholic hero   37

3.1 Physics laboratory, Escuela de Ingenieros Mecánicos y Electristas   49

3.2 Auto shop, Instituto Técnico Industrial   50

3.3 Physical education for young women, Escuela Nacional de Enseñanza Doméstica   53

3.4 Puericulture class, Escuela Nacional de Enseñanza Doméstica   55

4.1 The UDCM general council, May 1925   79

5.1 The SEP's image of primary education   96

5.2 Escuela Primaria "Horacio Mann"   97

5.3 La moda en París   111

6.1 Class of domestic economy at the Escuela de Arte Industrial Corregidora de Querétaro   126

6.2 Batik class at the Escuela de Arte Industrial Corregidora de Querétaro   127

7.1 Library at the Miguel Lerdo de Tejada Commercial School   150

7.2 Physical education for young men   163

8.1 Los deberes de una niña   192

8.2 El bautizo de mi hermanito   193

Maps

1   Mexico City, showing selected sites and colonias,
    ca. 1926   xxiii

2   Vocational and Workers' Night Schools between 1923
    and 1925   46

Tables

2.1 Schedule for Municipal Primaria Elemental Schools, 1921 24

2.2 Schedule for Municipal Primaria Superior Schools, 1921 26

6.1 Enrollment in SEP's Men's Vocational Schools, Mexico City, 1925 116

6.2 Enrollment in SEP's Women's Vocational Schools, Mexico City, 1925 116

7.1 SEP-Sponsored Films between 13 June and 30 November 1922 155

Acknowledgments

The research and the writing of this book would not have been possible without the generous financial support of the Overseas Research Students Awards Scheme; the Oxford Inter-Faculty Committee for Latin American Studies; the Oxford Committee for Graduate Studies; the Oxford Modern History Faculty's Arnold, Bryce, and Read Funds; the St Antony's College Raymond Carr Fund and Stahl Fund; and the University of Manchester School of Modern Languages Staff Travel Fund. I am particularly grateful to the Cañada Blanch Foundation for funding the costs associated with the reproduction of images and the making of maps. For allowing me to reproduce images in their collections, my thanks go to the Acervos Históricos de la Universidad Iberoamericana, the Archivo Histórico de la Secretaría de Educación Pública, the Bancroft Library, the Hemeroteca Nacional, and the Instituto de Investigaciones Dr. José María Luis Mora.

For their guidance, patience, and dedication to the pursuit of historical research, I am indebted to the staff at the Acervos Históricos de la Universidad Iberoamericana, the Archivo General de la Nación, the Archivo Histórico de la Ciudad de México, the Archivo Histórico de la Secretaría de Educación Pública, the Archivo Histórico Plutarco E. Calles y Fernando Torreblanca, the Archivo Histórico de la Secretaría de Salud Pública, the Bancroft Library, the Centro de Estudios Históricos Condumex, the Centro de Estudios Sobre la Universidad, the Hemeroteca Nacional, the Instituto Mora, and the Instituto Nacional de Antropología e Historia. The staff at the Secretariado Social Mexicano and the Seminario Conciliar welcomed me into these private collections. For that welcome and their subsequent guidance in the research I am indebted. I am also grateful to the staff at the Archivo Histórico del Arzobispado, especially Rebeca Ortega Pantoja, who guided my work during our daily tea breaks. In Oxford, Ruth Hodges and Laura Salinas at the Latin American Centre helped me obtain the books I needed, when I needed them.

First and foremost, my thanks must go to Alan Knight for his guidance, advice, and always insightful criticism both in the doctoral version of this work and its transformation to a book. It is simply not possible to list all the benefits from the many conversations I had with him, during and after my time as a doctoral student. Alan Angell and Guy Thomson, my doctoral examiners, both helped me begin the process of revision from dissertation to book and Guy's advice has made the publication stage less daunting. Mary Kay Vaughan has been extremely supportive, offering comments and critiques of my work, while introducing me to colleagues with similar interests. Lawrence Levine has offered me advice on the practice of history and his belief that I could become a historian since I was an undergraduate. I am grateful to Jon Beasley-Murray, Jérôme Bellion-Jourdan, Katherine Bliss, Ann Blum, Kristina Boylan, Keith and Claire Brewster, Robert Curley, María Teresa Fernández-Aceves, Elizabeth Hutchison, Brigitte Koenig, Monika Lütke-Entrup, Stephanie Mitchell, Jocelyn Olcott, Ariel Rodríguez Kuri, Nina Staehle, Nadia Tires, and Ruth Watson for insightful comments, gentle criticism, plenty of laughter, and necessary encouragement. Thanks also go to Helen Frost for her help during the revision process. I am particularly indebted to Gabriela Cano for clues to the background of Dolores Angela Castillo Lara, to Sarah Buck for sharing documents on Castillo's firing, and to Martha Eva Rocha who provided me with a copy of Castillo's veteran's file. The suggestions and comments of two anonymous readers for the University of Arizona Press have proved invaluable in guiding my revisions. My thanks also go to the Department of Spanish and Portuguese Studies at the University of Manchester for providing a stimulating intellectual environment in which to finish the manuscript. Finally, thanks to the University of Arizona Press, especially editors Patti Hartmann and Al Schroder, Design and Production Manager Anne Keyl and copyeditor Kirsteen E. Anderson for their hard work to turn a manuscript into a book. As those mentioned did their best to root out mistakes, I take full responsibility for any that may remain.

Throughout the research and writing of this book, I have had the support and commiseration of the two doctorates in my family — my stepfather and stepmother. Thank you. I also wish to thank my mother, the teacher, and my father, the priest, for their endless encouragement. All four are somewhere in these pages. Richard Fabian deserves more thanks than I can possibly give for his financial and emotional support, which made so much of this work possible. The Castillo family kindly took me in and took excellent care of me during research in Mexico City. My thanks go also to Evelyn Ferguson for encouraging my love of history; as is often the case with wonderful teachers, she has changed my life in ways never anticipated. Arturo Castillo has been a constant source of strength, always believing in me and this research, to which he turned his critical eye in both the dissertation and book stages. I will always be grateful.

Finally, I wish to acknowledge the generosity and support of my late grandmother Lorraine Wills, who died while I was finishing this manuscript. Because of the generation into which she was born, my grandmother was not able to become a journalist or writer as she had wanted. Yet her volunteer work with the Junior League and Planned Parenthood, her work as a newsletter editor, and her writing for the Junior League group Scribblers all pay tribute to her commitment to finding meaningful work within the limits of her era. As I wrote this book, I was constantly aware that the women of her generation and her daughters' generation enabled the women of my generation to have the choices that we do. I hope that she would have found this book worthy of her legacy.

Introduction

In 1924, a socially oriented magazine in Mexico City called for a campaign against illiteracy because "obtuse, simplistic, and ignorant" people were vulnerable to manipulation. Demands like these for widespread public education had emerged from the Mexican Revolution (1910–1917). Yet this demand for a literacy campaign came not from a revolutionary source but from the Catholic magazine *Acción y Fe*. The author went on to remind readers that literacy alone was not sufficient, because the newly literate often stumbled "on the morality scale." Thus, literacy had to be paired with religious instruction.[1] In response to concerns that public education did fail on the "morality scale," in 1925 the government introduced a morality code. Children were taught to be good citizens; kind toward others; and loyal to family, nation, and humanity. This morality code even included a mandatory examination of conscience each month.[2] These two examples demonstrate how revolutionaries and Catholics after 1917 not only shared concerns that the poor were ignorant and immoral, but through these concerns mixed up the supposed territories of church and state. Catholic social activists and the revolutionary governments identified the same problems in society, including poverty, vice, and illiteracy, which they sought to ameliorate through education. Both groups believed that the poor and working classes needed refashioning into either loyal, patriotic Mexicans or loyal, patriotic, Mexican Catholics. From the end of the armed revolution into the presidency of Plutarco Elías Calles (1924–1928), not only did church and state exist in relative accord on a variety of levels, but the institutions also worked toward common goals, occasionally cooperating in their efforts.

During this brief moment between the cessation of hostilities in 1917 and the start of the Cristero Rebellion in 1926, education provides a particularly clear optic through which to compare the wider social programs of church and state. This period represents an era of relative freedom for Catholic social work because the anticlerical articles of the 1917 Constitution had not yet been enforced on a national scale: In this period Catholic primary schools were tolerated and sometimes supported. Although the educational programs of church and state agencies promoted similar goals, revolutionary anticlericalism was incompatible with a socially active church. Moreover, the church's success threatened the nascent state. Clashes between the institutions started in 1925, eventually prompting armed conflict and making common goals immaterial. Because this study demonstrates common ground between church and state educational programs, it stops in 1926, the abrupt end of the period during which church and state worked toward similar ends.

As this study crosses several boundaries related to both subject matter and approach, it draws upon and contributes to various historiographies. Since the revolution, participants and historians have either analyzed the work of the Catholic Church or the nascent state, artificially dividing postrevolutionary Mexico into Catholics and revolutionaries. Initially, this division was caused by the strong partisan feelings of many of the authors, firsthand witnesses to events. Subsequent generations of analysis have projected the tensions of the Cristero Rebellion and its aftermath backward, looking for telltale signs of the violence to come. Yet in examining state and church at the same time, out from under the shadow of the Cristiada, their shared goals and approaches become apparent.

This study fits within a growing tendency to examine the revolution's impact at the local level and to question the capacity of postrevolutionary institutions to impose their programs on the population. In the historiography of education, scholars including Mary Kay Vaughan and Elsie Rockwell have turned away from an earlier emphasis on curricula that were at best only partially implemented. Through focusing on education at a regional level, such recent studies instead depict schoolrooms as contested spheres in which complex negotiations took place as local groups molded education to suit their needs.[3] While recent work has shown that examination of curricula offers limited insight into actual classroom activities, these programs still demonstrate goals and expectations of educators. As such, my own study combines examination of curricula with detailed discussion of classroom-level education to demonstrate that—even in the capital with all its resources—students, parents, teachers, and administrators had profound effects on the classroom.

The historiography of education has tended to focus on federal education, ignoring the fact that in this period the federal government could only aspire to an educational monopoly: States, municipalities, and private groups all offered education to Mexico's children and adults. Municipal education has been particularly maligned.[4] Yet local education was an important aspect of revolutionary demands for municipal rule, indicating the importance of municipal schools to communities. In this study, I demonstrate that Mexico City's municipal schools combined Porfirian and revolutionary curricula, offering a view of how the revolution had transformed the expectations and goals of Mexico City educators. In addition, municipal educators had to confront problems precipitated by the revolution, ranging from dire epidemics to an increase in streetwalkers. Their reactions to these changed circumstances offer a view of both life after the revolution and life as a result of the revolution.

Like municipal schooling, Catholic education has received little scholarly attention, and the limited studies have focused on fee-charging Catholic schools and schools run by religious orders.[5] Yet lay participation in Catholic education was integral to Catholic social activities. This study examines a wide variety of Catholic schools, from fee-charging schools that offered instruction in public speaking to free Catholic schools for working children, run by lay organizations. Examining the wide range of schools, it becomes clear that Catholic education was as diverse as Catholic responses to the revolution.

Like the history of education, the history of Catholic social and political activism is an area of growing interest. Recent work has reinterpreted the Cristero Rebellion as resistance to federal encroachment on local autonomy.[6] While studies of the conflict have become more sensitive to its diverse character, historians have also moved away from an exclusive focus on the rebellion. Catholicism in the Porfirian and revolutionary periods has come under increasing scrutiny, including major works on the development of Catholic social action. These studies are characterized by a common approach that takes Catholic organizations and political dissent seriously, while firmly establishing Catholicism within the historiography of Mexico. This turn in the historiography has integrated the study of the church into the broader historical trends from which it had been excluded for political reasons.[7]

Both educational and Catholic endeavors were dependent on

women's labor. By the 1920s, women were teachers, inspectors, and school principals in schools both public and private, as well as students, mothers of students, volunteers, and administrators. The Catholic volunteer workers in Mexico City classrooms have been classed as conservative and left out of a historiography that has concentrated on "traditional" feminists.[8] Yet as Temma Kaplan argues, "[T]he nature of the sexual division of labor into which women are socialized predisposes them to political arguments about social issues," and even public actions of conservative women can have "revolutionary" consequences.[9] Kaplan's perspective allows historians to transcend the division between "feminist" and "conservative" women, to view all women's political activity as potentially revolutionary. Like the women Kaplan studied in Barcelona, most women in 1920s Mexico City accepted a sexual division of labor while using their gendered responsibilities to claim political and social rights. Thus, my study not only contributes to a broader understanding of women's activism, but also fits into the growing literature that addresses gender as integral to processes of state and nation formation.[10]

Debates about gender and educational curricula between 1917 and 1926 were influenced by experiences of the revolution. The people who sat, read, wrote, or dreamed in Mexico City classrooms shared diverse personal experiences of the revolution. Children entering primary school in the 1920s had lived their whole lives during or after the upheaval. Adults could remember the overthrow of the dictator Porfirio Díaz and the decade that brought inflation, food riots, disease, and armed occupation to Mexico City. The revolution had transformed society, and the new political elite could not ignore the recently mobilized population, but instead had to incorporate revolutionary demands into the process of state formation. The nascent state, unable to impose its programs, was forced to negotiate with a population that had been mobilized through a decade of warfare. Teachers and students brought behavior, expectations, and interests precipitated by the revolution into the classroom with them. Examination of classrooms in Mexico City and its surrounding areas (see map 1) addresses the social impacts of the revolution, demonstrating that students and communities had their own ideas about what the revolution meant to their everyday lives. Even if the school programs implemented had Porfirian origins, Mexico City was no longer Porfirian.

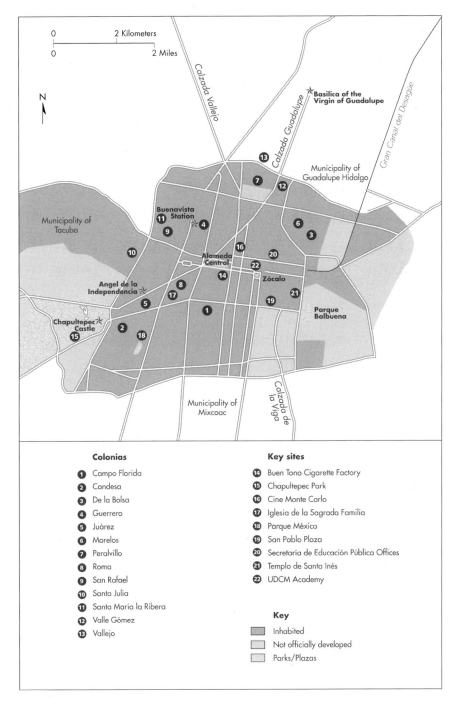

Colonias

1. Campo Florida
2. Condesa
3. De la Bolsa
4. Guerrero
5. Juárez
6. Morelos
7. Peralvillo
8. Roma
9. San Rafael
10. Santa Julia
11. Santa María la Ribera
12. Valle Gómez
13. Vallejo

Key sites

14. Buen Tono Cigarette Factory
15. Chapultepec Park
16. Cine Monte Carlo
17. Iglesia de la Sagrada Familia
18. Parque México
19. San Pablo Plaza
20. Secretaría de Educación Pública Offices
21. Templo de Santa Inés
22. UDCM Academy

Key

- Inhabited
- Not officially developed
- Parks/Plazas

Map 1. Mexico City, showing selected sites and colonias, ca. 1926. (Map by Ann Kennedy, Mapping Specialists, Ltd.)

Recent literature has begun to investigate the urban contribution to the revolution and the impact of the upheaval on cities.[11] My focus on Mexico City has emerged from a personal, long-standing fascination with and affection for the capital. It is also a logical regional focus for a study of early federal education and anticlericalism: If federal programs had been successfully implemented anywhere, it would have been in the capital city where resources and administrative oversight were concentrated. For the population of Mexico City, as well, the postrevolutionary period presented opportunities for taking a hand in national and local reconstruction. An increasingly militant working class, recent migrants fleeing violence, revolutionary generals looking to consolidate their positions, prostitutes catering to sexual needs, and Catholic ladies determined to save souls all jostled for position in the capital. The postrevolutionary period also witnessed transformations brought about because of technology and the media. Motorcars racing around made streets increasingly dangerous for pedestrians, some of whom sported the latest flapper fashions and bobbed hair. Teachers and students knew that they were witnessing a moment of transformation, a remaking of Mexico after a decade of destruction. Catholics and revolutionaries alike grabbed the opportunities of the 1920s, opening schools, teaching night courses, sponsoring films, and starting unions.

Chapter 1 provides the historical context, discussing the situation of the church and educational programs during the second half of the nineteenth century and the revolutionary era. While nineteenth-century conflicts cast a long shadow over church-state relations, in education each successive reform erased official memory of the previous one, and no reform overcame endemic material shortages. Chapters 2 and 3 discuss and compare the curricula in Catholic and public schools, looking at the values promoted, such as a strong work ethic and particular gender roles, as much as at academic subjects. While educational reforms in the 1920s were often built on nineteenth-century programs, curricula were altered by the educators who implemented them. As such, chapter 4 discusses the teachers, inspectors, volunteers, and priests whose work was integral to this project of education. Even when they were from radically different backgrounds and belief systems, these people shared a conviction that education was the first step to individual improvement and national development.

Once the set and cast are in place, chapters 5 and 6 describe and analyze the classroom experience. No matter how well designed educational programs might have been, the crushing poverty of some schools and students hindered implementation of educational reforms. In fact, shared problems in classrooms brought church and state education closer together, as both institutions struggled with inadequate supplies and hungry students. Moreover, students — both adults and children — had their own reasons for attending school, reasons that did not necessarily coincide with the goals of the state or church. Contemporary reports indicate that adult students, while in theory enthusiastic for schooling, would drop out of school or skip classes that were irrelevant or boring. Children, although less autonomous in their decisions, also dropped out, arrived late, and skipped classes to grab a smoke. Because church and state recognized that successful education needed community support and could actually transform entire communities, both sponsored public events, from films to poetry recitations. Chapter 7 discusses these federal and Catholic programs aimed at moralizing the working class. Because Catholics explicitly linked moralization, education, and unionization, this chapter also discusses Catholic unions.

Projects of education, community improvement, and unionization were developed and implemented amid increasing tension between church and state, tension caused in part by a fundamental disagreement over who had the right to control the education of Mexico's children. As such, chapter 8 examines church-state relations under Presidents Alvaro Obregón and Plutarco Elías Calles, and the impact of the church-state conflict on Catholic primary schools. After Catholic primary education was officially banned, priests became clandestine educators while federal education inspectors pretended not to see crucifixes still in place. The cutoff point for this book, 1926, in no way reflects an end to these debates on morality, religion in public life, and gender roles. Thus, the book concludes with a brief discussion of church-state relations in the age of mass media and miniskirts.

Abbreviations Used in the Text

CNCT	Confederación Nacional Católica del Trabajo
CROM	Confederación Regional Obrera Mexicana
DETIC	Departamento de Enseñanza Técnica, Industria y Comercial
EAOH	Escuela de Artes y Oficios para Hombres
EAOM	Escuela de Artes y Oficios para Mujeres (later Escuela de Artes y Oficios para Señoritas)
EAOS	Escuela de Artes y Oficios para Señoritas
PAN	Partido Acción Nacional
PCN	Partido Católico Nacional
PRI	Partido Revolucionario Institucional
SCNM	Sociedad Católica de la Nación Mexicana
SEP	Secretaría de Educación Pública
SIPBA	Secretaría de Instrucción Pública y Bellas Artes
SSM	Secretariado Social Mexicano
UDCM	Unión de Damas Católicas Mexicanas

Church and State Education
in Revolutionary Mexico City

1 Church Politics and Educating Mexicans

A Background

From the colonial period until the middle of the nineteenth century, the Catholic Church not only dominated Mexican religious life, but also played a prominent role in politics and the economy, particularly through landowning and money lending. From the 1840s onward, successive liberal governments sought to do away with these remnants of colonial privilege, which liberals believed impeded progress. Liberal legislation abolished clerical immunity from civil and criminal prosecution, forced the disentailment of religious properties, and prohibited the church from acquiring additional properties. Further legislation prohibited charging fees for baptisms, weddings, or burials for the poor, resulting in enormous losses of revenue for parish priests. These attacks on the church, known as the Reform, prompted a civil war (1857–1860) between conservatives, allied with the church, and liberals: The liberals won. When the liberal government refused to honor conservative debts, creditors France, Britain, and Spain invaded (December 1861–January 1862). Britain and Spain quickly withdrew, but France, with support from conservative Mexicans and the Catholic Church, crowned Archduke Maximilian of Austria as emperor of Mexico in 1864. The Second Empire survived only as long as it was backed by French troops: Maximilian died in front of a firing squad in 1867. The possibility of the conservatives regaining power died in front of the same firing squad. The conservatives and the church had fatally disgraced themselves through their alliance with the foreign invader and support for the empire. Well into the twentieth century, opponents of the church harkened back to the empire as proof of the church's treacherous nature.

Liberal attacks on church privilege stopped under President Porfirio Díaz (1876–1911). Díaz presided over an era of political stability, increasing industrial development, and centralization of power in Mexico City. Foreigners saw Mexico as a model of economic prosperity and stability; however, the wealth of the regime came at the expense of the vast majority of the population. As agricultural interests became more powerful, peasants were forced off their land and into the wage economy. The growth of industry was built upon the labor of the nascent working class, who toiled for long hours in dangerous conditions. Moreover, foreigners and things foreign were given preference over domestic goods and mentalities. The success of the Porfirian modernization project was only a veneer. By 1900, cracks had begun to show in its surface.

For the Catholic Church, divested of its property and legal privileges, détente with the Porfirian government provided a welcome respite. The period is known as the re-evangelization because Díaz permitted the growth of Catholic institutions, including new dioceses, new seminaries, and more religious orders.[1] These orders founded hospitals, schools, and orphanages, giving the church greater influence among both the middle classes and the poor. Nonetheless, because the Reform Laws were still intact, the church, divested of most of its property, could not return to its earlier levels of economic power. Without legal protection, its position depended upon the continued personal goodwill of Díaz.

The stance of Mexican Catholics toward the Porfirian government shifted between opposition and cooperation. Historian Manuel Ceballos Ramírez describes the period between 1867 and 1892 as a time when "intransigent" Catholics, who promoted a political and social program designed to compete with the liberal program, dominated church policy.[2] These intransigents were so called for their refusal to adapt to a secular society with religious toleration. Liberal Catholics, who supported the government's laissez-faire economic policies and were willing to work with government institutions, increased their influence between 1892 and 1900. Meanwhile, the Vatican published Pope Leo XIII's 1891 encyclical *Rerum Novarum*. The encyclical, which condemned socialism, liberalism, and class struggle, nonetheless promoted just wages, protective labor legislation, and the formation of Catholic unions. Until the early twentieth century *Rerum Novarum* and its proponents remained on the periphery of Mexican Catholicism. But at the turn of the century, some Catholics began to take public stances on social issues, criticizing the inequality of Porfirian prosperity and adding their voices to the growing chorus of concern over the country's political future. Thus, from 1900 onward,

Mexican Catholicism, building upon existing organizations founded by the intransigents, focused on social activism and criticism of the regime.[3]

Education in the Nineteenth Century

In the post-independence period, charitable organizations like the church founded and ran the schools the state could not afford. Liberal educational reforms in 1833 mandated that the church open free parish primary schools. Although the mid-century Reform did not restrict religious schools, after the French intervention the liberal state sought more control over education, limiting Catholic schools and making state education more available. An 1867 law prohibited for the first time the teaching of religion (or religion disguised as morality) in public schools. Free education offered by charitable organizations was no longer sufficient for the state's purposes. Instead, the state had to offer its own primary education that instilled the values of the incipient secular nation.[4]

Although restrictions on education specifically targeted the church, in 1874 primary education was a municipal, not a church, endeavor.[5] Municipalities had offered primary education since the late colonial era, and the 1867 legislation required the municipalities of the Federal District to establish and maintain primary schools in sufficient number for local needs. These municipal schools were characterized by staid pedagogy, material shortages, and general disorder. As the central government gradually increased its presence in education, municipal schools became targets for regulation and eventually elimination.[6]

Joaquín Baranda, Díaz's minister of justice and public instruction (1882–1901), was the first to aspire to the creation of a national education program. Because his ministry did not have national jurisdiction, his project partially relied on well-trained and enthusiastic teachers, working from a standardized curriculum. Baranda promoted professionalization, state licensing of teachers, and an increase in teacher training (normal) schools: from twelve in 1878 to thirty-six in 1910. Mexico City became home to a normal school for men, founded in 1887, and one for women, founded in 1890.[7] The two institutions in the capital city were supposed to train not only Mexico City residents, but also provincial students who would return home to help standardize education across the country.

While normal schools for women were expected to create more employment options for the poor, it was instead primarily middle-class women who took advantage of the institutions; poor students were less likely to have fulfilled the admission requirement of completion of primary school.[8] The profession was also transformed by increasing numbers of women in teaching, a profession previously dominated by men without means. In 1895, approximately half of Mexico's teachers were women; by 1910 that figure had risen to 65 percent. As women entered the profession in increasing numbers, salaries declined.[9] Lower salaries, in turn, made teaching less attractive to men, creating a cyclical process to the detriment of women teachers.

For Baranda, improving teacher training was just one aspect of standardizing the national curriculum. Baranda used the national educational congresses held during the 1880s to promote a uniform primary curriculum; standardized texts and teaching methods; and the principle of free, lay, and obligatory primary education. (In the 1880s, lay teaching was "neutral" rather than explicitly antireligious.) These reforms were codified in the 1888 federal law of primary instruction, a law that applied only to the Federal District and territories but became the model for state legislation.

The 1888 law divided primary school into *primaria elemental* (lower primary school, years one to four) and *primaria superior* (upper primary school, years five and six). Healthy children who lived within reasonable distance of a school were legally required to attend primaria elemental. Parents were responsible for their children's attendance, and those whose children were delinquent faced fines or imprisonment. The law also prohibited the teaching of religion in public schools and the employment of either ministers or priests as teachers in public schools. For the first time, too, private schools were subject to official inspection. Through the 1888 law, the government claimed for itself responsibility for overseeing the education of Mexico's children. Nonetheless, the law was difficult to enforce, in terms of both school attendance and religious content.[10]

Initially, municipal governments, which received limited federal subsidies, provided the principal funding for and administered the facilities of these primary schools, observed by federal inspectors. Yet, municipal education stood in the way of a national education project: In 1896, primary education in the Federal District and territories was taken over by the federal government. Although the action affected only the Federal District, some states had anticipated the move and others soon followed suit. Baranda's nationalization project was well under way.[11]

The 1888 law encouraged the integration of subjects across the curriculum and learning through observation, as well as contributing to nation building by making children aware of their place in society and their loyalty and duties toward the state. The program emphasized punctuality, generosity, and self-control in an attempt to "better" the lower classes and to train loyal, productive workers. In theory the new curriculum was to be implemented through the simultaneous teaching method. In this method, students were grouped into grades and then ability groups. Each grade had one teacher, who worked with one group at a time while the other groups listened or worked silently. Yet, as most primary schools employed only two teachers, the use of the simultaneous method remained an ideal, not a widespread reality.

Baranda's work raised the profile of education, culminating in the reorganization of the Ministry of Justice and Public Instruction in 1901. It was divided into two subministries, separating education from justice. Justo Sierra, previously a writer, journalist, and history teacher, was appointed minister of public instruction. In 1905, when a completely independent ministry of public education was founded (the Secretaría de Instrucción Pública y Bellas Artes, or SIPBA, the Ministry of Public Instruction and Fine Arts), Sierra became its head. The new ministry oversaw primary, normal, preparatory, and professional schools in the Federal District and territories. It also oversaw libraries, museums, and scientific societies, as well as historic and archaeological monuments. Although critics complained that there was no point in having a national ministry with jurisdiction only in the Federal District and territories, proponents responded that education in the Federal District served the nation because all regions of Mexico sent students to the capital to study.[12]

In 1902, Sierra outlined the educational reforms that he believed would forge regional and ethnic differences into a single Mexican identity. Sierra was particularly concerned about integrating indigenous communities into Mexican society and forming the national consensus that was necessary to protect Mexico from U.S. expansionism. Finding the curriculum of primaria elemental adequate, Sierra turned his reforming zeal to the program of primaria superior. Whereas before only primaria elemental had been obligatory, Sierra increased primaria superior from two to four years and made the first two years obligatory for all children. The first two years of primaria superior continued the course of general education, while the newly created last two years were to give children practical, technical skills. Education remained sex segregated in the program and, whenever possible, in reality. For boys, technical skills included mining, industrial, commercial, or agricultural training. For girls, technical skills included industrial, crafts-making, or commercial training.

The 1908 education law incorporating these reforms emphasized practical instruction as a fundamental component of primary education. For instance, in rural areas students would learn agricultural skills. Girls would learn to garden and cook, while in science classes children would raise plants and animals for study. Overall, the 1908 educational reform continued the work of the 1888 education law, which had sought to integrate subjects, inspire patriotism, and promote national progress through uniform primary education. The biggest difference between the two programs was the latter's promotion of practical skills.[13]

While Sierra believed that his educational reforms addressed the needs of both students and the larger society, his expectation that children could attend school for six years was unrealistic: Educational authorities frequently complained about low graduation rates. At the 1910 congress on primary education, one delegate noted that most children finished only first grade.[14] Educational authorities, hoping to improve attendance, offered poor children inducements, such as food and clothing, to attend classes. Other schools operated half-time in order to accommodate students who needed to work. While maintaining student attendance was a problem, many other children had no primary school available at all: There were simply not enough of them.[15]

Educational efforts were not directed only at children, but also at adult women and men. Municipal and federal agencies offered training for adults in night schools or full-time secondary schools. Generally, schools for adults taught students whom we would consider adolescents or young adults. Fourteen was the minimum age of admission, and students tended to be between fifteen and twenty-five years old. By 1910, Mexico City was home to forty-six night schools with 5,353 students: 3,364 men and nearly 2,000 women.[16] Adults could also enroll in daytime vocational schools, such as Mexico City's Escuela de Artes y Oficios para Hombres (School of Arts and Trades for Men, or EAOH), founded in 1869, which offered full-time technical training for adult men. Modeled on the curriculum of a Parisian technical school, the Mexico City EAOH offered courses including trigonometry, foreign languages, basic engineering *(rudimentos de mecánica)*, and chemistry. Since not all prospective students had attended primary school, in 1877, the EAOH added primary education courses and more practical courses, like carpentry. In order to improve attendance, the EAOH donated clothing and food to its poor students. The EAOH also sold the goods that students manufactured, with the accrued profits being used to purchase tool sets given to students upon graduation.

The Escuela de Artes y Oficios para Mujeres (School of Arts and Trades for Women, or EAOM) was founded in 1872 as a charitable institution to train poor women. Student enrollment doubled from 510 in 1872 to more than 1,000 ten years later, a promising result at least partially due to dedicated staff. Both educators and students preferred classes that gave women wage-earning skills. On the whole, business courses proved more popular than courses in handicrafts. A flexible enrollment policy, which allowed women to take as many or as few classes as they wished, was also popular with students. Nonetheless, as in the women's normal school, it was middle-class women, not poor ones, who tended to enroll at the EAOM.[17]

Catholics and the Social Question

Adult education was one response to the "social question," a euphemism describing the problems associated with rapid industrialization and urbanization, such as poor sanitation, overcrowded living conditions, and low wages. The social question was one of the prime preoccupations of Mexican Catholics at the turn of the century. During the first decade of the twentieth century, a series of congresses (1903–1907) held to discuss solutions to the social question created the framework for Catholic social action. Laity, clergy, and some bishops called

for improved wages paid in cash, medical services, educational opportunities for workers, and Catholic workers' organizations to improve
urban working conditions. The congresses, however, were better at
diagnosing problems than solving them,[18] and individual Catholics began to implement the above-mentioned resolutions to ameliorate the
plight of industrial and rural workers. For example, Catholic workers'
circles — essentially mutualist societies — provided savings programs
and insurance in case of industrial accidents or death. Some workers'
circles offered night schools, bands, and recreation centers for members.[19] Rather than limiting their activities to the poor or working class,
Catholics sought to incorporate individuals into the church structure
by gender and age, including organizing the so-called *clases directoras*
or ruling classes. These programs were corporatist and, like the work of
the intransigents before, offered a Catholic alternative to secular social
programs.[20]

From the turn of the century onward, attempts to address the social
question included founding more Catholic schools.[21] Overall, the number of private schools (Catholic, Protestant, and lay), and the enrollment in these schools, increased during the last years of the Porfiriato.
Mary Kay Vaughan attributes the rise in private-school enrollment to
increased social stratification and income inequality.[22] Not all Catholic
schools, however, charged tuition, and throughout Mexico free Catholic schools enrolled students of diverse socioeconomic backgrounds.
By the turn of the century, parental pressure had begun to eliminate
some of these free schools. Well-off parents, who wanted their children
to attend exclusive schools, asked religious orders to institute tuition as
a barrier to the "wrong sort" of children. Tuition also generated much-
needed revenue for the religious orders. Some orders, such as the La
Salle Brothers, used the tuition from their fee-paying schools to subsidize their free schools.[23]

Most Catholic primary schools combined primaria elemental and
primaria superior levels, offering all grades together. In terms of curriculum, Catholic schools tended to adhere to the official program,
offering Spanish, math, natural history, Mexican geography and history, handicrafts, singing, civics, and morality. Additionally, Catholic
schools offered courses in religion, sacred history, and foreign languages. Generally, Catholic education was as modern as its lay coun-
terpart, teaching science, national history, some practical skills, and

Catholic activism.[24] Thus, *Rerum Novarum* and liberalism had both penetrated Catholic classrooms.

Catholic orders, particularly the Salesian Brothers, also offered education and technical training for adults. The Salesian school in Mexico City's Colonia Santa Julia, a middle- and lower-class neighborhood in the city's northeast, offered training in carpentry, printing, shoemaking, baking, and bookbinding, combined with primary education. By the turn of the century, Mérida, Oaxaca, Chilapa, Puebla, Mexico City, Morelia, Zamora, Zapotlán, Guadalajara, and Aguascalientes each had at least one Catholic technical training school. In Mexico City, for instance, the Salesian Sisters ran schools for girls in the Colonias San Angel, Santa Julia, and Jesús María. The school in Santa Julia could accommodate three hundred young women. In these technical schools, women learned skills considered appropriate for their gender, such as managing a household.[25]

Catholics and the Revolution

In 1908, Díaz made the tactical error of suggesting in an interview that he was ready to step down. Both the opposition and his own camp took the remark seriously, and organizing quickly began for the 1910 election. Francisco Madero, a member of a prominent Coahuila family, became the most important opposition candidate, running under the banner of the Anti-Re-election Party. Catholics in the social action movement greeted the Madero candidacy with optimism. Although his Plan de San Luis Potosí upheld the 1857 Constitution and the Reform Laws, Madero gave an interview to *El País* that raised expectations he would grant the church a larger public role. In this interview, Madero said he supported religious liberty and assured Catholics that he had no plans to persecute them. Later, after he assumed the presidency in 1911, he even hinted that he was interested in abrogating the Reform Laws.[26]

Bolstered by the opposition movement, Catholics organized their own party. The Partido Católico Nacional (National Catholic Party, or PCN), founded in 1911, initially showed great promise. The PCN platform championed fair elections, no re-election, democracy, labor reform, and the application of Christian principles (expressed by *Rerum Novarum* and the Catholic congresses) to society's problems. During

the 1911 presidential campaign, the PCN supported Madero nationally, while successfully running its own candidates in local and state
elections. In Jalisco, the PCN won a majority of seats in the state legislature as well as the governorship. The PCN also won a majority of
seats in the legislatures of Michoacán, Colima, Puebla, Chiapas, Querétaro, Mexico state, and Guanajuato.[27] During the Madero presidency
(1911–1913), Catholics continued to organize lay society through
groups such as the Asociación de Damas Católicas (Association of
Catholic Ladies), founded in 1912. In the 1920s, this women's association became a pillar of Catholic social action, struggling to maintain a
public space for the church.

The brief moment of democracy ended abruptly in 1913, when
Madero was overthrown and assassinated, and his betrayer, Victoriano
Huerta, became president (1913–1914). Huerta was a product of the
old regime, and his presidency was joyfully received by elites, among
them Catholics and the church hierarchy, who wanted a "strong man"
ruling Mexico. The PCN leadership, composed of Mexico City elites,
had old ties to the Porfirian regime and decided to support Huerta's
coup. A *Te Deum* was sung in Huerta's honor at the cathedral, and similar joy was expressed in other churches throughout Mexico. Huerta
represented a return to order and stability for the Catholics, including
socially active ones and members of the PCN, who collaborated with
the regime.[28] Moreover, the loan that Archbishop of Mexico José Mora
y del Río was forced to give Huerta provided revolutionaries with
further reason to include the church among their enemies. Nonetheless,
there were also a few Catholic voices opposing the coup, including
Archbishop of Morelia Leopoldo Ruiz y Flores, who immediately published a condemnation.[29] The alliance of prominent political Catholics
with Huerta provoked a fierce anticlerical response from the Constitutionalist revolutionary faction (so called for their support of the 1857
Constitution), which had taken up arms against Huerta. Although the
social action wing of the church had shared goals with the revolutionary factions, such as the promise of fair elections, the institutional
church supported the Huerta government and did not aid the revolutionaries. Thus, from 1913 onward, the church was increasingly denied
a voice among decision makers, and Catholics were forced to the margin of revolutionary politics.

The ferocity of the northern revolutionaries' attacks on the church —

which included the occupation and desecration of churches and convents as well as confiscation of church wealth — further polarized
stances. These attacks were designed not only to despoil the church, but
to humiliate it. Anticlericalism combined with the violence of the period
drove the episcopate and many clergy into exile. Beleaguered Catholics
banded together, pushing proponents of social action into an alliance
against the revolutionaries with whom they actually shared common
goals. The church was not a monolith actively seeking to overthrow the
revolution; it was divided between the clergy and the laity, the ecclesiastical hierarchy and the lower clerics, and supporters of Catholic
social action and conservatives. But in response to the church's recent
public support for Huerta and the historic role of the church in Mexico,
including suspicions lingering from the Catholic alliance with the Second Empire, anticlerical revolutionaries defined the entire church as a
barrier to progress and an incubator for reaction and superstition.

The Constitution of 1917 codified the anticlericalism of the victorious revolutionaries. Constitutionalist leader Venustiano Carranza
specifically prohibited former members of the PCN and other defeated
factions, such as the Zapatistas, from attending the 1916–1917 constitutional convention in Querétaro. Yet even without the participation
of PCN members, the 1917 Constitution included articles that could
have been inspired by earlier Catholic congressional resolutions. Jorge
Adame Goddard compared passages from constitutional Article 123,
which deals with labor issues, with Catholic congressional resolutions
and Catholic press commentary, finding notable similarities. For example, both Article 123 and Catholic sources sought to prohibit children
under twelve from working, and excluded women and children from
nighttime or hazardous work. Catholic congresses proposed a minimum wage, as did Section 6 of Article 123. According to Article 123,
this minimum wage was to be sufficient to meet "normal" needs, including education and entertainment, so that a working man would be
able to support his family alone. Catholics promoted a similar concept,
known as the family wage. Article 123 and Catholic sources concurred
that salaries were to be paid in legal tender and that workers should
have accident indemnity protection, the right to form unions, and the
right to strike.[30]

Although the constitution promoted social and economic reforms in
line with Catholic proposals, it restricted the ambit of the church's

work in these realms while denying the church juridical existence. The 1917 Constitution did not recognize religious vows, prohibited religious organizations from obtaining or holding property, and nationalized actual church holdings. Clergy were to be utterly excluded from politics, not even allowed to vote. Meanwhile, the state retained the right to register all practicing clergy and to regulate the number of churches in a given area. Perhaps the most contentious article of the constitution was the third, which prohibited the teaching of religion in private and public primary schools. Article 3 also prohibited religious orders or members of religious orders, ministers, or priests from founding or running primary schools. These constitutional measures, which attempted to remove the church from public life, spelled the end of direct and legal Catholic participation in politics.

Nonetheless, the wave of Catholic activism that had started in the last decade of the Porfiriato and flourished under Madero emerged again in the postrevolutionary period. Regulating legislation for the constitution had not been created, and enforcement was left to the discretion of regional and local leaders. Moreover, the revolution had left a power vacuum as national leaders struggled to consolidate their positions and regional *caudillos* (strongmen) negotiated with national and local military leaders to maintain control of their areas. Without a strong central government, Catholics were able to resume the organizing that had been so important to the church before the revolution.[31]

The upheaval of the revolution also broke down established social mores and hierarchies. Although the military revolution had ended in 1917, the cultural revolution began in earnest in the 1920s. For this cultural revolution, the Catholic Church was as well placed if not better placed than the government, because it still had Catholic social action organizations as a foundation upon which to build. Since the goals of the social action movement and the social goals of the revolution overlapped, the church presented a serious political and cultural threat to the revolutionary state-in-formation. To counter this Catholic political, social, and cultural offensive, the government eventually sought to define revolutionaries as inherently anticlerical, although the situation was not as clear-cut as it was portrayed. While Villista and Obregonista troops had engaged in anticlerical pillaging, arguably the most radical of the revolutionary factions, the Zapatistas, went into battle behind the flag of the Virgin of Guadalupe.

Yet the church was at a disadvantage as well; while Mexico was nominally a Catholic country, many Mexicans were cultural Catholics rather than political Catholics. Cultural Catholics believed in church teachings and followed Catholic rituals but would not defend their church against attacks on its juridical existence. So the task of the social activists was to turn cultural Catholics into political ones who would be willing to defend the church against state encroachment.[32] Ironically, in their struggle to protect the rights of the church, Catholics used inherited nineteenth-century liberal arguments about individual freedoms: Citizens should be free to choose and practice their religion without government interference.[33]

Schooling and the Revolution

The revolutionary years also profoundly changed the federal government's role in education. In spite of years of effort to standardize education during the Porfiriato, at the outbreak of the revolution, there was still no national system or curriculum, as the Secretaría de Instrucción Pública y Bellas Artes had legal jurisdiction only in the Federal District and territories. Nonetheless, using the SIPBA, Madero presided over limited improvements to education, including raising teachers' salaries. The opening of *comedores escolares* (school cafeterias), where children could eat for free or at a low cost, was another Madero project. Finally, Madero modified the school calendar, so that the academic year began on 1 February and students had their long holiday over Christmas and New Year.[34]

The Huerta coup brought little benefit to education. In educational matters, Huerta's policy ignored rural and poor areas in favor of rich, urban regions and he reduced the number of comedores escolares. Like Madero, Huerta did attempt to better teachers' material conditions, stating that it was absolutely necessary to improve the economic situation of teachers, in order to allow them more dignity and job stability.

Policy changes had little impact when the disruption caused by revolution made it difficult for schools to operate regularly and many schools closed because of the danger. Precarious financial circumstances further lowered attendance; families needed their children's labor to survive. While the revolutionary upheaval made it difficult for any school to function regularly, Catholic schools were particular targets of revolutionary hostility. Anticlerical revolutionaries closed many Catholic schools, and fear of violence alone prompted some schools to close their doors. Nonetheless, in Mexico City most Catholic schools continued to operate without problems.[35]

Mexico City witnessed its first revolutionary violence during the Decena Trágica (tragic ten days), which culminated in the assassination of Madero and the presidency of Huerta. Yet after the coup, residents had more to fear from Huerta's *leva* (press-gang tactics) than revolution. Because Huerta could not find sufficient volunteers for his army, even patients at the general hospital became a source of recruits. Anyone on the street at night, from vagrants to those heading home after a visit to the local cantina, was a target. The rich, however, could still attend balls and eat at the best restaurants; as late as 1914, their social life was unaffected by the upheaval in the countryside that surrounded them.

In August 1914, the revolutionaries occupied the capital for the first of many times. This time it was the Constitutionalists with Alvaro Obregón, who had no fondness for the city, in command. He declared martial law and closed the cantinas. The occupying troops took over the city's elegant homes and commandeered cars for joyrides along the tree-lined, once placid, streets, while favored groups received confiscated buildings. Donations of former elite sanctuaries to the working class demonstrate how the revolution changed the relationship in Mexico City between social class and city space; they symbolized the reoccupation of these spaces by the urban poor, undoing Porfirian efforts to push the poor into marginal neighborhoods.[36]

Revolutionary confiscation of properties belonging to the church and religious orders meant that after the revolution, those organizations that were still financially viable had to purchase new properties. Because of these purchases, the church and religious orders no longer had the means to sustain free schools, thus earning criticism from revolutionaries that the church served only the elite. In spite of the social action emphasis on teaching the poor, Catholic private education became increasingly oriented toward the select few who could pay tuition, partially as a consequence of the revolution.[37]

Mexico City changed hands several times during the course of the revolution, and the instability made life a struggle for the capital's residents. Frustrated citizens became accustomed to waiting in line for everything and occasionally resorting to riots to procure food. Their paper currency lost value due to inflation. The dangers from war-related diseases, including typhus, malaria, and Spanish influenza, were exacerbated by the lack of public sanitation. Unemployment was another specter haunting the populace, and workers who had thus far avoided the upheaval enlisted to avoid slow starvation.[38]

Education in the capital also underwent profound transformations during the revolutionary period. Félix Palavicini, Carranza's minister of public instruction (1914–1916), dismantled the SIPBA and returned educational responsibility to local governments, partially in response to Carranza's promotion of municipal education. Municipalities in the Federal District administered primarias elementales, night-school primarias superiores, and kindergartens, while the government of the Federal District administered the preparatory, technical, and normal schools. Yet the municipalities were not adequately equipped or funded to run these schools, as they had no new revenue base to balance the extra expenditure. After Carranza's overthrow in 1920, municipal education lost its most powerful supporter. For President Adolfo de la Huerta and his successors, federal education was both a vehicle for national unity and a popular mandate.[39]

While the centralization of education was a top-down imposition, serving to curb the power of both the church and local governments while moralizing the masses, access to education was a bottom-up demand. From the 1900s onward, greater educational opportunities had figured among working-class demands, along with better housing, shorter working hours, and respect. Demand for increased educational opportunity came not only from the working class but also from the middle class and campesinos (peasants).[40] Groups in Mexico City demanded schools and then expected to have a hand in what was taught there.

As the first step toward a federal education system, De la Huerta transferred jurisdiction of schools that had been under the government of the Federal District, such as normal schools, to the National University and rector José Vasconcelos. Vasconcelos already had aspirations beyond the university. In May 1920, he had launched the one-teach-one campaign, in which anyone who could read was to teach anyone illiterate how to read. The hugely successful project caught the national imagination and helped garner support for the federal ministry of education. In September 1920, a presidential decree gave the university, and its rector, the task of creating a national education system. Primary schools in the Federal District were to pass to university control. A year later, in October 1921, the federal Secretaría de Educación Pública (Ministry of Public Education, or SEP) was inaugurated with three departments. Assurances were offered to doubters, like teachers in state schools, that federal education would not replace state or local provision of education, but rather would complement that provision and offer education in regions that were too poor to support schools. The project of a federal ministry of education was presented as compatible with the larger goals of increased educational opportunity and better wages for teachers.

At first, the SEP's priorities were primary, vocational, and rural education. Throughout the country, the SEP, in cooperation with the states, founded schools that were either solely SEP-administered or jointly administered. The SEP also subsidized or provided loans for state education, covering the cost of schooling or smaller costs such as materials and building repairs. Even at this early stage, the tendency was toward centralization of education, and the SEP preferred to administer its own funds rather than subsidize state education.[41]

The ministry was initially divided into three sections: schools, libraries, and fine arts. The schools under study here — including primary, technical, vocational, and normal schools — all fell under the Departamento Escolar (School Department). The Library Department oversaw the expansion of the public library system and the establishment of thousands of small libraries all over the country, stocked with books published under the SEP's editorial department. The Fine Arts Department was rooted in a nineteenth-century belief in the arts as uplifting; it also reflected the growing interest in forging a new national culture. Under Vasconcelos, the Fine Arts Department patronized a flourishing cultural program, including public performances of dance and music, training in the arts for students, and public art. The SEP also operated the literacy campaign and the Department of Indigenous Culture, but these were considered to be separate and temporary sections of the SEP.[42]

Vasconcelos resigned in July 1924, ostensibly to run for governor of

Oaxaca but actually due to his increasing disagreements with President Obregón and frustration at budget limitations.[43] The new education minister, José Manuel Puig Casauranc, was a political appointee with more interest in tightening administrative control than uplifting Mexicans through education. The reorganization of the SEP, which he oversaw, was intended to make the department more efficient on less money. A department of administration and statistics was added, while the Departamento Escolar was divided up: Technical and commercial schools were put into the Departamento de Enseñanza Técnica, Industria y Comercial (Department of Technical, Industrial, and Commercial Training, or DETIC), while the primary schools were under the new Departamento de Enseñanza Primaria y Normal (Department of Primary and Normal Training), which had responsibility only for Mexico City. The cultural programs of the Vasconcelos era were curtailed as the SEP's priority shifted toward rural education.[44] Moreover, the SEP budget was dramatically reduced. The budget allocation fell from 52,363,000 pesos in 1923 to 25,593,000 pesos in 1924 and remained at about that level throughout the presidency of Plutarco Elías Calles.[45] Spending on education as a percentage of the national budget also fell during the Calles presidency. In 1923 and 1924, educational spending was 9.3 percent of the national budget, in 1925 it was only 6 percent, and it rose to 8 percent by 1928.[46]

From the late nineteenth century throughout the Mexican Revolution and its aftermath, two themes emerged that were to prove critical to church-state relations and education during the 1920s. The first was the centralizing tendency evident during the Porfiriato, which continued (with the exception of Carranza) during the revolutionary years. In the nineteenth century, education had been offered by a variety of municipal, religious, and private organizations. Initially, the national government promoted this diverse approach to education, aware that its capacity to educate the population was limited. Basic literacy and numeracy were the goals, as public and private agencies worked together to educate Mexicans. During the Porfiriato, however, education became a tool for national unification and the federal government its ideal regulator, if not its provider. During and after the revolution, the emphasis on a national education system would continue, except for the brief period during which primary education was returned to municipal control. Education had become an indispensable tool for creating a unified Mexico.

The second theme involved attacks on the Catholic Church that resulted from attempts to bolster the power of the national government. In the postrevolutionary period, the church was one of the few organizations capable of offering effective national opposition to the government. Yet because church and state responded to each other's actions, the relationship shifted depending on specific historical circumstances. While some liberals had attacked the church during the Reform, Díaz, ostensibly a liberal, allowed the re-evangelization of Mexico, during which time the church began to regain its temporal powers. During the revolution, the political wing of the church flourished under Madero, until the complicity of PCN leaders in the Huerta coup cemented the lasting ire of the Constitutionalists. The relationship depended upon individuals as well as institutions, and shifted along a spectrum ranging from staunch government anticlericalism to unofficial tolerance. The period between the end of the revolution and the war of the cristeros began with unofficial tolerance of the church and gradually shifted to the hostility of the Calles years.

2 Primary Education

Programs and Pedagogy

In the postrevolutionary era, primary-school programs were designed to mold patriotic citizens who were prepared to work for national economic development. Between 1917 and 1925, reforms to both municipal and federal curricula promoted skills of observation, experimentation and, in schools run by the Secretaría de Educación Pública, training in manual, agricultural, and domestic skills. Attempts by educators and pedagogues to integrate subject matter across the curriculum and ensure practical application carried over from Porfirian education. The 1888 federal law, Sierra's 1908 law, the municipal reforms of 1917, and the SEP reforms of 1922 and 1923 all moved toward these goals. Yet as each subsequent reform was proposed, the previous curriculum was criticized as staid, traditional, and disciplinarian. This chapter begins with a discussion of the 1917 primary curriculum reform and municipal primary programs in Mexico City. Next, it examines the SEP curricula, including the 1923 action-pedagogy-based reforms and the abandonment of action schools in 1925. Examination of programs and teaching methods in Mexico City's Catholic schools follows, demonstrating that government and Catholic curricula and methods were similar.

Municipal Primary Programs

By 1915, Constitutionalist leader Carranza was already planning to dismantle the Secretaría de Instrucción Pública y Bellas Artes and had organized the Dirección General de Educación Pública (General Directorate of Public Education) to replace it. When the SIPBA was dismantled in 1917, the primarias elementales were assigned to the various municipal governments. The Dirección General had jurisdiction only over Mexico City's primarias superiores, normal schools, and preparatory schools. With regard to primarias elementales, the jurisdiction of the Dirección General versus that of the various municipalities in the Federal District is unclear: At the very least the Dirección General offered advice on texts and curriculum; meanwhile the municipal authority dealt with school administration, such as hiring and funding. In 1917, the Dirección General promulgated curriculum reforms for both primaria elemental and primaria superior levels. The new program was to be nationalistic and practical; students were to observe natural phenomena, study life cycles of plants and animals, collect specimens, and draw their own conclusions from their work, using textbooks only as an aid. The curriculum was to refer to Mexico and things Mexican as much as possible, in order to foster a sense of national identity. Yet there are no indications as to whether and how the reform was introduced in Mexico City municipal primary schools, as these schools were not directly under the jurisdiction of the Dirección General. Nonetheless, like the 1917 Dirección General curriculum, the municipal curriculum focused on practical education, especially regarding rural living, and used education to foster a sense of nationalism.[1]

In the first and second years of primary school, the curriculum covered Spanish, natural sciences, arithmetic and geometry, handicrafts, gymnastics, choral singing, and in girls' schools, "female labors." In the third and fourth years, history and "civic education" were added to the academic curriculum, while in the fifth year students started learning a foreign language. Tables 2.1 and 2.2 show the municipal primary-school schedule in 1921. For all the grades, the day was divided into morning and afternoon sessions. The class periods were shorter for younger students and lengthened in the higher grades. During the break, students returned home for a long lunch.

In first and second grades, both Spanish and math classes incorporated basic morals but offered children training with little practical application. Readings suggest that Spanish classes taught children generosity, patriotism, self-sacrifice, obedience, and the importance of family. The teachers appear to have lectured to stationary children, using Porfirian pedagogic techniques including verbal descriptions of *estampas* (illustrated cards), memorization, and recitation of poems or literary passages. In first grade, "The Generous Prince" was one story read, while poems included "The School," "Hidalgo," and "To Columbus." Second graders examined and described an estampa entitled "Moral through Example" and copied sentences which their teacher read aloud. Stories for second graders focused on "moral" topics, as exemplified by "The Disobedient Son," "The Envious Girl," and "The

Martyr's Mother." Although Spanish classes included units on how to write a message or a letter, overall the curriculum promoted socialization and virtues rather than practical skills.[2] Mathematics classes had a bit more practical application than Spanish classes did but still tended to teach abstract theory divorced from function. Although first graders were taught how to measure using the metric system, counting and problem-solving exercises, particularly dealing with geometric figures, appeared most frequently. Moreover, counting was not taught in relation to denominations of money, learning to tell time, or another practical skill.[3]

The science curriculum was tied into students' lives and suggests that the capital shortly after the revolution blended both urban and rural characteristics. Drawing from their own experiences, students in science classes examined the everyday natural world. In first grade, science classes addressed common animals and insects—such as cows, dogs, ants, and fleas—and common plants, including corn, beans, wheat, and daisies. Science classes also offered students an opportunity to gain agricultural skills. Second-year students were to learn about planting and cultivation. In the third year, students were supposed to observe a garden, paying special attention to fruit trees, and to learn to prepare the earth for planting. Thus, the science program assumed that Mexico City children were not only familiar with natural phenomena but needed agricultural skills in order to be productive adults.[4]

Science teachers not only gave their students practical training, but some did so through lively, interesting teaching. The curricula suggest that teachers took their students outside to examine actual plants in a natural setting. Variations among individual teachers' plans further suggest they were given wide leeway in how to present the material. While Felisa Torix took her students outside to observe plant and animal life, Guadalupe Jiménez lectured to her students on the same material.

This agricultural training for Federal District children was not limited to municipal primary schools: SEP and Catholic primary schools, discussed later, also taught agricultural skills. Although one of the lasting effects of the revolution was mass migration to cities, Mexico was still a predominantly rural country.[5] Many schools on the outskirts of Mexico City and in surrounding communities had access to arable land. Even schools in central Mexico City could garden in their patios.

Table 2.1. Schedule for Municipal Primaria Elemental Schools, 1921

Time	Subject
First and Second Years: Monday, Wednesday, Friday	
9:30–10:00	Assembly
10:00–10:20	Elements of Natural Sciences
10:20–10:50	National Language
10:50–11:10	Recess
11:10–11:40	Arithmetic and Geometry
11:40–12:00	Industrial Work and Application Exercises [*Est. Trab. Ind. y Ej. de Apl. (sic)*]
12:00–12:20	Gymnastics
Break	
4:00–4:20	Drawing, Manual Work (and Female Labors)
4:20–4:40	Choral Singing
4:40–5:10	National Language
5:10–5:30	Recess
5:30–6:00	Industrial Work and Application Exercises
First and Second Years: Tuesday, Thursday	
9:30–10:00	Assembly
10:00–10:20	Elements of Natural Sciences
10:20–10:50	National Language
10:50–11:10	Recess
11:10–11:40	Arithmetic and Geometry
11:40–12:00	Industrial Work and Application Exercises
12:00–12:20	Gymnastics
Break	
4:00–4:20	Industrial Work and Application Exercises
4:20–4:40	Drawing, Manual Work (and Female Labors)
4:40–5:10	National Language
5:10–5:30	Recess
5:30–6:00	Arithmetic and Geometry

Third and Fourth Years: Monday, Wednesday, Friday	
9:30–10:00	Assembly
10:00–10:30	Elements of Natural Sciences
10:30–11:05	National Language
11:05–11:25	Recess
11:25–12:00	Arithmetic and Geometry
12:00–12:30	History and Civic Education
12:30–1:00	Gymnastics and Military Exercises
Break	
4:00–4:30	Drawing, Manual Work (and Female Labors)
4:30–4:50	Choral Singing
4:50–5:25	National Language
5:25–5:35	Rest
5:35–6:00	Industrial Work and Application Exercises
Third and Fourth Years: Tuesday, Thursday	
9:30–10:00	Assembly
10:00–10:30	Geography
10:30–11:05	National Language
11:05–11:25	Recess
11:25–12:00	Arithmetic and Geometry
12:00–12:30	Industrial Work and Application Exercises
12:30–1:00	Gymnastics and Military Exercises
Break	
4:00–4:30	Drawing, Manual Work (and Female Labors)
4:30–4:50	Industrial Work and Application Exercises
4:50–5:25	Arithmetic and Geometry
5:25–5:35	Rest
5:35–6:00	Industrial Work and Application Exercises

Source: L. Ortega, oficial mayor, 18 March 1921, Archivo Histórico de la Ciudad de México, Instrucción Pública 2664/4 "1917–1921 Circulares, disposiciones."

Table 2.2. Schedule for Municipal Primaria Superior Schools, 1921

Time	Subject
	Fifth and Sixth Years: Monday, Wednesday, Friday
9:30–10:00	Assembly
10:00–10:40	National Language
10:40–11:20	Arithmetic and Geometry
11:20–11:40	Recess
11:40–12:10	History and Civic Education
12:10–12:50	Elements of Natural Sciences
12:50–1:20	French and English
Break	
4:00–4:35	Drawing, Manual Work (and Female Labors)
4:35–5:15	Industrial Work and Application Exercises
5:15–5:25	Rest
5:25–6:05	Physical and Military Exercises
	Fifth and Sixth Years: Tuesday, Thursday
9:30–10:00	Assembly
10:00–10:40	National Language
10:40–11:20	Arithmetic and Geometry
11:20–11:40	Recess
11:40–12:10	Geography
12:10–12:50	Industrial Work and Application Exercises
12:50–1:20	Music and Singing
Break	
4:00–4:35	Drawing, Manual Work (and Female Labors)
4:35–5:15	National Language
5:15–5:25	Rest
5:25–6:05	Industrial Work and Application Exercises

Source: L. Ortega, oficial mayor, 18 March 1921, Archivo Histórico de la Ciudad de México, Instrucción Pública 2664/4 "1917–1921 Circulares, disposiciones."

Training students to garden and raise livestock, however, related not only to students' needs, but also to the values of those designing the curriculum. The curriculum indicates that educators in Mexico City imagined a future in which children would contribute to their own upkeep through farming. The municipal curriculum not only trained students in industrial work — which would be the nation's future — but also prepared children for Mexico as it was: predominantly rural. Considering the plight of the capital's residents during the revolution, when hunger was the order of the day, these science classes taught municipal primary-school children important survival skills. Finally, even if children never used their agricultural training, their knowledge might give them some respect for campesinos, helping create national unity. Not far from the capital, peasants were still fighting and dying for village rights to land.

Besides moralizing children while evoking an ideal rural life, municipal school curricula promoted class-biased health and hygiene rules. Many of the hygiene problems targeted were a result of poverty and inadequate infrastructure, rather than personal slovenliness. While any child could stop gnawing on pencils or cleaning objects with saliva (advice included in the curriculum), advice pertaining to living conditions was harder to implement. For instance, children learned that multiple people living in a room was unhealthy, but the poor crowded together out of economic necessity, not by choice.[6] Poor diet was also a result of poverty not choice. The courses further suggested that children eat fruit and drink plenty of water, ignoring the fact that poor children had little control over their diet. Children were also told not to drink the alcoholic beverage *pulque,* yet alcohol consumption was high among the poor because of water shortages and contamination. Moreover, pulque was relatively low in alcohol and had nutritional benefits.[7] Ironically, many teachers would themselves not have been able to follow these health and hygiene suggestions because of their meager salaries.

Municipal education combined attempts to improve not just body but soul. One municipal inspector prepared a guide that teachers were to use to rate the character improvement of their students. Teachers were to look for evidence of courtesy and urbanity; clean, precise work; regular, punctual school attendance; and control over "lazy" impulses. Personal appearance also counted toward character improvement.[8]

Again, the poor were at a disadvantage because children from prosperous families would have had less difficulty living up to these ideals. For instance, well-off children who could afford to dress nicely also attended school more regularly because they did not have to contribute to their family finances.

Not content to better children's manners and characters, municipal educators promoted physical education as a means to better health and discipline. Students' gender, however, determined the ways in which they exercised. In 1917, Carranza directed that boys were to receive military training instead of general physical education, in order to ensure that Mexico's young men were ready to defend their nation should the need arise. While boys practiced being soldiers, in girls' schools students were supposed to receive nursing training so that they could serve Mexico by curing wounds.[9] As the schedules in tables 2.1 and 2.2 show, students in the lower grades played games for their physical activity, while older students participated in military exercises. How students exercised also depended on who taught them. Whereas first graders in María Portugal's class played games, such as "the cat and the mouse" and "the poppies," Ana de la Fuente's second-grade students marched and practiced breathing exercises. According to municipal educators, both games and military training had a moralizing effect, because any sort of physical exercise was a wholesome pastime that would eventually turn children away from centers of vice and prostitution. Militarization was not limited to physical education; students were also supposed to execute a military salute when an adult entered the classroom. The military salute was abolished in 1921 and replaced with standing at attention.[10]

After physically preparing to battle invaders, children were supposed to learn of past military exploits in history classes. The point of history and civics classes was to teach children about the moments that defined Mexico and what their duties were as Mexicans. History curriculum included study of pre-Columbian civilizations such as the Aztecs and the Toltecs. Students appear to have skipped the colonial period to go straight to the independence era, at which point Miguel Hidalgo, José María Morelos, and Agustín Iturbide all received mention, although Iturbide only briefly. The mid-nineteenth century was depicted as an era of foreign interventions, which included war with Texas and the Guerra de los Pasteles (War of the Cakes). Benito Juárez then emerged as the national hero. Through teaching about events such as the defeat of the French at Puebla on 5 May 1862, the sacrifice of the *niños héroes* (boy heroes), Independence Day, and Hidalgo's execution — all addressed in the curriculum — educators sought to forge national ties based upon a common historic foundation.[11] Yet the interpretation of history depends on factors such as familial, social, religious, and economic backgrounds. Children learned just one narrative of the past out of many possibilities, serving to alienate any other narratives or loyalties children had been taught at home: Even "national" heroes could be controversial. For instance, Juárez was not a hero to many Catholics. Perhaps because of the partisanship and divisions of history, in particular recent history, the municipal curriculum ignored the Porfiriato and the revolution. Municipal education built nationalism upon the distant past, which teachers and students could not remember personally, while ignoring recent events that were more controversial.

Geography courses were another means of inculcating nationalism while offering students the practical skills necessary to find their way around the capital. In the first years, the curriculum was based on students' immediate environs and young children were taught how to orient themselves, easy enough to do with the snow-capped volcanoes Popocatépetl and Iztaccíhuatl sleeping southeast of their city. Gradually, geography lessons moved beyond the immediate vicinity to the larger neighborhood and the capital itself. Lessons on Mexico City included borders, communication systems, and the geographic characteristics of the valley, such as its mountains, lakes, and canals. Students were to memorize the size and capital of each of the municipalities in the Federal District. Expanding upon the themes from science classes, the curriculum addressed products cultivated in the region as well as which plants were poisonous, beneficial, or medicinal. Again, the municipal curriculum suggests that these urban children were closely tied to the natural world or, if they were not, that knowledge of nature was still considered fundamental to a basic education. The geography curriculum also included study of urban features such as the factories, churches, theaters, hotels, and cemeteries of Mexico City.

While more advanced students were supposed to learn to locate Mexico on a map and to know which countries bordered it and their importance, the primary focus of geography classes remained Mexico itself.[12] More advanced geography classes were designed to persuade children of the existence of a national "imagined community" called Mexico.[13] Tools such as wall maps that provided a visual representation of the abstract concept of nation were essential to this endeavor. The geography curriculum, however, focused on the city of Mexico rather than the nation of Mexico, perhaps a legacy of Porfirian centralization. Under Díaz, Mexico City had become a showplace and symbol for the nation, particularly after the building and hygiene campaigns undertaken for the 1910 independence celebrations.[14] The primacy of the capital in the geography curriculum could have been intended to teach young citizens about the glory of the nation's political and cultural seat, as well as giving them, as residents, a source of civic pride. On the other hand, this focus could also have been parochial, reflecting municipal pride.

SEP Primary Programs

Like in municipal schools, in SEP primary schools children attended class in the morning, had a long lunch break, and resumed classes in the late afternoon. In 1921, schools operated Monday through Saturday with half days on Wednesday and Saturday. In the first and second years of primary school, children learned math, Spanish, singing, physical and natural sciences, physical education, drawing, and manual labors or, for girls, domestic tasks. In the upper grades, history, civics, geography, military exercises, and a foreign language were added to the curriculum. Although the school day was longer for the upper grades, all children began the day with games and sports, and had breaks for both rest and recess. Each day before classes began, there was an assembly, although it is not clear whether this was for the entire school or individual classes.[15] By 1928, the school schedule had been altered to *tiempo corrido,* meaning that there was just one school session, ending in the early afternoon.[16]

In 1922, having federalized much of the primary education in the Federal District, Minister of Education José Vasconcelos reorganized the primary-school curriculum there. Vasconcelos wanted education to reach the "humble," to create a nation of producers rather than consumers, and to form citizens with analytical capacity. Characterizing earlier educational programs as making students passive, Vasconcelos designed the 1922 program of studies to promote hands-on learning. The program gave teachers leeway to interpret the curriculum according to student and community needs. Given a new autonomy, teachers were to consider students' interests and their lives outside school when adapting the curriculum, so as not to overwhelm them with unnecessary information. Moreover, teachers were to minimize their use of punishment, to create an atmosphere of affection.

According to Claude Fell, the 1922 program formed the basis of the 1923 reorganization of primary schools in the other regions under SEP authority.[17] In contrast, Mary Kay Vaughan devotes her attention to action pedagogy and the 1923 reforms.[18] John Dewey, a professor and philosopher at Columbia University, was the original proponent of this teaching method, which was supposed to prepare children to be productive members of society. Dewey criticized traditional education as being static and having no relation to the present. He also criticized traditional schools for imposing adult expectations, rules, and learning styles upon immature people. Dewey wanted education to be centered on children and their interests and to be grounded in practical experience, which he believed was the basis of education. Dewey promoted a mode of education in which experiences were linked to each other and teachers used local history, economy, and topography in planning classes.[19] He suggested that children could understand society and their contribution to it only by doing the work that was fundamental to civilization. Dewey exhorted, "We must conceive of work in wood and metal, of weaving, sewing, and cooking, as methods of life not as distinct studies." While Dewey's training could prepare children for future work, that outcome was of secondary rather than primary importance: Of primary importance was the link to their daily lives and the emphasis on cooperation, group learning, and exchanging ideas. "The aim is not the economic value of the products, but the development of social power and insight."[20] Dewey was convinced that education could bring about societal reform. In contrast, critics worried that the emphasis on technical training would transform primary schools into little more than workshops. Substantiating critics' concerns, action schools in Mexico emphasized the economic potential of the products the schools manufactured. Action schools became children's first contribution to Mexico's economic and industrial development.

In theory, the practical training offered in action schools meant that the schools were tailored to students' environments and local needs. For instance, rural schools were supposed to promote agricultural skills. Boys in rural schools were trained to become providers, while girls in rural schools were to be trained for unpaid domestic work and motherhood. In contrast, urban primary schools for boys were to instruct students about the "commercial transactions of industrial artisans." Based on the assumption that boys would one day work in factories and workshops, their study of the natural world was to be limited to investigation of raw materials necessary for industrial production. Urban girls, who would one day oversee the domestic sphere, were to learn to care for home and family.[21]

Skills training for students was also a means to integrate disparate academic subjects. When making a table, for instance, students could use skills in drawing, geometry, and calculus. A geography lesson could address where the wood for the table originated and how it was transported to the city. Giving students academic information within the context of a project was also supposed to help them retain their knowledge. Handicrafts production itself would make students feel competent, and the activity would be good for their physical development.[22] The introduction of action pedagogy built upon an established but never acknowledged base: Municipal education had encouraged study of local environments, while municipal teachers integrated subject matter and observed nature.

Also like its municipal predecessor, the SEP requested that schools cultivate crops for consumption and public sale. Teachers, principals, and students were authorized to spend up to three hours daily in school gardens, which were to serve as outdoor classrooms. Teachers and inspectors were supposed to ask neighbors for donations of materials, suggesting that the SEP provided little practical support for gardening. The SEP also suggested that students cover the costs of the garden by forming a cooperative and donating a few *centavos* each. At the end of the year, the profits were to be divided. When the crops were ready to be harvested, the SEP suggested that students with the most economic need should receive the most produce.[23]

It is difficult to determine how many Federal District schools actually had gardens. The SEP divided its primary schools in the Mexico City area into four types: ordinary, academic centers, open-air, and semiurban. The academic centers, which enrolled between 1,400 and

1,500 students, and the open-air schools, also large, had ample space for playgrounds and gardens. The semiurban schools were located in towns around Mexico City that were close enough to the capital to have a metropolitan influence but still remained essentially rural. In 1925, there were seventy-one semiurban schools in the Federal District. Almost all the semiurban schools had fields to cultivate, some of which belonged to the school and some of which belonged to local residents. Moreover, in 1925, 15 of the 174 primary schools had annexed fields for cultivation. Thus, a sizeable number of schools in the Federal District, and even some in Mexico City, had gardens or fields for cultivation.

Although the action schools were supposed to integrate subjects and allow children's needs to direct the teaching, the SEP still mandated certain academic subjects and priorities within primary education. The subjects were Spanish *(lengua nacional)*, arithmetic, geometry, natural science *(estudio de la naturaleza)*, hygiene, Mexican geography and history (both included more general themes as they related to Mexico), crafts *(trabajos manuales)*, drawing, singing, games and sports, and (for girls only) puericulture and domestic arts. All these subjects had to be taught, even in rural schools, but the SEP permitted subjects to be adapted as discussed previously. Schools that did not offer the full course of subjects would not be permitted to issue SEP-recognized certificates of completion, and their students would have to finish their primary schooling elsewhere before continuing their education.[24]

Although the SEP promoted Dewey's action pedagogy, a variety of circumstances limited the program's implementation. The 1923 De la Huerta rebellion sapped federal funding, and the SEP did not have the resources to equip schools with necessary supplies. Because of the rebellion, teachers' salaries were suspended, reducing their enthusiasm to institute reforms. Some teachers were unwilling to alter their teaching method or curriculum, while others lacked the training or materials to undertake these experiential projects. Finally, the SEP complained that the majority of its teachers had been educated in traditional pedagogy and were not prepared to include modern methods in their classrooms.[25]

Under the new administration of Puig Casauranc, SEP priorities shifted away from action pedagogy. The new SEP priorities became education designed to promote national economic progress and rural schools that would help improve agricultural production. Following the confusion over action pedagogy and unrelated financial difficulties, Puig's SEP sought the return of the disciplined and orderly classroom. Textbooks became more important and the SEP introduced U.S.-modeled standardized tests to measure IQ and academic performance. Because of students' poor performance on these tests, the SEP renounced integrated education and promoted memorization for arithmetic and reading.

Under the new curriculum, however, the twin goals of morality and nationalism remained unaltered. A pledge of allegiance was introduced in 1925: During an Independence Day celebration at the National Stadium, fifty thousand children swore allegiance to the Mexican flag under the gaze of President Calles. Also in 1925, the SEP introduced a new school calendar that commemorated patriotic festivals, such as the births and deaths of Juárez and Madero, as well as important military events, such as the start of the revolution. In marked contrast to municipal education, which had ignored the revolution altogether, this new calendar made the revolution equal to independence as an event in the making of Mexico. Primary schools continued to emphasize individual morality and a morality code was introduced in 1925. Responding in part to Catholic criticism that secular education could not impart moral values, the code promoted behavioral rules similar to those of the Ten Commandments and the Catholic catechism. For instance, the morality code instructed children to be charitable and kind to others. It also encouraged cooperation and self-control in thought, word, and deed. The code included a monthly report card, so that teachers could assess students' progress. The SEP distributed ten thousand copies of the code to primary- and secondary-school children.[26]

The morality code is but one example of increasing SEP encroachment upon the realm of parents that occurred under Puig Casauranc. A 1926 leaflet describing the rights of children provides another example of SEP intrusion into the family. All children had the right to love, a clean home, a separate bed, and three meals daily. No child should be allowed to drink stimulants, such as tea, coffee, or fermented beverages. In terms of clothing, every child needed clean apparel and undergarments, a nightshirt, and something warmer for winter. Children had the right to play areas at home, as well as access to playgrounds.

Every child had the right to attend school and, in order to ensure sufficient time for rest and play, should not be encumbered with more than three hours of domestic tasks daily.[27] In this declaration of rights, the SEP did not acknowledge that many parents could not provide these amenities to their children. Instead, the rhetoric turned poor parents into negligent parents.

Catholic Primary Curricula

The SEP curriculum had much in common with that of the Catholic schools. By the 1920s, Catholic primary schools were technically illegal because Article 3 of the 1917 Constitution stated that all primary education was to be secular. Until February 1926, however, the regulation of Article 3 was left to state and local governments. Moreover, private schools, Catholic or otherwise, were necessary to ease the SEP's burden, so the SEP allowed Catholic primary schools to operate. Of the two hundred private schools in the Federal District in 1923, more than one hundred were free Catholic schools. Of the remaining schools, some were Protestant while others probably catered to the language needs of Mexico City's foreign communities. Of those 200 private schools, 143 were incorporated into the SEP, meaning that they followed the official program.[28] For practical as well as political reasons, religious primary schools continued to operate in Mexico City without major interference until 1926, and many of these schools operated within SEP guidelines and received regular visits from SEP inspectors, as discussed later.

Unlike SEP and municipal primary schools, Catholic schools offered diverse curricula and programs for students ranging from homeless paperboys to elite daughters from Mexico City suburbs. What all these schools shared was an alternative vision of Mexican nationalism. For Catholics, Catholicism was an essential aspect of national identity that served to unite Mexicans from different regions and ethnic backgrounds. This alternative nationalism was promoted in the religious celebrations that took place in schools, such as Christmas festivities and pilgrimages to the Basilica of the Virgin of Guadalupe. Catholics also had alternative national heroes, including Hernán Cortés and Agustín Iturbide, who were probably included in the history curriculum of Catholic schools (fig. 2.1). Even characterizing the Catholic approach as alternative is misleading: Catholics believed that their nation was Catholic, and the state was seeking to impose an alternative nationalism on the people against their will.

Although united by nationalism and approach, Catholic primary schools can be divided into four overlapping categories based on tuition and status: Catholic schools either charged tuition or were free and, after 1921, they were either incorporated into the SEP or completely independent. Incorporated schools had to conform to the SEP program and were subject to SEP inspection and monitoring of exams. These schools usually added courses in catechism, sacred history, and religion to the SEP curriculum. If a private school was not incorporated into the SEP, its students could not continue their education in SEP schools later, because their qualifications would not be recognized. Yet the SEP's capacity to inspect and regulate private schools was limited, allowing incorporated Catholic schools substantial independence. Moreover, the quality of education was more important to the SEP than content. An inspector who visited a primary school in Tacuba run by the Salesian order reported that not only did priests teach the classes, but the school also used its own textbooks and curriculum. Because of the caliber of the education offered, however, the SEP did not punish the infractions, but merely reminded the staff not to teach religion.[29]

Most of the schools considered in my study were associated with the Unión de Damas Católicas Mexicanas (Union of Mexican Catholic Ladies, or UDCM). In 1922, the UDCM Sección de Escuelas (Schools Section) agreed upon the requirements that schools for poor children had to meet in order to receive UDCM sponsorship: Schools had to be Catholic, to be incorporated into the SEP under a religious name — in clear violation of constitutional Article 3 — and to follow the SEP program, with the additions of catechism, sacred history, and morality. The school was to accept UDCM inspection and not make major decisions without consulting UDCM members. Because UDCM schools were incorporated into the SEP, official inspectors presided over exams and oversaw the curriculum. Nonetheless, as the preceding example demonstrates, good schools could get away with bending the rules, and inspectors had a great deal of leeway to punish or not as they saw fit. Interactions between the UDCM school staff, individual *damas,* and

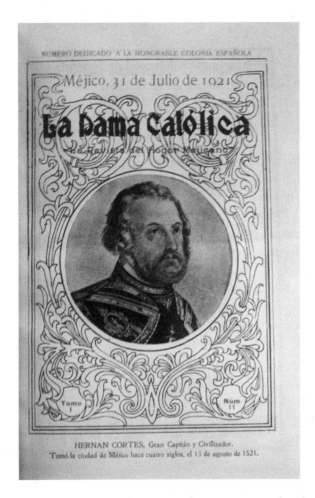

NÚMERO DEDICADO A LA HONORABLE COLONIA ESPAÑOLA

Méjico, 31 de Julio de 1921

La Dama Católica

La Revista del Hogar Mejicano

Tomo I

Núm 11

HERNAN CORTES, Gran Capitán y Civilizador.
Tomó la ciudad de Méjico hace cuatro siglos, el 13 de agosto de 1521.

Figure 2.1. The Catholic version of Mexican nationalism had its own heroes, as shown in this cover of a Catholic periodical. The caption reads, "Hernán Cortés, Gran Capitán y Civilizador. Tomó la ciudad de México hace cuatro siglos, el 13 de agosto de 1521." (Hernán Cortés, the great captain and civilizer, took Mexico City four centuries ago, on 13 August 1521). For Catholic organizations like the UDCM, Cortés was a hero because he brought Christianity to Mexico. They believed that their work of opening Catholic schools, sponsoring first communions, and offering catechism classes was a continuation of his evangelizing mission. (Courtesy of the Hemeroteca Nacional, Mexico City)

inspectors were cordial, suggesting that the UDCM schools were of acceptable quality and conformed to the SEP curriculum. Even in 1926, after Catholic primary education was prohibited and UDCM schools hid their religious character, members of the UDCM did not find SEP inspection detrimental to their work.[30]

Visits that damas made to UDCM schools and their correspondence with school employees provide indications of the curricula at Catholic primary schools. The Colegio del Sagrado Corazón de Jesús (School of the Sacred Heart of Jesus), founded by a married Catholic woman, received financial support from the UDCM. Located in the Colonia Vallejo, a poor neighborhood on the pilgrimage route to the Basilica of Guadalupe, the school of approximately one hundred students taught the SEP program, including English and French, with the addition of religion. In SEP schools, French and English were taught only to students in primaria superior, not younger children. An interested dama volunteered to teach students music, music theory, and how to play the piano. As was typical in Catholic schools, the students sat for two exams: one for the government and one for their school. Damas presided over some of the exams, while the UDCM spiritual director, Father Leopoldo Icaza, presided over religion exams.[31] An inspector from the SEP would also have presided over the official exam.

Materials used in UDCM schools offer further suggestions as to curricula and teaching methods. The Schools Section bought ten zoological maps with text (*mapas zoológicos con texto,* probably maps indicating animal species found in Mexico), a chart of the metric system, six maps of Mexico, one physical map, and four spheres on stands (*esferas con repisa*) for a school they founded.[32] The animal maps, the metrics chart, and the Mexican maps were obviously for study of math and geography. The spheres could have been globes for geography lessons. Use of maps of Mexico suggests that for Catholic as well as SEP schools, national geography promoted students' sense of an identity linked to the nation of Mexico.

Damas also inspected the schools to which they gave financial support. During a visit to the Sagrado Corazón de Jesús School, UDCM members heard the children recite in English, French, and Spanish. Students, balancing on their tiptoes to reach, copied dictation onto the blackboard and impressed the damas with their handwriting. The older students, who were still not more than ten years old, demonstrated their ability to multiply fractions, use exponents, and solve basic algebraic problems quickly and correctly.[33] This visit to the Sagrado Corazón de Jesús School suggests that, regarding pedagogic method, teachers relied upon recitation and memorization. Children probably spent most of the day sitting on their benches listening to lectures and repeating the lessons. An occasional trip to the blackboard to work out a problem would have broken the monotony. The Sagrado Corazón de Jesús School did not offer skills training or orient the subject matter toward practical application.

Other UDCM schools, however, did focus on practical training. The UDCM shared with the SEP a belief in the importance of agricultural training, founding the Escuela Granja (Farm-School) in the Colonia Vallejo for the express purpose of training children to be agricultural workers. The UDCM wanted the training to be "scientific" and "efficient" so that students could obtain optimal results with minimal expenditure of time and money.[34] The damas' use of the term *scientific* belies the stereotype of Catholics, particularly Catholic women, as conservative and reluctant to incorporate new ideas. The damas used the term to mean training that incorporated a modern method of approaching problem solving, a method that had been proven to be the best, most efficient, and most rational. In using the term, they were also countering the anticlerical revolutionary perspective that their religious beliefs were incompatible with modernity. Unfortunately, records are not specific enough to determine what sciences the school taught or what perspective it used, although the courses would probably have been based on the prescribed science curriculum.

The women of the Schools Section were not the only Catholics to recognize the importance of science as a field of study. At the 1922 UDCM national convention, a resolution called for increased literacy so that knowledge of religion, science, and the arts would become more widely available.[35] Training for members of the central committee of the UDCM at the coordinating center of Catholic social action, the Secretariado Social Mexicano (Mexican Social Secretariat, or SSM), included study of the encyclical *Ubi Arcano Dei* by Pius XI on Catholic action, followed by training in geography, natural history, and public speaking.[36] Other Catholic schools found ways to incorporate science into their worldview. María Teresa Fernández-Aceves has written about the informally Catholic Aquiles Serdán School, which was founded in Guadalajara in 1937 with both church and SEP support. (It was incorporated into the SEP in 1939.) This school for women, run by women, had the motto, "Science, Work, and Virtue."[37]

The UDCM Escuela Granja promoted practical as well as scientific education. Students raised rabbits and cured their skins, raised chickens and doves, cultivated silkworms, and worked with straw (presumably to weave hats or mats). In addition, the school offered primary education and religion. Later, the school added classes in English, stenography, hatmaking, and machine embroidery.[38] Another Catholic school that offered technical training was founded by Father José Castillo y Piña. The girls' Colegio-Casa Nazaret (Nazaret Home-School) taught Spanish, math, geography, Mexican history, natural sciences, civics, drawing, physical education, choral singing, and hygiene. The school curriculum promoted feminine work such as embroidery, growing flowers, and raising poultry.[39]

While Catholic and SEP schools show obvious affinities in curriculum, Catholics were present in federal education just as the federal government had a presence in religious schools. The sharp division between Catholic and public schools that I have made in this chapter ignores the fact that religious faith was not limited to teachers and students in Catholic schools. SEP schools were targeted by religious agents asking children for donations, as described in one SEP circular.[40] It is unlikely that these religious sympathizers would have entered schools without knowing that some members of staff felt affinity with their cause. (When the visits came to the attention of the SEP, a circular immediately reminded inspectors of the Article 3 restrictions and their duty to enforce them.[41]) Teachers also brought their personal beliefs into the classroom, or so the SEP feared, as Catholic teachers were required to sign loyalty pledges when the church-state conflict began in earnest and risked losing their jobs if they refused to sign them.[42] At the same time, private schools evidently adhered to the SEP curriculum and employed teachers who had been trained at the National Normal School, as had the headmistress of the Sagrado Corazón de Jesús School. At least a few SEP teachers were also members of the UDCM, again suggesting overlapping identities and loyalties.[43] Thus, neither the schools nor the society in which they functioned was segregated into clear camps of Catholics and revolutionaries.

This examination of primary-school curricula demonstrates the common priorities and approaches in municipal, Catholic, and federal schools. Municipal education emphasized practical training in its science classes (in which students learned agricultural skills) and integration of subject matter particularly between science and geography. Frequent physical education classes, as well as recess, suggest an interest in the health of children's bodies as well as their minds. The reforms introduced in SEP schools, especially action pedagogy, had a similar focus on integrated education guided by children's interests, experimentation, and observation. The strong emphasis on practical training and the decision that primary education should provide children with marketable skills, however, indicates the primacy of skills training. Focus on skills training also recognized the situation of many Mexican children, whose poverty did not allow them the luxury of years of study before starting to work. If primary education could provide children with marketable skills, they would be better prepared to provide for themselves and their families. When Calles became president, however, primary curricula returned to the basics of reading, writing, and mathematics, with examinations to rate students' progress. Nonetheless, the focus on patriotism and on fostering national unity through schooling increased.

As the examples in this chapter have shown, Catholic schools could be just as innovative, forward thinking, and practical as SEP ones. Catholic schools that were incorporated into the SEP used the authorized curriculum and received visits from SEP inspectors, resulting in relative standardization of programs. While the overall focus of the education was similar, Catholic schools promoted their vision of the world through additional courses in religion, sacred history, and often catechism. Catholic schools, like SEP and municipal schools, also promoted separate worlds for boys and girls, in which boys protected and provided for the family, while girls made and supervised the home with their love and skill. Because there was more variety in Catholic schools — some were operated by religious orders, some by lay organizations, and others by individuals with a mission — they did not reflect a Catholic consensus on what education should be, but rather reflected the ideas of their individual founders. For instance, the damas wanted their own skills and values to be present in the schools they supported, so some UDCM schools taught music appreciation. Whatever differences might be present among the various schools, however, a comparison of the municipal, SEP, and Catholic schools of the Mexico City area shows a broad consensus on the problems facing Mexican society and on the role of education in solving them.

3 Vocational Education

Training Hearts and Hands

The vocational education programs of the Mexico City municipality, the SEP, and various Catholic organizations emerged from and expanded upon Porfirian education. Regardless of their origins, the schools and their courses provide evidence both of continuity between pre- and postrevolutionary Mexico and of adaptations to profound changes in society brought about because of the revolution. Examination of vocational programs sponsored by Catholic and governmental agencies indicates that these institutions offered similar courses, each preparing students to play a role in society based upon their gender and class. This chapter addresses first municipal schools for adults, then SEP schools, both vocational schools and workers' night schools, and finally Catholic adult education. Because information on municipal adult schools is scarce, a brief discussion of municipal adult education in practice is included here.

Municipal Adult Education

Municipal night schools for adults originated during the Porfiriato, and by 1918 the Mexico City municipality reported that it operated thirty-nine single-sex night schools. As with municipal primary schools, there are no indications that the municipal government imposed a standard curriculum or program. The schools were to provide adults with basic primary education skills, such as literacy and mathematics. Textbook inventories suggest that the teachers also promoted civics, hygiene, and morality, as well as virtues and responsibilities specific to men and women. For instance, textbooks at schools for men addressed citizenship, while textbooks used in women's schools discussed the domestic sphere. *La mujer en el hogar* (the woman in the home), by teacher Dolores Correa Zapata, continued to be used in night schools for women even though by the postrevolutionary period her work was considered out of date. Correa Zapata's works, including also *Moral, instrucción cívica y economía doméstica* (Morals, civic instruction, and domestic economy), were written to instruct women on their domestic and societal duties. Other texts, such as *Alcoholismo y tabaquismo* (Alcoholism and tobacco addiction), *Enfermedades infecciosas* (Infectious diseases), and *Cuidado de los dientes* (Dental care) indicate that municipal night schools taught personal and community hygiene, as well as moralizing against popular customs, such as drinking and smoking. Workers' night schools also used children's textbooks, such as *Corazón, diario de un niño* (Heart, a boy's diary) and *Rosas de la infancia* (Roses of childhood), probably for Spanish classes.[1] These texts, as well as more recent works like José M. Bonilla's *Derechos civiles* (civil rights) and Daniel Delgadillo's *Adelante* (Forward), promoted liberal and positivist ideologies, presenting indigenous cultures as barbarous. They encouraged submission to a strong central government and emulation of Europe and the United States. The books were oriented toward students from the elite and middle classes and ignored any social gains resulting from the revolution.[2] These textbooks suggest that municipal education sought to moralize the working class, while improving their health and instructing them in their duties as citizens, more than to teach them their rights as citizens. The books also suggest that adult education had changed little from the prerevolutionary period.

The staff at these schools confronted the same material scarcities that municipal primary schools faced. Classrooms were sparsely decorated with portraits of Mexican heroes Juárez and Hidalgo and maps of the nation and the Federal District. Buildings ranged from merely rundown to outright dangerous; teachers had to make do with what was available and use their creativity in designing courses and getting materials. For example, night-school principals María Téllez Escalante and Emilio Bravo worked together to obtain free tickets to cinema showings with which to reward students who had good attendance. The principals also asked the municipality to persuade local newspapers to donate subscriptions to their schools.[3] The initiative of these principals demonstrates that poor conditions and inadequate supplies notwithstanding, with good teachers and principals, municipal adult schools could help educate working adults.

Federal Schools for Adults

Like municipal adult schools, many SEP schools had originated in the Porfiriato, and these schools formed the base of the SEP's adult education program in the 1920s. Although the capital had contributed neither ideology nor faction to the revolution, it was among the first regions to receive the benefits of the upheaval because it was the seat of authority and because instituting changes was easier in the capital than in the provinces. Mexico City was the "laboratory of the [federal] revolution" because it was one of the first places to experience revolutionary reforms, particularly in terms of education and religion.[4] Minister of Public Education José Vasconcelos hoped to reform and update the vocational system that he had inherited while expanding technical education for adults. He believed that technical education could modernize Mexico, improving the nation's industrial base by training skilled workers.

Roberto Medellín, Vasconcelos' "most constant collaborator,"[5] was in charge of the SEP's Departamento Escolar, which administered technical as well as primary and normal schools. Having inherited the schools from the previous governments, Medellín sought to reform their programs, limit duplication of classes, and provide them with better equipment. In 1922, the SEP operated seven vocational schools in the Federal District, offering free business, industrial, and crafts education. An additional eight institutions were planned, including schools for railroad and textile workers, and a normal school that would offer skills training for primary-school teachers. Although for Vasconcelos and Medellín, men's schools were a higher priority than women's schools, in the 1920s there were more schools for women than for men, and women's schools tended to enroll more students. By 1926, out of thirteen vocational schools in Mexico City, nine were for women. (Map 2 shows the locations of the principal vocational schools discussed in the text and the distribution of workers' night schools throughout the capital.) In the same year, there were 8,280 men enrolled in vocational schools compared to 13,050 women. These vocational schools offered courses during the day for full-time or part-time students, and at night for part-time students only. In addition, the SEP administered night schools aimed specifically at the working class.[6]

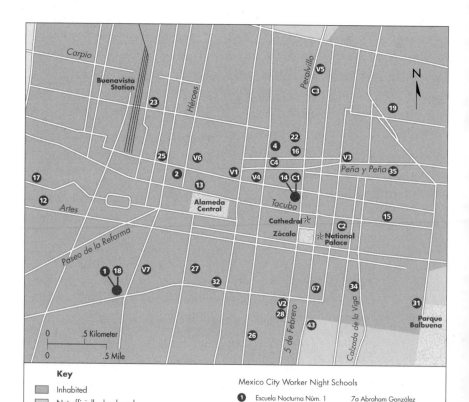

Key

- ▨ Inhabited
- ▧ Not officially developed
- ▨ Parks/Plazas

Vocational Schools and Worker Night Schools

Vocational Schools

V1	Escuela de Arte Industrial Corregidora de Querétaro	1a Mina Núm. 1
V2	Escuela de Artes y Oficios para Señoritas	5 de Febrero 90
V3	Escuela Nacional de Enseñanza Doméstica	1a Aztectas Núm. 1
V4	Escuela de Ingenieros Mecánicos y Electristas	Allende 38
V5	Escuela Hogar Gabriela Mistral	Peralvillo 124
V6	Escuela Hogar Sor Juana Inés de la Cruz	Sadi Carnot 63
V7	Escuela Técnica Nacional de Maestros Constructores	Tres Guerras 27

Centros Nocturnos Industriales

C1	Centro Industrial Nocturno Núm. 1	Rebública de Cuba 95
C2	Centro Industrial Nocturno Núm. 2	Capuchinas 135
C3	Centro Industrial Nocturno Núm. 3	Peralvillo 51
C4	Centro Industrial Nocturno Núm. 4	Esquina Avenida Honduras y Ciprés

Mexico City Worker Night Schools

1	Escuela Nocturna Núm. 1	7a Abraham González
2	Escuela Nocturna Núm. 2	6a Mina y 2a Héroes
4	Escuela Nocturna Núm. 4	5a del Ciprés 132
13	Escuela Nocturna Núm. 13	Avenida Hidalgo 91
14	Escuela Nocturna Núm. 14	República de Cuba 95
15	Escuela Nocturna Núm. 15	Mixcalco 10
16	Escuela Nocturna Núm. 16	Paraguay 28
17	Escuela Nocturna Núm. 17	Velázquez de León 61
18	Escuela Nocturna Núm. 18	7a Abraham González
19	Escuela Nocturna Núm. 19	Mineros 23
22	Escuela Nocturna Núm. 22	Panamá 52
23	Escuela Nocturna Núm. 23	Mosqueta 247
25	Escuela Nocturna Núm. 25	Zaragoza 64
26	Escuela Nocturna Núm. 26	13a de Bolivar 162
27	Escuela Nocturna Núm. 27	6a Luis Moya 99
28	Escuela Nocturna Núm. 28	Cinco de Febrero 135
31	Escuela Nocturna Núm. 31	Juan de la Granja 16
32	Escuela Nocturna Núm. 32	Arcos de Belem 45
34	Escuela Nocturna Núm. 34	Talavera 20
35	Escuela Nocturna Núm. 35	Peña y Peña 57
43	Escuela Nocturna Núm. 43	Calzada San Antonio Abad 38
67	Escuela Nocturna Núm. 67	Avenida Pino Suarez 60

Worker Night Schools outside of Mexico City (not featured on the map):

Escuela Nocturna Núm. 33	Porfirio Díaz, Milpa Alta
Escuela Nocturna Núm. 89	Rancho de Arbolillo, Guadalupe Hidalgo

As I mentioned in chapter 1, in 1924 the SEP underwent a dramatic shakeup, with Vasconcelos' abrupt resignation, a new presidential administration, and departmental reorganization. As a result of the reorganization, vocational education, rather than being administered with primary and normal education, was administered separately through the Departamento de Enseñanza Técnica, Industria y Comercial (DE-TIC). Despite the creation of an independent department, vocational training was less important to the new SEP administration; the schools were seen as potential profit makers rather than agents for social improvement. SEP vocational education had been free until President Obregón declared (on 22 July 1924) that all vocational-school students who were financially able to pay fees were thereafter required to do so. Even though impoverished full-time students who had a minimum grade of "very good" in their studies were eligible for grants to offset the tuition charges, the vast majority of students paid fees because only a tiny number of grants were available. Obregón also mandated that profits from the sale of goods manufactured in technical schools were to be divided between the students and the new DETIC. The DETIC was to use these fees and profits to found new vocational schools and to improve the facilities at existing schools.

Under the new administration, vocational education for men remained a higher priority than education for women because skilled male workers would contribute to Mexico's economic growth. Vocational schools trained male workers, upon whom Mexico's industrial development depended, to understand production, the market, and transport costs.[7] Upon finishing vocational education, these men were expected to found the modern workshops and factories that would create economic growth. In contrast, women's technical education had a dual and contradictory purpose, as the programs at the two types of

---

Opposite **Map 2.** Locations of vocational and workers' night schools between 1923 and 1925. This list was compiled from the Secretaría de Educación Pública, Noticia Estadistica sobre la Educación Pública de México correspondiente al año de 1925 (México: Talleres Gráficos de la Nación, 1927), p. 174; "Lista de las Escuelas Dependientes de la Dirección de Enseñanza Técnica y Comercial," 13 Feb. 1923, AHSEP DE 63/5/24; "Lista de las Escuelas Nocturnas," 12 April 1923, DETIC 72/18/5. (Map by Ann Kennedy, Mapping Specialists, Ltd.)

women's schools were at odds with each other. Women's technical training in commercial schools, of which there were few, prepared students to earn a living as typists or clerks. Vocational schools, on the other hand, trained women to produce goods in their homes for sale or family consumption.[8] The two types of women's education indicate that the SEP did not have a single vision of how women would be integrated into the postrevolutionary economy, yet more investment went into women's domestic education than commercial education. Regardless of whether women worked inside or outside their homes, the SEP viewed women as the educational and moral force in the family. Through educating one woman, the SEP expected to reach her entire family.

Schooling Men

Technical schools for men were oriented toward developing and rebuilding both industry and infrastructure after a decade of destruction. The SEP inherited its most prestigious men's vocational school: the Escuela de Ingenieros Mecánicos y Electristas (School of Mechanical Engineers and Electricians). Founded in 1869 as the Escuela de Artes y Oficios para Hombres (Arts and Trades School for Men), it was essentially a training ground for artisans. By the turn of the century, the school had added modern technical courses in key industries such as railroads and electrical power. In the Carranza period, the Escuela de Artes y Oficios was renamed and became more technical in its orientation; the school trained machinists, auto mechanics, electricians, and electrical and mechanical engineers (figs. 3.1 and 3.2).[9]

Besides inheriting Porfirian schools, the SEP also founded its own schools, including the Escuela Tecnológica para Maestros (Technological School for Teachers), established to train young men to be technically knowledgeable primary-school teachers. Teachers with technical training were essential if the SEP was to impart practically oriented primary education. Although more women than men were primary teachers, the SEP's approach to adult education consistently emphasized education for men over that for women and thus ignored the demographics of primary teachers probably from a desire to increase the number of male teachers combined with a perception that technical

Figure 3.1. The physics laboratory at the showcase Escuela de Ingenieros Mecánicos y Electristas. The combination of whirring devices, serious expressions, and formal dress are all meant to convey the importance of the training these young men were receiving, training that was to be the foundation of Mexico's industrial development. The SEP under Vasconcelos promoted technical careers, like those taught at this school, as a respectable option for middle-class and elite men. (Courtesy of the Instituto Mora)

training was masculine. The Escuela Tecnológica para Maestros was closed in 1927 due to lack of funding.[10]

When the SEP planned to found a railroad school (Escuela de Ferrocarrileros) in 1922, it was with the hope of training workers who would improve the communication and transportation infrastructure, laying tracks and running trains to bind the nation together. During the Porfiriato, the United States had dominated the railroad industry, which ferried goods and materials to and from U.S. markets. The network's infrastructure was badly damaged during the revolution, and the school was envisaged as part of its reconstruction. Moreover, the school was intended to provide Mexico with the expertise necessary to

Figure 3.2. Auto shop at the Instituto Técnico Industrial. Opened in 1924, the Instituto Técnico Industrial offered training for modern careers, such as auto mechanic, as well as more traditional areas, such as blacksmith. Under Puig Casauranc, vocational education in schools like this focused more on skills training and less on theoretical training. (Courtesy of the Instituto Mora)

finally rid the industry of foreign (mostly U.S.) railroad workers. Male students would learn to plan freight and passenger movements, as well as to operate the rolling stock and telegraph as machinists or engineers. These industrial and economic goals were not without their political uses, particularly in consolidating the state's role as arbitrator of industrial conflict.

When the railroad school was proposed, the independent Confederación de Sindicatos Ferrocarrileros (Confederation of Railroad Unions) protested that the SEP school would undermine its role in training apprentices, breaking its training monopoly and creating a reserve force of potential strikebreakers. Railroad workers were among the largest sector of the organized working class to remain independent from the government-allied Confederación Regional Obrera Mexicana (Mexican Regional Workers Confederation, or CROM), and this independence threatened both the government and the CROM. Whereas Vasconcelos did not want any union involvement for the school, the railroad confederation asked that the school be under its supervision. Finally, against the wishes of both the railroad confederation and the SEP, the Cámara de Diputados (Chamber of Deputies) ceded administration of the school to the CROM. The school was expected to open near Mexico City's central Buenavista Station, attracting students from the Colonias San Rafael, Santa María, and Guerrero. Due to financial problems, however, work on the school was suspended and never resumed.[11]

The physical destruction of the revolution prompted the SEP to found the Escuela Técnica Nacional de Maestros Constructores (School of Construction Site Foremen) in 1922. Examination of the graduation requirements indicates that while the SEP promoted swift, practical training in its rhetoric, it also offered arduous and lengthy degree courses. To become a construction site foreman or oilfield technician, students had to complete four years of study and a yearlong apprenticeship. The shortest course available lasted two years. For those able to complete the full course, the rewards could be great: One graduate was earning more than a thousand pesos a month working for the Bank of Mexico. Yet the SEP hoped that even the school's dropouts would have improved their job prospects.

While promoting a strong work ethic, the Escuela de Maestros Constructores also sought to train a docile workforce. The school's code of honor taught students that questioning superiors was a sign of cowardice. The young men attending classes were told they had a duty to work as hard as possible, respecting the sacrifice their parents and the nation had made for their education. The school also prepared its students to live in "civilized" middle-class comfort.[12] Thus, the Escuela de Maestros Constructores promoted class harmony and the status quo: Workers who never questioned their superiors would not resort to disruptive industrial action. SEP vocational schools were to prepare skilled workers, but more importantly, workers who cared about upward mobility, not working-class militancy.

Schooling Women

Women, too, had their role to play in this project of national reconstruction and learning. Whereas vocational education for men was justified on the basis of economic development, vocational education for women was justified because of women's influence on future generations. Humanity was supposedly in "women's hands" and educating women would result in a better society.[13] Although the SEP offered limited commercial and business training for women, even at some vocational schools, for SEP policymakers, women's most important role continued to be that of mother and homemaker.[14] Focus on a professionalized domestic role was part of a broader ideological shift toward "modernized patriarchy," in which the male breadwinner would be sober and industrious, his children would be patriots educated in a public school, and his wife would maintain a tidy home and healthy family. The family — thus linked to the state through education, welfare, and agrarian policies — was to be the base of national development. Women in particular were pivotal to this modernization project because of their responsibility for creating an orderly, rational home and bringing up productive citizens. Thus, whether aimed at the well-to-do housewife or the poor working woman, most technical education for women offered through vocational schools and courses concentrated on the domestic sphere. Courses in *trabajos manuales* (domestic tasks) encompassed everything from mending to ironing, washing to childcare — basic skills that both Catholic and SEP educators agreed that women needed in order to run a household. In addition to running the household, women could also earn pin money through artisanal or crafts production. Women had learned similar skills since the colonial period, yet the ideology behind these courses was completely modern. The SEP courses professionalized domesticity, teaching women to attack household problems from the scientific perspective of a career housewife.[15] Ernesto Meneses Morales notes that women graduates could open their own workshops with their manual skills, yet all the primary sources emphasize that these tasks were to be done in the home.[16] Thus, the SEP encouraged women's economic activity as long as it did not transgress established gender norms: Women could manage their own homes, and do occasional piecework, or work to keep up someone else's home.

The Escuela de Artes y Oficios para Señoritas (Arts and Trades School for Young Ladies, or EAOS) had been founded as the EAOM in 1872, to train poor women, offering them an alternative to prostitution.

Figure 3.3. Physical education for young women, emphasizing grace and beauty, at the Escuela Nacional de Enseñanza Doméstica. Women's vocational schools frequently emphasized that their physical education programs took place outdoors, in the fresh air. Women's physical fitness was doubly important because of their future contribution to the nation as mothers. (Courtesy of the Instituto Mora)

Classes at the EAOS included cooking, flower arranging, clothing design, and hairdressing. All full-time students practiced physical education on the "ample terrace," which was covered to protect the young women from direct sunshine (fig. 3.3).[17]

The Escuela de Arte Industrial Corregidora de Querétaro (Corregidora of Querétaro Industrial Art School), named after a heroine of Mexican independence, was founded in 1910 and had been inaugurated as part of the centennial celebrations Díaz hosted. The building boasted an interior patio, with a fountain and carefully tended garden. Classroom wall murals combined abstract designs with art deco depictions of provincial Mexican scenes: prickly pears in bloom and barefooted, beautiful women. Offering both full-time degrees and individual courses, the Querétaro School was supposed to prepare single young women or housewives to become economically independent—

again based from their homes. Students in degree courses were required to take five hours of Spanish and arithmetic weekly.[18]

Named for the Chilean poet, the Escuela Hogar Gabriela Mistral (Gabriela Mistral School Community), founded in 1922, also trained women for domestic life. The skills students gained were intended to give them the means to earn a living and to better their intellect and character. The school that bore Mistral's name promoted her philosophy of domesticity, one admired by both Vasconcelos and members of the UDCM. The Mistral School crest showed a woman nursing a baby in one arm while holding a toddler in the other. With time, however, the Mistral School became more supportive of women as professionals; by 1928, the charter emphasized that prominent businessmen were to be invited to the school to give talks to the students on how to open their own enterprises.[19]

The Escuela Nacional de Enseñanza Doméstica (National School of Domestic Instruction) was to train women as modern housewives or teachers of domestic economy. One of the courses available at the Enseñanza Doméstica School was puericulture: the "scientific cultivation of the child." Originating in late-nineteenth-century France, the science of maternity treated mothers and children as national resources. Following this logic, intervention in prenatal care, childbirth, and care for young children was essential for the nation's future. Mexican puericulture was slightly different in focus, emphasizing infant and toddler care, rather than a selective approach to human reproduction and prenatal care. Because there were no appropriate textbooks available in Mexico, the teacher's personal experience became invaluable, and she was given ample freedom to design her course. During field trips, students visited the Casa de Cuna, a state-run orphanage, to practice bathing and playing with the orphans (fig. 3.4). The inclusion of puericulture classes in women's vocational education is one of the first indications of the shifting view of women and their role in society. Throughout the 1920s, women were increasingly tied to the state and objects of state intervention because of their biological and maternal roles in making and raising citizens. The political importance of motherhood, in turn, allowed women to argue for greater rights and justify their action in the public sphere using maternalist rhetoric.[20]

Full-time students at the Enseñanza Doméstica School could also

Figure 3.4. Puericulture class at the Escuela Nacional de Enseñanza Doméstica. Students watch as the dolls are gently bathed. Listed on the blackboard are the correct temperatures for bathing babies by age and important considerations in selecting clothing (uniform warmth, freedom of movement and circulation, cleanliness). Modern childrearing was to be based on scientific principles and formal study. (Courtesy of the Instituto Mora)

specialize in housewifery, learning about "good manners" and the "moral home." Courses were designed to teach future housewives to make beautiful homes on a shoestring budget.[21] A pleasant home environment was considered important to keep men at home, rather than loitering on the streets or visiting cantinas. Housewifery students also learned to be educated consumers who knew how to select the best produce, as careful shopping was another characteristic of the professional homemaker.

At the Escuela Hogar Sor Juana Inés de la Cruz (Sor Juana Inés de la Cruz School Community), named for Mexico's famous poet, students could also train to be housewives. Housewifery students listened to lectures about "daily budgets," "the importance of plants in the dining room," "washing and ironing men's shirts," and "general rules on how to behave inside and outside the home."[22] Again, the emphasis was on forming a moral home, operated in an orderly, hygienic, and rational manner.

The courses offered at SEP vocational schools promoted contradictory visions of women. Courses trained women for a life at home in which they would paint porcelain and worry about which plants to place where in the dining room, while simultaneously training them to keep house and family on a tight budget. Women were trained to be educated consumers who at the same time could make soap, jams, and clothing for home use or for sale, thus reducing their dependence on manufactured goods.

This emphasis on the domestic sphere occurred at a time when middle-class women were working outside their homes in greater numbers, as schoolteachers, nurses, and journalists, and also making their presence felt in the public sphere. During the revolution, women had participated in mass mobilizations against stockpiling of food and had demanded social services from the government. Perhaps stressing the home as women's proper place was an attempt to depoliticize them after the tumult of the revolution, in the hopes of keeping them out of politics and the professional workforce. A similar stressing of the domestic occurred in the United Kingdom and the United States after women's mass paid employment during World War II.[23]

For both men and women, courses mixed traditionalism and modernity: Men learned saddlery and woodworking alongside auto mechanics and electrical engineering. It appears that the SEP curriculum designers did not deliberately provide students with out-of-date skills, but simply did not understand the economic, political, and social changes Mexico was undergoing. While men's vocational schools modernized, teaching skills essential for national industrial development, both men and women continued to train in small-scale crafts and artisanal work, learning to run a workshop or to do piecework from home. Even if these skills still had market value, it was diminishing as machine-made goods entered the Mexican market and consumer desires.

Night Schools

Full-time vocational education was not an option for those who worked to support themselves and their families. A school inspector expressed popular sentiment when he wrote that the state, while not having a legal obligation to educate the working class, had a moral obligation to offer literacy training and to help workers improve their trade skills.[24] The vocational schools discussed previously frequently offered evening courses, and the SEP also opened night schools that offered primary education and skills training to allow working men and women to better their economic situations. No matter which courses they offered, these night schools required minimal expenditures from the SEP because they operated in primary-school buildings and used relatively inexpensive equipment.

In 1924, there were fifteen SEP night schools for working men and ten for working women. In these centers men learned artisanal crafts while women learned domestic skills and crafts making similar to the courses taught in the vocational schools. In addition, there were four Centros Nocturnos Industriales de Cultura Popular (Nocturnal Industrial Centers of Popular Culture) for women. These educational centers offered women workers primary education and also a marketable skill, such as hatmaking, shorthand, typography, sewing, or bookbinding, so that they could earn a living. By 1928, the SEP reported that there were only ten remaining workers' night schools and two Centros Industriales para Obreros (Industrial Centers for Male Workers) in the Federal District: Nonetheless, night schools still imparted primary education and such technical skills as cooking for women and carpentry for men.[25]

While some night schools were closed down, the remaining schools were subject to increasing regulation and expectations. For the early 1920s, I have found no examples of standard curriculum, while in the late 1920s, the SEP gave teachers detailed plans. In civics classes, male students were to learn about their constitutional rights; appropriate behavior during "games, meetings, and public events"; and about the "legal benefits of marriage." At the same time, civics classes discussed capitalism and the various forms of socialism defined as "laborism, agrarianism, cooperatism, and communism." Later on, civics classes addressed legitimate and illegitimate children and the issues involved in the recognition of illegitimate children. In hygiene classes, students were warned away from alcohol, tobacco, marijuana, and "irritating drugs" because of their dire consequences. Physical education, accompanied by singing, was intended to attract students, developing their bodies and minds while keeping them away from bars and cabarets. Through night schools, then, the SEP promoted a version of middle-class domesticity in which legal marriage and parenting, rather than cohabitation and illegitimacy, were ideals and in which students entertained themselves by singing rather than drinking.[26]

Catholic Adult Education

After the revolution, government agencies were not the only ones to respond to adults' demands for greater educational opportunities: Various Catholic organizations, operated by both lay and religious Catholics, opened facilities to teach working men and women skills and literacy. These vocational education centers generally offered Catholic doctrinal instruction, including catechism, and access to Catholic rituals such as baptism, first communions, and weddings. Since adult students sought skills training for immediate use and would not require certification to attend further education, there was no need for Catholic vocational institutions to incorporate into the SEP and thus no SEP regulation of the courses offered. Moreover, Article 3 did not apply to adult schools, giving these institutions more long-term security.

While my research suggests that Catholics offered technical training to women more frequently than to men and the focus of this section is on women, this inequality could reflect a lacuna in the archives rather than a genuine tendency. Religious orders, such as the Jesuits, had run vocational schools for men during the Porfiriato, and some of these schools might have continued to operate in the postrevolutionary period. If Catholic educators did favor women's training, it was because they saw women as the moralizing force in the family, making women's moral education more important than men's. Additionally, men's work required more specialized equipment: It was less expensive to found a sewing center for women than to equip a center for auto mechanics or electricians. Women's educational opportunities may also have been a response to demand: Men, more likely to learn trades in apprenticeships, had less need for such education. Finally, women's traditional support for and reliance upon the Catholic Church could have prompted Catholic educators to focus on them. A demographic consideration may have applied as well: In Mexico City at the time, there were more women than men, especially among young adults who typically attended vocational schools.[27]

The UDCM was among those organizations that trained working women, in direct competition with SEP schools, which were considered "dangerous" because they did not offer religious instruction.[28] The UDCM's Academy for women workers and office employees offered classes in clothing and hatmaking, machine embroidery, embossing, cooking, and singing. At the Academy, nurses from the general hospital, unionized through the UDCM, could take advantage of massage classes or train to become pharmacists. Similarities to SEP courses can be found on both a general level, i.e., the types of classes available, and in the ideals promoted. For instance, UDCM cooking courses included training in hygiene, theory and practice of food preparation and presentation, nutrition, diet based on age and health, and setting a pleasing table. In cooking classes, women were to plan a budget and keep their spending within it. All these topics were also covered in SEP cooking classes.

The UDCM Academy, however, offered more cultural courses than the SEP did, including piano, mandolin, singing, and drawing courses for the workers and white-collar employees who attended it.[29] It appears that the damas modeled these courses on their own ideas of appropriate leisure-time activities. Like the SEP, which sought to transform working-class and poor homes into models of modernity and hygiene, the damas not only promoted hygiene and modern homemaking, but appear to have modeled their courses on their own well-organized homes and lifestyles. Similar to the SEP courses discussed previously, most of these classes encouraged women to remain in the domestic sphere, using their skills to supplement their husband's family wage. Yet the courses offered by the UDCM in Mexico City diverged from both the teachings of *Rerum Novarum* and the resolutions of the Catholic congresses. While the church preached against women entering the labor force, the UDCM trained women to earn a livelihood through traditional means (such as crafts making and domestic service) and nontraditional means (such as pharmacist and masseuse). The damas likely knew that the poor depended upon multiple wage-earning households to survive, and they were certainly aware that the industries in and around Mexico City, including the textile and tobacco industries, depended on a female workforce. In their own homes, damas would have hired domestic workers. So rather than blindly following Catholic teachings on women's duties, the damas offered practical training to meet women's needs.

Nonetheless, the damas still held the home to be women's primary responsibility and most appropriate sphere. But the damas worried that women in the postrevolutionary era no longer knew how to manage their homes and needed to be taught how to make inexpensive, attractive, and healthy meals; to wash and mend; and to attend ill children. Training in domestic tasks also ensured that the damas would be able to find skilled domestic workers for their own homes. For instance, in 1913, the UDCM's predecessor organization, working with the religious order of María Inmaculada, opened a school for maids that offered courses on cleaning and managing someone else's home.[30] The school later helped graduates with job placement.

Of all the "honorable" means (meaning other than prostitution) to earn a living, factory labor was the most distasteful to the damas because of sexual threats from male supervisors. While SEP educators did not express the same distaste for women working in factories, they did not promote such work either, indicating another parallel in the education of adult women. The damas' horror at factory labor and promotion of domestic service as an alternative reflect their willing ignorance to dangers within their own homes and their dependence upon a ready supply of domestic labor. UDCM rhetoric made reference to the dangers of the factory bosses' appetites for women, without paying heed to the same dangers behind their respectable doors. In Mexico, rape was a common but seldom punished offense, and poor women were most vulnerable to this aspect of the sexual double standard. Delegates at the constitutional debates of 1917 joked about having raped their domestic workers. During the 1920s, Mexican feminists spoke out against the prevalence of rape and the leniency with which judges and juries treated it. With the new fight against sexually transmitted diseases, the sexual double standard became an issue of health and politics.[31] Yet the UDCM refused to confront the double standard, continuing to promote domestic labor for young women while ignoring the fact that respectable men could also have violent intentions.

As the 1920s progressed, the UDCM appears to have become even more accepting of women entering the workforce. Rather than attempting to return them to the domestic sphere, the UDCM sought to improve women's working conditions through unions, discussed in chapter 7, and the mothers' center. In 1926, the UDCM planned to found the Centro de Madres de Familia (Center of Mothers of Families — perhaps a play on the oft-heard phrase *padres de familia*) in Mexico City. The center was designed to offer working mothers a support group while training them in domestic economy and hygiene; yet the program was to be flexible and mold courses to members' needs. When writing the proposal for the center, the dama author used language now associated with the then-young profession of social work and techniques of psychology and criminology. For instance, center volunteers were to classify women as cases and gather information about family life and children for the subjects' files. This information would help the group leader understand the needs of members in light of their personal situations.[32] The proposal for the mothers' center came at a moment when the state, through social services, medical inspection, and increasing regulation of child welfare, was becoming a stronger presence in poor homes.[33] It was also written at a time when the state was limiting the legal, public presence of the Catholic Church and claiming for itself the role of arbitrator of public morality and well-being. Even as the state's rhetoric accused the church of being a barrier to progress, Catholic social actors sought out modern solutions to modern problems.

The Unión de Damas Católicas Mexicanas was not the only Catholic organization to reach out to the adult poor through vocational training. The Congregación de Nuestra Señora de Guadalupe y San Luis Gonzaga (order of Our Lady of Guadalupe and Saint Aloysius Gonzaga) operated a workers' center in the Campo Florida, an industrial region south of downtown. The young women teachers were referred to as *señoritas catequistas*, likely volunteers but perhaps nuns.[34] The center offered academic and vocational training, a savings plan, and recreational activities for working women. Vocational courses were similar to those already mentioned, including making artificial flowers, hats, ceramics, and desserts.[35]

The UDCM was joined by other Catholic organizations in promoting domestic service as an honorable occupation for women who needed to work outside the home. The Congregación de Nuestra Señora de Guadalupe administered the Casa de la Niña Obrera de [*sic*] Señor

San José (House of the Girl Laborer of Lord Saint Joseph) in Tlalpan, a picturesque suburb south of the city that had once hosted the Porfirian elite in its exclusive restaurants. The Casa de la Niña Obrera, located in this restful site, was to educate girls as domestic servants, work viewed as appropriate to their class.[36] Upon finishing their course, students found employment with the patrons of the center; in effect, the sponsors paid to train their own domestic workers. The center's founders believed it would benefit both the rich and the poor. The rich benefited by having a ready supply of moral maids while poor (men) benefited from a supply of well-trained Catholic women to court and marry. How the young women themselves might benefit was not of apparent concern to the organizers; however, since the Casa de la Niña Obrera fed and clothed its students, there was an economic incentive for girls to enroll.

Classes offered in Catholic vocational centers generally trained women to sanitize and moralize their homes but did not offer skills that enabled significant economic betterment or class mobility. For the most part, the poor were educated to become decent poor. Father José Castillo y Piña, when he founded a school for young women, made this static view of class explicit. A seminary professor, Castillo y Piña believed in class-segregated education in which school facilities matched the social and economic background of the students.[37] According to Castillo y Piña, class-segregated education protected the poor from having unrealistic expectations; he wanted his students to avoid the disillusionment and disappointment that he had observed in poor students who returned to their homes with ambitious goals after being educated amid material comfort. Some UDCM members, like the damas who moaned that uppity working-class women were dressing beyond their station, probably would have agreed with Castillo y Piña. Overall, the UDCM supported education appropriate for the socioeconomic status of the students, such as domestic training for working-class women. It is important to remember, however, that the SEP's action pedagogy trained children to be content with their social station in order to promote future class harmony. They were to join the ranks of the industrious poor who did not strive for social mobility, but rather supported the nation's collective progress, allowing for the wealth of the few.

Comparisons are easy to make between the programs of the Catholic Church and the SEP, particularly regarding the place of women. Many proponents of Catholic social action and key SEP figures would have agreed that women's primary duty and preferred place was in the home. Jesuit priest Alfredo Méndez Medina, the de facto leader of Catholic social action during the first half of the 1920s, noted that fostering domestic industries would contribute to the betterment of working-class families while keeping women at home.[38] Castillo y Piña concurred, training young women for the domestic sphere at his Colegio-Casa Nazaret. Meanwhile, SEP educators trained women to "conquer their economic independence" from the home while working as servants, housewives, or office workers, but none of the schools trained women for factory work. Both Catholic and SEP agents trained young women to manufacture luxury consumer goods that were of little use to the poor, and both sectors viewed the education of women as key to moralizing the entire home. Because I have not found sufficient records on Catholic education for men, I cannot make a clear comparison between SEP programs for men and whatever Catholic men's education might have existed. The SEP certainly hoped that skilled male workers would provide the engine for Mexico's economic development. Moreover, in SEP vocational education, men not only perfected their skills but also learned that obedience and trust were due to their superiors. Both church and state emphasized the importance of earning a living through socially acceptable work, which the Catholic Church also sanctified through Jesus' work as a carpenter.[39]

SEP schools responded to a toned-down version of revolutionary goals, a version that did not threaten capitalist development or industrial relations. Variations on the revolution's radical demands — including land redistribution, public ownership of natural resources, improved wages, and access to education — were all offered as gifts by a benevolent government. The national government used these reforms to bind individuals to the state through gratitude and loyalty. In Mexico City, increased educational opportunities not only responded to revolutionary demands, but also offered male students an avenue to obtain bourgeois respectability through technical training. The Porfirian middle class in particular had decried its lack of opportunity for advancement. The more conservative face of the revolution evident in Mexico City sought not only education, but also professional opportunity and access to the modern world of goods. These desires for an improved personal standard of living coincided with the goals of the victorious northern revolutionaries, many of whose leaders came from this professionally stunted group. When the Constitutionalist faction took Mexico City during the armed phase of the revolution, they commandeered the cars and homes of the elite not to destroy them but to enjoy them. After this faction triumphed, it invited the backbone of Mexico's economic development, male industrial workers, to join in this respectability. Students accepted the invitation. Photographs of students in the vocational schools depict serious young men, self-consciously facing or ignoring the camera but sharing a preference for starched shirts, plastered-down hair, and polished shoes.

While the virtues promoted in the vocational curricula were generally conservative, some students would remember only the armed phase of Mexico's history — not the *pax porfiriana*. No doubt some of the students in adult education were among those migrants who had fled violence and hunger in the countryside; perhaps students in vocational schools had fought, followed the troops, or participated in street mobilizations in Mexico City. One of the primary interests of church and state was to instruct students who had lived through the revolution that the time for settling grievances through violence was over. Education was a tool of social control, made more important because control had only recently been re-established and, in some quarters, that control was still tenuous. But for education to be an effective tool of social control, church and state needed loyal teachers. The next chapter discusses the teachers who both implemented and altered programs of primary and vocational education.

4 Urban Missionaries

Teachers, Priests, and Volunteers in Classrooms

The programs discussed in chapters 2 and 3 provided the outline for school activities, but teachers also molded curriculum to suit the communities in which they served and their own goals. Thus, an understanding of who these teachers were and the lives they led is crucial for any examination of education. After a brief discussion of teachers during the Porfiriato and revolution, in this chapter I study the working conditions and problems of municipal teachers between 1917 and 1921, afterward addressing similar questions for teachers working under the new SEP. The high profile of education under the revolutionary governments did not improve working conditions or status for teachers, and they continued to grapple with the same difficulties that municipal teachers had faced. Catholic teachers faced similar problems under even more uncertain circumstances because of the precarious political and financial situation of many Catholic schools. This chapter closes with an investigation of the volunteers and priests whose work was essential to running Catholic primary schools.

Porfirian and Municipal Teachers

During the Porfiriato, teachers' living and working conditions reflected the low status and pay that had been accorded the profession throughout the nineteenth century. Although demand for teachers increased with Minister of Public Instruction Joaquín Baranda's emphasis on their importance, salaries and working conditions remained abysmal. Luz Elena Galván de Terrazas has used teachers' letters to Díaz to demonstrate their dire circumstances. Teachers asked Díaz for various forms of basic aid, even clothing, because they could not afford to dress properly. Mexico City teachers generally lived among the poor in cramped quarters under stairwells or in small rooms in tenement housing. They had entered teaching hoping to improve their economic circumstances, only to find themselves struggling to survive. Justo Sierra lamented that teachers were expected to be martyrs, and he called for salaries that would allow teachers to meet their basic needs.[1] Unfortunately, his humane call was ignored and teachers continued to earn a pittance throughout the period under investigation and afterward.

Low wages and even lower social standing gave teachers ample reasons for discontent, and historians point to teachers as active participants in the revolution. A combination of ideological and practical considerations, as well as teachers' status as community leaders, propelled them into the revolt. Teacher participation in the revolution was not limited to a particular geographic region or to a particular revolutionary faction. In rural Tlaxcala at the end of the Porfiriato, teachers were involved in local anti-reelection clubs; Tlaxcalan teachers who had studied in Puebla also maintained ties to radical groups in that city. At the men's normal school in Mexico City, eighty-five students participated in the armed struggle and nineteen died. Various teachers at the women's normal school collaborated with Carranza against Huerta, as nurses or secretaries. Women teachers also acted as messengers for the Villistas and Zapatistas. Even teachers who remained in their classrooms used their position to promote the revolution.[2]

While individual teachers played important roles in the armed struggle and former teachers participated in revolutionary governments, those who returned to their classrooms found that their meager salaries were still late and their status still low. Claude Fell blames teachers for allowing themselves to be martyrs rather than struggling to better their conditions, yet teacher participation in the revolution and their later attempts to unionize undermine his conclusions. I suspect that the low wages and social stigma of teaching were partially a result of the high proportion of women in classrooms. Without improvement to the profession, there was little incentive for men, who had more lucrative and respected opportunities open to them, to become educators.[3]

If anything, conditions deteriorated under municipal governments, which controlled primary education after 1917, because the federal government did not offer the municipalities any extra funding to cover the new expenditure.[4] Difficult working conditions were public knowledge and helped garner support for teachers. One group of angry mothers complained to the Mexico City municipality that teachers' poverty forced them to work multiple jobs, leaving insufficient time for classroom preparation and perhaps harming children's education. Other groups in Mexico City supported the teachers: In July 1918, students and industrial workers staged a joint demonstration demanding that municipal teachers receive preferential payment of their salaries over other municipal employees.[5]

Even though municipal authorities were aware of the problems that teachers faced, including the need to work several jobs just to survive, teachers were nonetheless banned from holding multiple positions in May 1918. Although it is doubtful that the ban was enforced, it does indicate lack of sympathy with the teachers' plight.[6] Financial instability eventually prompted Federal District teachers to ask the various municipalities to alter their school schedule to one long session rather than separate morning and afternoon sessions. Teachers said that they could not afford to eat enough to work effectively in both the morning and afternoon and, with the afternoon free, they would be able to look for other positions. While the municipalities considered the change, in October 1918 President Carranza made the federal government responsible for paying teachers' salaries, thus ending the rationale for altering the school schedule.[7]

The first teachers' associations in the Federal District date from this period: The Liga de Profesores de la Ciudad de México (League of Mexico City Teachers) was founded in 1919 and endorsed the federalization of primary education as a remedy to municipal difficulties. The problems the teachers' league faced were exacerbated when the federal government announced that after 10 May 1919 it would no longer pay salaries. Of all the municipalities in the Federal District, only San Angel was able to pay its teachers. Caught between these governmental bodies were the frustrated and desperate teachers. The Liga del Distrito Federal (Federal District League — it is not clear whether this was another union) sent a list of demands, including regular and timely payment of wages, to the various municipalities. The municipalities of Coyoacán, Mexico City, and Tacubaya, delinquent employers all, did not even respond to the league's demands. With few remaining alternatives, the Liga del Distrito Federal resolved that teachers, except for those who worked in Mexico City night schools, would suspend classes for five days. The organization probably exempted night-school teachers to garner working-class support, and they certainly courted the press. Various unions affiliated with the CROM, including the unions of newspaper workers and typesetters, supported the league's suspension of classes. Other workers threatened to strike in solidarity if teachers' requests were not granted, while the law faculty and the Preparatoria Nacional (National Preparatory School) suspended their classes in support of the two thousand municipal teachers who had walked out of their schools. Students at the normal schools also supported the teachers' walkout.

Although suspension of classes looked like a strike, the league denied that it was one; rather, it claimed the suspension of classes was a break to give all sides time to reach a solution. The municipalities, nonetheless, dismissed all the teachers who walked out. Teachers who had not walked out continued to work in the same difficult conditions. On 20 August 1919, the Federal District municipal presidents said that they could not continue to pay teachers' salaries and they would be forced to close some primary schools. They appealed to the federal government for subsidies to avert the crisis. It is not clear if the municipalities received federal aid, but salaries certainly remained unpaid. Even when the SEP took over municipal education in 1921, Obregón's minister of finance, Adolfo de la Huerta, noted that he was still responsible for delinquent salaries.[8]

In discussing the financial plight of teachers, it is important to note the gendered aspect of the problem: More women than men were teachers, and women teachers — whether from the middle, lower-middle, or working class — appear to have earned even less than their male counterparts. It was not until 1920 that municipal women teachers (in theory) received equal pay to men teachers. Yet women teachers were much more dependent on their profession than were their male counterparts. With the exception of nursing, women had few professional careers open to them. Both men and women trained at normal schools, yet more women than men entered the classroom. Men who enrolled in normal schools often followed other careers, using the normal school for professional training and making useful personal connections.[9]

The people who observed at close hand the difficulties facing classroom teachers were the school inspectors, whose position had emerged at the turn of the century as part of the standardization of primary education. Inspectors were to observe teachers and principals at work, enforce school attendance, and communicate between the school and the administration. According to a 1921 municipal regulation, inspectors had to be qualified teachers, more than twenty-five years old, with at least six years of experience working in Federal District schools. Besides visiting at least two primary schools daily, municipal inspectors were also responsible for visiting the homes of truant children to scold their parents. Educational authorities also wanted inspectors to improve the social and professional circumstances of the teachers under their charge, while inspiring teachers to professional excellence. There were strict rules regulating their behavior to prevent corruption. Yet because inspectors played a key role in hiring and firing, as well as levying fines and promotions, they could easily abuse their authority and teachers often resented them.[10]

In 1918, with the revolution winding down, the Mexico City municipality began to enforce an ideal of teachers as chaste, dedicated young women like the nuns upon whom education had depended for so long. The Mexico City municipal Comisión de Instrucción Pública (Commission of Public Instruction) acknowledged the many requests from inspectors to dismiss married women teachers and sought to clarify the regulations on the matter. Municipal authorities were aware that dismissing married women might seem strange but added that when the needs of the students were put first, it was often "just" to dismiss married women teachers. According to municipal authorities, married teachers were often distracted by domestic concerns and could not concentrate on teaching. Even if they seemed to handle both duties without problems, that was only an illusion. Marriage and teaching were incompatible, as both required full-time dedication, and home life was a higher duty for women than working. The commission continued that most of the time, as was "customary" in Mexico, married women did not need to work because a husband could support his family. Yet anecdotal evidence regarding the poverty of municipal teachers and their recourse to unionization belies the claim that married women teachers did not need to work.

While the commission consistently referred to married women in its regulations, the term was used as a euphemism for sexually active women, and the commission's concerns had more to do with pregnancy and motherhood than marriage. Thus, the regulations concentrated on women who were most likely to become pregnant or were already pregnant. The commission resolved that women in their first year of marriage, pregnant women, and breastfeeding women were all to be dismissed. Married women without children, those with older children, and women who were separated or widowed could retain their positions.[11] Yet in practice there were approximately six women primary teachers for each man and the municipality could not do without married women teachers. Therefore, the regulation gave the commission the right to make exceptions. One of the unintended results of this ban appears to have been that married women teachers lied about their civil status in order to keep their positions. A few years later, a Mexico City doctor remembered that women teachers hid their marriages because they needed to work.[12] The question of married women teachers also concerned the SEP, as discussed later.

SEP Teachers

Revolutionary rhetoric exalted teachers as missionaries bringing the fruits of the revolution to all of Mexico. In a typical passage, Vasconcelos proclaimed that President Obregón was trading soldiers for teachers and barracks for schools. Discursively, teachers had become the new soldiers in the campaign against ignorance, illiteracy, filth, and superstition. Teachers were lay saints and superheroes. They were to be knowledgeable about their subject matter, able to enforce discipline, and eager to improve their teaching skills. They would attend class regularly and punctually and exhibit exemplary conduct outside of school. To their students, teachers were to be modern crusaders, both wise guides and surrogate parents.[13] Yet exalted rhetoric was free and Vasconcelos was not able to increase teachers' salaries substantially or to improve the low social status of the profession; the position of SEP teachers was only marginally better than that of municipal teachers.[14]

SEP statistics provide a general profile of its teachers. Whereas most teachers nationally had little formal training, in the Federal District in 1926, 71 percent of primary-school teachers had a normal-school degree. Up to 80 percent of teachers in Mexico City had graduated from normal school, while in municipalities such as San Angel and Coyoacán, 70 percent of the teachers had. In rural areas within the Federal District, about 20 percent of the teachers had degrees. Teachers in SEP workers' night schools, however, were a different case. In 1926, only 32 percent of workers'-night-school employees, including principals and teachers, had graduated from a normal school.

In both day and night schools women continued to dominate the profession: In the early 1920s, women primary-school teachers outnumbered men nationally by nearly three to one. In 1926, among the primary-school teachers with normal-school degrees in the Federal District, there were 1,276 women and 321 men. While the majority of teachers were women, men were more likely to teach in higher education or to occupy positions of authority. For instance, in 1926 in vocational schools male teachers (813) outnumbered women (701). Regardless of their gender, teachers tended to be young, generally between twenty and forty years old.[15] A typical Federal District SEP teacher, then, was a young woman who had come of age during the last decade of the Porfiriato or during the revolution itself and who had completed normal school.

The SEP, like the municipality before, regulated women's employment based upon their capacity to reproduce, justifying its regulations as protecting mothers and children. SEP regulations insisted that married women would not pay sufficient attention to their students; teachers needed to be independent and able to give all their energies to their position. A woman might be an excellent teacher while single, but once married her work would automatically suffer due to the extra responsibilities of home and husband. Nonetheless, the SEP claimed that married women teachers with normal-school training could handle the double duties of work and home. This caveat to the SEP's policy effectively negated it. Since most of the teachers in the Federal District had normal-school training, the ban on married women in the classroom affected very few teachers. This exemption provided the SEP with a convenient way to balance practical considerations with ideology.

Like the municipal regulations, the SEP regulations had more to do with women's reproductive potential than with their civil status. In the May 1922 regulation on the matter, visibly pregnant women, women about to give birth, and women who had recently given birth were suspended due to their "delicate state." Teachers in earlier stages of pregnancy were allowed to work only in schools for women or girls. Pregnant women also had six months of maternity leave, three months of which was to be paid. To earn maternity leave, a married woman had to inform the SEP that she was pregnant by her sixth month. Teachers had to visit the Servicio Médico Escolar (School Medical Service) to be given instructions in hygiene during pregnancy, birth, and lactation. If a teacher miscarried or if her infant was stillborn, she could return to work immediately after receiving authorization from SEP health authorities. A teacher who completed her six months' leave was given permission to return to work if the SEP Department of School Hygiene reported that she was capable of teaching without harming her infant. Unmarried teachers who became pregnant had to resign as soon as they realized that they were in "an interesting state."[16]

After the 1922 regulation was issued, two doctors whose opinions could not have been more divergent were asked for their professional views.[17] Dr. Rafael Santamarina favored the employment of mothers as teachers because their practical experience could be an advantage in teaching hygiene and puericulture. During the first four months of the baby's life, Dr. Santamarina recommended that teachers be allowed to breastfeed twice daily at school. These nursing teachers would offer an educational opportunity for puericulture classes. After studying the regulation, he expressed his concern about the clause on stillbirths and miscarriages, believing that if a pregnant woman lacked moral fiber, the clause might tempt her to end the pregnancy or harm her infant. But on the whole, Dr. Santamarina urged the SEP to trust its married women teachers. For him, the situation of women teachers who left children at home was comparable to that of a male teacher leaving family members at home. Santamarina believed that young married women teachers were generally better mentors than single women of the same age and would train their students to form honorable homes. He continued that the SEP had to choose between the profession losing valuable teachers or women sacrificing their private lives to the detriment of their work. Dr. Santamarina concluded that, since women teachers were already entrusted with Mexico's children, they should be trusted with their own children as well. Dr. Alberto Román, unlike his colleague, confidently reported that it was impossible for women to combine marriage, pregnancy, and motherhood with teaching. He admitted that married women could work in factories without a problem, because these workers were not in a position to influence children. Román believed that the SEP should employ married women only if a medical examination proved them sterile. After receiving these divergent reports, the SEP amended its regulation. The amended regulation required women teachers to inform the SEP if they married. Moreover, pregnant teachers could return to work only after a miscarriage or stillbirth that had not been caused intentionally. Paid maternity leave was reduced from three months to one.[18]

Although women's health remained a high priority because of their reproductive capacity, beginning in 1926, all teachers were required to carry sanitary booklets, recording regular medical examinations by school doctors (médicos escolares). The regulations, which principally dealt with verification of sickness, appear to have been a response to a suspicion that teachers feigned illness. Essentially, SEP doctors had to confirm a genuine illness, through visits to the home if necessary, for teachers to be given sick time.[19] Teachers were not singled out, for during the 1920s, the SEP expanded its sphere of authority and intruded upon the private lives of students, employees, and their families.

While regulations grew ever more intrusive, salaries stayed low and public debate continued to focus on this issue. Between 1923 and 1924, salaries fell 10 percent as a result of SEP financial problems precipitated by the De la Huerta rebellion. In 1924, Universal reported that teachers even found paying tram fares a financial burden. Teachers returned home for the main meal in the middle of the day, thus paying four single journeys. Again, a single-session school day was proposed as a solution to reduce teachers' travel cost and time.[20]

Besides commuting to and from work twice daily, schoolteachers taught and prepared for classes and were under increasing pressure to receive more training. The SEP organized various courses of further education for teachers that, it claimed, would benefit them, their students, and society at large by updating their knowledge. This further education was available through a variety of means, including day and night courses at the normal schools, intensive courses in the winter and fall, lectures, recitals, museum visits, and "cultural missions." A mandatory lecture series for primary-school teachers included topics such as the role of teachers in children's play.[21] Another short course offered for working teachers was about the pedagogy of physical education. Most further education had limited SEP funding: Neither the vocational teachers, who taught many of the courses, nor the primary teachers who attended the courses were compensated for their time or materials. The headmistress of the women's vocational Querétaro School wrote that even though the teachers she supervised were living in desperate financial circumstances, they were asked to give extra classes and provide materials without compensation. In addition to the occasional expense of further education, teachers routinely spent their salaries on classroom supplies and materials. An inspector of night schools remarked that principals used their own money to solve their school's financial problems.[22]

For all the SEP's attempts to turn teachers into missionaries of the revolution, teachers still had their own ideas about what they wanted to do in their classes. A circular from 1921 reminded teachers not to organize inappropriate dances, even though children might enjoy them, because these dances warped moral development. Teachers were also warned not to use "erotic" reading material in the classroom, use re-citations from public theaters, or sing the national anthem with ribald lyrics. These behaviors apparently were common enough to merit a general circular. Additionally, the SEP complained that teachers left their classes without permission, which was justification for dismis-sal.[23] Problems were certainly not limited to Mexico City or to the 1920s, but were widespread in time and place. During the Cárdenas era, the SEP reprimanded educators in rural Michoacán for teaching their students songs such as "La Borrachita" (the drunken maiden), which according to authorities, encouraged alcoholism.[24]

Considering the long hours, low pay, and flurry of regulatory circu-lars dictating behavior, it is not surprising that teachers believed they had few allies. The Asociación Nacional de Maestros Normalistas (Na-tional Association of Normal-School-Trained Teachers) commented that "the humble classes of our society, and especially our workers' organizations, see us with scorn to the point of labeling us reaction-aries. Our intellectuals, who are the most capable of [helping us] find justice, consider us to be encyclopedic pedants who have Methodology as an idol, but are fasting from science. The true bourgeois classify us among their servants, as simple preceptors." Perhaps worse than the conviction of low public regard was the disdain of inspectors and ad-ministrators. The association continued, "In the perception of the im-mediate school authorities, the primary teacher is an employee with little honor, who has to be watched up close by a numerous Corps of Inspectors so that he will fulfill his duty."[25] Teachers, in turn, resented both inspectors and school administrators for their lack of experience in the classroom, personal biases, and arbitrary decisions.[26]

The SEP, like Baranda had earlier, promoted good teacher training as

a solution to these problems. Until 1925, Mexico City had three separate normal schools: one for women, one for men, and a coeducational
night school. The night school, for working teachers who had no previous formal training, offered a six-year degree. The day schools offered
the same degree in five years. When the normal schools were reorganized in 1925, the day schools, which served the more prosperous students, benefited the most. The biggest change was the merger of the
men's and women's facilities, because a coeducational normal school
"better reflected society." The new institution trained rural teachers,
missionary teachers, technical teachers, and primary-school teachers.
The new normal school also included laboratories, sports fields, and
space to raise animals. In these improved facilities, students studied agriculture and crafts as well as pedagogy. According to John Dewey, the
school was "housed and equipped in a way equal to any in the world."
As well, the new normal-school facility included a kindergarten and
primary school, offering students practical experience. Other students
were placed in schools throughout the Federal District for practice.[27]
After the merger, increased attendance brought the normal school to
nearly five thousand students total and, although class size increased,
the SEP claimed that these larger classes somehow represented daily life.

In 1926, the normal school added a new specialty called *visitadora
del hogar* (home visitor). This new specialization blurred the distinctions between teacher, social worker, and nurse. Home visitors were
trained for two years to work in the poor neighborhoods of Mexico
City, teaching everything from hygiene to cooking.[28] These young
women would teach the poor how to prevent venereal diseases and
what composed a good diet. They would inoculate and instruct pregnant women on prenatal health. They were responsible for the children
who played in Mexico City's streets, and were to inspect recreation
areas to ensure that they were moral and safe. Home visitors were
supposed to go into the homes of the poor to teach them how to relax,
sleep, bathe, and solve their conflicts without violence. At neighborhood meetings, they were to give lessons on history and civics.

Catholic Primary Teachers

Records for teachers in Catholic schools are not nearly as rich as those
for either SEP or municipal teachers. The limited sources available,

however, indicate that Catholic primary-school teachers grappled with issues similar to those mentioned previously, including low salaries, lack of respect, and an atmosphere of mistrust. For instance, assistant teachers (laymen) at Catholic schools in the Archdiocese of Mexico requested a 50 percent pay increase to offset the high price of necessities; they noted that they would be content with a loan, to be repaid once peace was restored, rather than a raise. The teachers did not individually sign the letter because their supervisor fired anyone who asked for a raise. Days later, their request, although acknowledged as valid, was rejected on the basis of declining church income. The teachers' fearful petition suggests that favoritism, blacklisting, and vengeance firings occurred in Catholic schools as in SEP schools.[29]

It is also important to recognize that these teachers were men, unlike most teachers in public schools. Before the revolution Catholic schools preferred to hire men. After the revolution, Catholics were more accepting of women in the classroom. The Sociedad Católica de la Nación Mexicana (Catholic Society of the Mexican Nation, or SCNM) hired men to teach in its schools during the early 1920s, while women teachers staffed UDCM schools for either boys or girls. By then acceptance of women as teachers had reached official levels. A memorandum from the archdiocese regarding the education problem refers to the need for a Catholic normal school in Mexico City that would train female educators. In this memorandum, probably dating from the mid-1920s, the writer also suggests that the students should be prepared to be tested by the government for professional recognition, if necessary.[30]

The need for a normal school was a frequent concern among Catholics. Yet the large and sustained financial outlay such a school would require made it difficult for Catholic lay organizations to tackle the problem. The concern was not limited to the capital: A report from the UDCM regional center for Yucatán called for the foundation of teaching centers to prepare Catholic teachers. According to a 1924 national report, the UDCM had only two centers for training Catholic teachers, which prepared a total of seventy women students nationally. In 1925, the SEP reported that there were seven normal schools run by private interests, but it is not clear how many were Catholic. Catholic teachers were also trained in seminaries and in convents, although these teachers did not receive SEP titles. Low salaries further contributed to the problem of staffing Catholic schools with good, well-trained Catholic teachers. A report for the 1923 UDCM National Assembly noted that there were many trained Catholic teachers, but that Catholic schools paid so badly that fully trained teachers could not afford to work in them. Thus, Catholic schools had to rely upon staff with less training.[31]

For both women and men, conditions remained difficult. The men employed in SCNM schools frequently complained about their low salaries and poor living conditions. The SCNM members decided to provide a five-peso monthly housing subsidy to alleviate the problem, yet the subsidy was of little help. For comparison, a priest whom the members considered hiring for catechism classes wanted five pesos *per class*. In 1923, SCNM teachers earned sixty pesos per month, principals, one hundred pesos, and aides, thirty. Only a year later the municipality reported that apartments in Mexico City rented for between eighteen and four thousand pesos monthly, with an average rent of twenty-nine pesos.[32] While no one in education fared very well in terms of salary, Catholic teachers generally had lower salaries than SEP or municipal teachers.

Unión de Damas Católicas Mexicanas

Catholic schools also relied upon a network of volunteers to keep classes going. Members of the UDCM supervised examinations, planned parties for students, volunteered to teach classes, and distributed prizes at the end of the school year. Their attitudes and goals were incorporated into the educational programs of their schools, even when damas did not teach the courses. Some historians have both minimized the UDCM's prominence and charged that it was a puppet organization operated by the clergy,[33] but as I discuss later, the archival record indicates otherwise.

Most sources agree that Archbishop Mora y del Río appointed Jesuit Carlos Heredia to found the Asociación de Damas Católicas (Association of Catholic Ladies, the precursor of the UDCM) in Mexico City in 1912. Mora y del Río, an important proponent of Catholic social action, was made archbishop of Mexico in 1908. An active participant in the social action congresses during the first decade of the century, he continued to support Catholic involvement in Mexico's political arena throughout the turbulent 1920s.

The Asociación de Damas Católicas was founded to aid the poor and working classes, in particular through educational activities. The damas sought to restore Catholic values in society at large, while staying within the realm that the church assigned to women: charity, children, and home. The damas promoted their vision as a "reasonable" feminism in which women — rational, thinking beings — sought solutions to social problems.[34] One article that appeared in the UDCM magazine, *La Dama Católica,* advised Catholic women to stop being "beautiful animals" and to demonstrate their right to think by entering the debate on the social question. This call to action for Catholic women might have been prompted in part by Protestant and liberal critics who accused the church of making women into toys for their husbands' passions.[35]

Although Catholic women were prepared to debate the social question, there were limits to women's public role. The UDCM did not suggest that women were ready to hold public office or vote: Women's entry into politics would occur under the tutelage of men at some unspecified future date. Nonetheless, as Temma Kaplan demonstrates for Barcelona, even when women were simply defending the rights of their gender, their conservative actions could have "revolutionary consequences."[36] In this case, Catholic women's mobilization had far-reaching political consequences for the church-state conflict, as women actively defended what they perceived as attacks on their liberties and their religion.

The UDCM was organized on three levels; a national office oversaw various regional centers, which in turn oversaw local centers. In 1924, the organization had 13,625 members nationally, and by 1926 it had grown to 22,885 members. Also in 1924, the Mexico City regional center grew from 1,404 to 1,714 members. Of course, active membership must have been much smaller: The documentary record frequently shows Father Leopoldo Icaza, supervisor of the Mexico City regional center, cajoling and pleading with damas to become more involved.[37] The fifteen sections under the Mexico City regional center encompassed different aspects of the union's work, such as schools, moralization of the press, and clothing donations for the poor (fig. 4.1).

Although membership regulations stated that the UDCM was open to all women who encouraged the promotion of Christian values in the home, the organization acquired the reputation of drawing members

Figure 4.1. The UDCM general council, May 1925. UDCM national president Elena Lascurain de Silva sits in the front row, left, and Father Leopoldo Icaza, supervisor of the Mexico City regional center, sits next to her. (Courtesy of the Archivo Histórico de la Unión Femenina Católica Mexicana)

exclusively from the upper classes. To the damas this was an unfounded charge, as different levels of membership allowed women to be active members without paying dues. Yet concern about the lack of socio-economic diversity promoted the creation of specific sections within the UDCM, such as youth and popular centers for young women, to attract the poor. Moreover, the UDCM proposed finding a few talented working-class women who could organize activities to appeal to the "humble." Even as they planned to study why working-class women did not join, however, members reminded themselves that quality was better than quantity.[38] It is likely that women from the working classes did not join the UDCM because of limitations on their time and energy, while the condescending attitudes of some damas must have further alienated women workers.

The activities in which *"clase humilde"* (humble class) women participated nonetheless demonstrate that the organization was in constant contact with working-class women who, while not rushing to membership, joined UDCM unions and attended UDCM schools. Concern that not enough working-class women were involved in the organization was a recurring theme, as was concern about the form their involvement should take. In the 1925 national congress, the damas admitted that although they wanted more working-class participation, class distinctions must be maintained because poor women had neither enough training nor enough "tact" to direct the organization's work.[39]

There are indications that UDCM membership in Mexico City was largely divided between upper- and middle-class women, although at least one member was a teacher and another was a headmistress in a federal school. Either of these women could have been lower middle class or lower class. Most members of the Mexico City center's Schools Section lived in the new middle-class colonias of Juárez and Roma, with their wide, paved streets and "splendid public fountains." A few damas continued to reside in the once-posh historic city center, suggesting that they were stubborn old money or only marginally well off. Some UDCM members were women of substantial means: National president Elena Lascurain de Silva, from a prominent Catholic family, was an owner of several properties. But there are other indications that some damas needed to work for a living. The UDCM offered its members training (cooking, French, typing, and the art of domestic economy) at the "good price" of a peso a course, while a book about typing and office skills was recommended to the damas as "very useful."[40]

These indications that the UDCM included women of different backgrounds notwithstanding, topics of concern to the damas — such as the moralization of female domestic workers or the problem of working-class women aping elite styles — reflect the prejudices of the privileged and the middle class. *La Dama Católica* offered the "Señora de la Casa" (lady of the house) a fashion page and recipes including beef in white wine, macaroni soup, and chocolate ice cream. One advertisement promoted a boarding school in the United States while another lauded automatic pianos from Kimball: "There are none cheaper." An advertisement for lots in the middle-class Colonia Condesa, "the first garden city of Mexico" lured prospective buyers with the promise of access to the most modern church around. Already 60 percent of the lots had been purchased, so readers were advised to inquire without delay.[41]

While their attitudes toward the poor mixed religious fervor with condescension, Mexico City damas, women who had witnessed a revolution, did go into disadvantaged neighborhoods to offer charity and aid, defying the spatial limitations of their class and gender. Their charity work took them to the "marginal city" of crowded tenements and pulquerías, inherently challenging the social boundaries imposed on them.[42] Responding to the social upheaval precipitated by the revolution, they opened soup kitchens for the "deserving" poor and donated clothing to orphans. When the epidemic of Spanish influenza swept the capital in 1918, damas rallied doctors and pharmacies to donate services or, when necessary, purchased medicines themselves. The damas congratulated themselves on their altruism in seeking out the poor. One dama, who had volunteered in Mexico City's Red Cross Hospital during the revolution, remembered how wounded soldiers became gentle, polite young men when faced with their generous volunteer nurses. Still, the revolution took its toll. During the difficult years, only eight women regularly attended general meetings while the association president fled Mexico between 1914 and 1919. The organization's economic situation grew precarious: The damas reduced service at the soup kitchens in November 1915 and, shortly thereafter, the treasurer suggested selling the organization's chairs to stave off financial crisis. Eventually, some of the damas sold their earrings to generate revenue. Nonetheless, the organization survived the lean years and, with the end of the revolution, was able to expand its work considerably.

These years of revolution had convinced the damas that if they did not address the social question, the future could only offer more violence. One dama remembered that Father Alfredo Méndez Medina had exhorted them in a series of lectures about women's influence on society that they could not be indifferent in the face of the threats that surrounded them. But in order to better things, they had to give up their pride and go to the people, people who would follow the damas' influence if the damas truly loved them.[43]

Méndez Medina, a prominent Catholic social action Jesuit, had studied social action organizations in Europe, attending classes in sociology and participating in Catholic congresses while abroad.[44] Among the Catholic social activists, he was unique in his training and methods. Between 1920 and 1925, Méndez Medina acted as the first director of the Secretariado Social Mexicano, which organized and guided Catholic social action. Determined to witness Catholic social action projects himself, Méndez Medina spent his first year as SSM director traveling throughout the country and speaking with laypeople and clerics about their work. Because the UDCM was an important national organization, Méndez Medina was also involved in its activities, including publishing articles in *La Dama Católica* and offering courses in UDCM schools and to damas about unionization.

Father José Castillo y Piña, who had studied at Mexico City's Seminario Conciliar (Theological Seminary) and in Rome, was another contributor to *La Dama Católica*. He lectured in Spanish, geography, cosmography, sociology, and church history at the Mexico City seminary.[45] A fervent believer in women's education, Castillo y Piña was nonetheless adamantly opposed to female employment outside the home. His ideas are demonstrated in the curriculum of the Nazaret School that he founded in Mixcoac in 1919.

As I noted previously, historians have depicted the UDCM as an organization dominated by the clergy. Laura O'Dogherty maintains that male ecclesiastical directors approved every UDCM decision and that the women followed instructions rather than creating a program that responded to their own concerns. O'Dogherty bases her conclusions in part on the fact that priests or laymen wrote the reports of new centers founded.[46] While these reports might have been written by men, reports on the work of the centers published in the *La Dama Católica* were always written by the damas themselves. Moreover, the Mexico City regional center had fifteen sections and Father Icaza would have been unable to oversee every aspect of the UDCM even if he so desired. Icaza was also the ecclesiastical director for the UDCM national center and a parish priest. Recognizing that Icaza was overburdened, in 1925 Archbishop Mora y del Río gave another cleric the UDCM national position.

Reading the minutes of the Mexico City regional center's Schools Section, it becomes clear that the damas directed the section, while Icaza ensured that their work was appropriate for a Catholic organization. Of the sixty-four meetings that took place between 1920 and

1926, Icaza was absent from twenty-nine. During the meetings that he did attend, he occasionally offered ideas that the damas accepted or rejected. But the damas themselves ran the Schools Section; they discussed how to proceed, sought sponsors, and founded new schools.[47]

When Méndez Medina acted as the ecclesiastical advisor to the first national UDCM congress in 1922, he presided over debates and the drafting of the new union's statues. Yet the newly constituted UDCM did not blindly follow Méndez Medina's wishes. Tellingly, the membership ignored the priest's suggestion that they change their name to the Unión Femenina Católica Mexicana (Mexican Feminine Catholic Union): They were damas and preferred to be addressed as such.[48] Every regional center and many of the local centers sent a delegation of at least one woman and usually several to the national conference. At the conference itself, eighteen women presented papers on various themes.[49] Moreover, individual damas clearly used the organization to realize personal goals and find some level of professional satisfaction. Thus, under the auspices of the UDCM, elite and middle-class women left the domestic sphere, organized projects, wrote and presented conference papers, attended meetings, and became public leaders. They also crossed invisible boundaries, entering into dusty neighborhoods with trash-filled streets to visit the schools discussed in the next chapter, where they witnessed the problems and successes of daily classroom education.

Although the revolution brought great changes to the lives of Mexicans, for teachers the struggle for daily survival remained the same. This profession — which women entered in increasing numbers, hoping for financial security, respect, and opportunity — remained underpaid and undervalued. Yet teachers' decisions were crucial in implementing any educational reform. Teachers were the link between programs of institutionalizing the revolution and the students who were its subjects. As educators and administrators knew, teachers had the greatest influence on education at the classroom level; as a result they came under increasing regulation and pressure for further training. A corps of inspectors, often resented because of their arbitrary use of power, linked municipal and later Catholic and SEP schools to the central educational administration. Their detailed and frequent reports are crucial to the reconstruction of day-to-day educational practices that follows.

Inspectors were also responsible for overseeing Catholic schools that were incorporated into the SEP. Catholic teachers suffered similar or worse professional situations, particularly if they worked for lay charitable organizations. Meanwhile, in the postrevolutionary period Catholics had come to accept primary teaching, in particular, as an appropriate profession for women. Women were also crucial to the work of Catholic lay social action organizations, especially that of the UDCM. Members of that organization were actively involved in charitable work that sought to address social needs resulting from the revolution, an overlap with the state's interests that pointed them toward eventual conflict.

5 Daily Life in Primary Schools

Moralization in an Immoral City

Teachers, inspectors, students, and their families implemented the programs discussed in chapter 2, altering them to suit local needs. Parents, teachers, and administrators did not necessarily agree on how to help children and their communities. Thus, everyday school activities were as much a result of negotiation as they were a product of official programs. Moreover, financial limitations hampered successful implementation of educational reforms. In this chapter I examine primary education from the years of reconstruction immediately after the Constitutionalist victory to the period of state building under Obregón and Calles. At the time of the Constitutionalist victory, municipal schools offered the only widespread education available in the Federal District. These were the first schools in which teachers promoted the new ideologies coming out of the upheaval. After examining classroom activities and problems in municipal schools between 1917 and 1921, I turn to the subsequent federal takeover of Mexico City's municipal schools. Municipal schools were replaced with SEP schools, which continued to face problems of poor attendance and lack of supplies. Examination of Catholic primary schools, indicating similarities and differences between public and private primary education, ends this chapter.

Municipal Primary Schools

The transfer of primary schools from federal to municipal jurisdiction in 1917 shifted political oversight and financial responsibility from one administering body to another; the municipality inherited an intact primary education system. Overwhelmed by the burden of these newly acquired primary schools and with no new revenues, the Mexico City municipality could not pay rent on the buildings, much less teachers' salaries. Classrooms were crowded, with one teacher responsible for up to one hundred children. Children sat on dirt floors, as their schools had no benches, while their teachers worked without desks. Overcrowding would have been worse were it not for high truancy rates.

Dull classes also lowered attendance, and schools had to compete with the sights, smells, and sometimes-lurid scenes of Mexico City that interested students more than school did. One principal expressed frustration that her girls skipped school to go to the cinema, with parental permission. Other truant children loitered in the capital's streets, gambling with their snack money or smoking.[1]

Regardless of why absences occurred, when they became a regular problem, the Mexico City municipality authorized the *policía escolar* (school police) to visit homes and encourage children to return to school. Yet the sheer number of truants made their task next to impossible. Meneses Morales estimates that in one year, 33 percent of the 96,000 students enrolled in Federal District primary schools stopped attending classes. Moreover, average enrollment in public and private primary schools fell from 92,415 students in 1917 to 73,614 in 1918, approximately a 20 percent drop. Cash-strapped municipalities were sometimes forced to close schools, so many children did not have a school available, even if their parents wanted them to attend school. In the Federal District, 191 municipal schools, of which 101 were in Mexico City, were closed.[2] School closures, moreover, contributed to the problem of overcrowding.

The reputation that municipal schools had for spreading the war-related diseases that ravaged Mexico City between 1915 and 1918 contributed to low enrollment and high truancy. Typhus, smallpox, malaria, and the Spanish influenza pandemic had all spread quickly through Mexico City's weakened population. While church leaders ordered masses to be held outside and authorities shut public buildings, municipal authorities, school hygiene inspectors, and teachers ignored these epidemics. Instead, they feuded about how to treat routine childhood ailments that were also epidemic but certainly not life threatening.[3] Municipal educational authorities' disregard for the role of schools in spreading disease no doubt contributed to the schools' bad reputation.

While apparently unconcerned about typhoid and smallpox, municipal school principals reported that brothels, pulquerías (dispensaries of pulque), public baths, and markets exposed their students to scandal, filth, and vice. Principal María Guerrero complained to an inspector that a small restaurant dispensing pulque had recently opened next to her girls' school and that her students were fascinated by the dive.

Guerrero assigned a teacher to monitor the school entrance, ensuring that students went directly home rather than loitering near the pulquería. Municipal authorities closed the pulquería within weeks in response to Guerrero's concern.[4] In other cases, schools were besieged by multiple threats to morality. A principal wrote to the municipality about the dreadful businesses that shared a building with his boys' school. The school was located south of the Zócalo on the San Pablo Plaza, an area that a fastidious foreigner described in 1911 as a "native ghetto where cleanliness is considered a sin and slothfulness a virtue."[5] The principal was disgusted to have a public bath open next to the school's entrance, while a pulquería operated in the same building. The bath created a health risk and the pulquería, a risk to morality, he claimed. Three months later, a hygiene inspector noted a brothel on the ground floor, in addition to the bath and pulquería. Why did the principal not mention prostitution on his earlier list? Perhaps he was not worried about the brothel's influence on boys, or perhaps limited time prevented him from updating the municipality. Because of generalized concern that pulquerías corrupted morals, they were eventually prohibited near schools, but as a 1922 complaint from residents in the Colonia Juárez makes clear, the legislation was only as good as its enforcement. Pulquerías continued to open and operate wherever there were sufficient customers to sustain them.[6]

Prostitutes also worked where their customers could find them. An inspector for a girls' school on Calle Allende in the city center complained that during school hours, streetwalkers threatened the girls' innocence. According to this inspector, every nook for three blocks around the school offered sanctuary to the sex trade. Although the school administrators wanted the prostitutes expelled, instead the school was transferred to another location. Prostitutes continued to practice in the city center and attempts to move them to *zonas de tolerancia* (tolerance zones) located on the fringes of the city met with opposition. The prostitutes feared a loss of clients, while the working-class residents of the receiving neighborhoods protested what they viewed as an invasion of vice.[7]

What, then, prompted principals to pen these horrified catalogues of sin to municipal authorities? Was it a shift in social mores precipitated by the revolution or a moral panic? Concerns about pulque and its immoral influences date back to colonial Mexico, but the Puritanism ushered in with the revolution added new urgency to these concerns. Sexual mores had also changed with the revolution. The upheaval had loosened sexual taboos as families were torn apart and more women were abducted, eloped, or lived with men without marriage. The revolution increased the population's mobility, both through military conflict and population displacement. This mobility fostered contact among various regions of Mexico and between the countryside and the city.

Besides fostering new behavior, the revolution and its aftermath introduced new pastimes and new fashions. Catholics, in particular, feared for the morals of young women who bobbed their hair, raised their skirts, and took up the tango. Nonetheless, brothels, public baths, and pulquerías had not emerged out of nowhere to colonize new areas. During the Porfiriato, too, municipal schools had been located in tenements and had operated under conditions like those just described. In the 1902 novel *Santa,* the story of a young woman's decent into prostitution, Santa's brothel is located across the street from a municipal school. Moreover, both before and after the revolution, children attended school close to home. The "bad examples" that children witnessed in the streets, pulquerías, and tenements around their schools were similar to what they saw near or in their own homes. These children were not entirely innocent either. Children began gambling and smoking while still in primary school. What may have caused principals to write to the municipality was a lower tolerance level toward vice, as revolutionaries looked upon these practices as degenerate leftovers from the Porfiriato. Moreover, public and private spaces were blurred in these neighborhoods. Matters that the well-to-do conducted behind closed doors, such as arguments or trysts, took place in the patios of *vecindades* (tenements) or the streets outside pulquerías. Reformers since the colonial period had been trying and failing to regulate public behavior, and these letters perhaps represent an attempt to shield children from viewing what their teachers and principals understood as private matters.[8]

While some principals worried about children's morals, parents and other school principals feared for children's safety as Mexico City residents perceived a wave of kidnappings, car thefts, rapes, assaults, and murders. Although crime rates in Mexico City began declining in 1916 and continued to do so until the 1990s, there was a generalized perception that the postrevolutionary period was a dangerous time. Crimes became increasingly anonymous and unpredictable, while the insecurity during the upheaval, the public nature of revolutionary violence, and the breaking down of social barriers all contributed to an atmosphere of sensitivity toward crime. For example, a principal informed the municipality that a gang of at least twelve men had attacked her school and the houses nearby. Her armed neighbors defended themselves but, as the school's porter had no gun, he was unable to protect them. The principal asked the municipality to arm the porter so that he could defend himself; the local school inspector agreed that the porter needed a gun. Principals were also worried about reported attempts to kidnap students, which caused attendance to decline. Inundated with complaints, the municipality declared "war" against these kidnappers. Local gendarmes were made responsible for the safety of children in transit to and from school, at school, and in the streets.[9] Parents particularly worried about their children's safety while walking to and from school alone. Although in Mexico City itself, crimes became less frequent after 1916, there was an increase in violent crime committed by strangers. Whereas before violent crime had often been between people known to each other and served to settle a dispute about honor, now violent death could come from a speeding car or a wild bullet.[10]

If a story in the Catholic magazine *Acción y Fe* can be believed, new forms of violence were present inside the classroom as well. The story tells of an unruly student, Valetín, who, upon being mildly disciplined, insulted his teacher. In response, the teacher hit Valetín, accidentally causing a nosebleed. Valetín ran home to tell his father, who returned to the school to threaten the teacher, accusing him of barbarism. The honor of both men was at stake, and when the father reached for his pistol the older boys in the class attacked him, forcing him to withdraw his threats and himself from the classroom. From the point of view of the author, the teacher, not the father, was in the right. The moral of the story was that discipline had broken down because of the revolution, and teachers were not even allowed to use corporal punishment when necessary. Even if the story is utter fiction, it speaks to a perception that when and where violence was acceptable had changed. While corporal punishment was now considered barbaric, quick recourse to the revolutionary pistol had become an anticipated behavior.[11]

One of parents' biggest concerns inside the classroom was coeducation. In Peñón de los Baños, west of Mexico City, parents attempted to
halt the merger of the local boys' and girls' municipal schools. Parents
saw no benefit for boys or girls in a mixed school; placed together, the
children would distract each other. They warned that if the merger
occurred, they would remove their children from school altogether and
illiteracy would be the result: "What is shameful to us is that today, in
these times of civilization, [our children] stay the same as our ancestors,
without knowing how to read, because of the despotism of past rulers
who occupied themselves with matters of transcendental interest, leaving the poor in obscurity." In this protest, the parents implicitly compared the past despots with the current municipality. These parents
even preferred to have their children work rather than attend a coeducational school. Although threatened with a boycott of the new school,
the municipality contended that coeducation was an "ideal form of
education." Actually, in 1918, single-sex education was not yet the
ideal, and the municipality was no doubt hiding economic considerations behind progressive rhetoric. Educators' preference for mixed
education did not begin to emerge until the mid-1920s; in 1925, the
first grade of all SEP primary schools became coeducational, to the
dismay of both parents and teachers. The next year the first and second
grades were mixed until, by 1928, years one through four were all
coeducational. That year the SEP was able to report that boys and girls
being in the same classes no longer caused upset.[12]

The municipal archives are certainly filled with complaints about bad
plumbing, low morality, and frequent theft, reflecting municipal inca-
pacity to maintain the schools. Nonetheless, records survive that demonstrate how Mexico City municipal schoolteachers attempted to im-
bue children with a sense of civic duty, patriotism, and the value of
work. These records also show how even in the most difficult circumstances, a good teacher could provide students with a sound education.

Teachers' plans indicate the values promoted in municipal primary
education. A poem for first graders to recite, entitled "When I Am Big,"
praised all forms of work, both rural and urban, in rhyming verse. The
teacher began the recitation by asking, "Pepe, Juan, Enrique, Tomás,
Luis . . . let's see, when you're big, what do you think you'll be?" In

response, Pepe explained why he wanted to be a farmer. In the following stanza, Juan was delighted at the prospect of becoming a blacksmith, while Enrique had ambitions to be a great carpenter. Tomás planned to be a teacher, telling stories to children and moralizing to adults. Luis hoped to be a printer in order to combine work with study, in that he would be able to read books before they became available to the public. The final stanza ended thus: "Work is life, work is peace, may each do what he's capable of. We all cultivate constant work, virtue, and honorability . . . WORK AND VIRTUE are the health of body and soul."[13] This poem promoted both artisanal labor and a strong work ethic, as well as revolutionary idealism about the value of education and its transformative potential.

The topics discussed at the monthly municipal school general assemblies combined revolutionary themes, particularly respect for others and love of the land, with Porfirian ideals. Perhaps the most traditional, and remarkable, among the topics was the Ten Commandments, discussed at the year's first general assembly. Students also heard a modified version of "love thy neighbor": Care for rural day laborers because they were the country's strength. Students at the assemblies were urged to extend respect to all living things and to the earth, cultivating a plot if they were able to do so. Although students learned about modern inventions, such as the airplane that improved mail delivery and El Buen Tono cigarette factory's dirigible, monthly assemblies still promoted agriculture as fundamental to Mexico's progress.

Under the theme of *la raza* (the race), the students learned that their race was Mexican, by virtue of their having been born in Mexico. Thus, in postrevolutionary municipal education, Mexican became a race that united different ethnic and class groups. Students were to love Mexico, starting with the place where they were born, because love of the Mexican earth was what defined Mexicans. The municipal rhetoric unified Mexicans across regional and ethnic boundaries, emphasizing equality and respect for all. Indigenous peoples were the students' "brothers," *mestizos* (people of mixed Spanish and indigenous blood) could equal and even supersede foreigners, while the campesino and the professional were of equal value to the nation. Within their school community, students learned that there were no differences between rich and poor children, who had the same duties and rights. Through a discourse of mutual respect and unified racial heritage, these assemblies were intended to unite the country after a generation of warfare and to erase the racial divisions wrought during centuries of history.

An emphasis on equality also provided students with a basis for understanding political equality. At these assemblies the students learned that in a democracy, while they could defend their convictions, they also had to respect the will of the majority. As loyal citizens, children would avoid recourse to arms except to repel foreign invaders. While arms were necessary for national defense, inside Mexico students learned to resolve their differences through civil institutions. Civics lectures included topics such as voting and the formation of political clubs and parties. Students learned that the press and mutualist societies were concrete examples of their freedoms of speech, association, and work.[14]

The assemblies also sought to impart a respect for authority, teaching children to work within the political system to effect change rather than resorting to arms. Moreover, despite the anticlericalism of the revolution, the Ten Commandments was the first assembly topic addressed. Yet for children who had grown up during the revolution, the simple idealism promoted in the general assemblies would have seemed hollow, as they knew that recourse to arms had been an efficient tool of political change. The children who attended these assemblies, in particular the older ones, would have remembered seeing Zapatista or Villista forces in Mexico City. These children would already be aware of the complicated political and social situation of postrevolutionary Mexico.

Civic education, not limited to assemblies, was also incorporated into classroom activities. Disenfranchised women teachers taught students about the political system in which boys would one day participate. Both female and male teachers taught groups of boys about the voting process and arranged mock elections. When elections occurred in Mexico City, the municipality encouraged its male teachers to vote and to explain the historic and civic importance of voting to students. Students practiced elections within the school, for instance electing classmates to the School Honors Board. Civics lessons were limited to the municipal level and ignored the federal government that sought to represent the revolution. Municipal educators used primary school as a place to inculcate support for local government, even as the future of both municipal rule and municipal education was in grave doubt due to the centralizing tendencies of the revolution in power.[15]

Federal Primary Education

In 1921, the newly founded Secretaría de Educación Pública took over primary education in the Federal District. On 11 January 1922, one hundred Mexico City municipal schools officially passed to SEP control, and negotiations were ongoing for the transfer of schools from other municipalities.[16] Minister of Public Education Vasconcelos had nothing but disdain for municipal education and believed that the public, sharing his low opinion of municipal schools, would support federalization. The process nonetheless was a difficult one because municipal teachers and authorities were loath to give up their schools. Under the auspices of federalization, the SEP physically occupied some primary schools, in spite of municipal protests and unsuccessful court appeals. Under orders from Obregón, the SEP informed all municipal schools renting federal buildings that they would have to leave. Municipal authorities and teachers, however, had no intention of giving up their schools, and in at least one case in the autumn of 1921, the police had to remove protesting teachers bodily.

At municipal school number 72, principal Dolores López Banealaria refused to abandon her school. In response, the SEP chained the doors and sealed the building as if it were condemned. Undeterred, representatives of the municipality smashed a window, opened the school's locked doors, and resumed classes. Because municipal representatives had broken the federal seals, Vasconcelos was justified in calling the police; twenty-two armed officers barged into classrooms during class to force the removal of the headmistress and teachers. The headmistress condemned the SEP's use of force, saying that there had still been opportunities for a peaceful resolution, while Municipal President Abraham González sent a telegram to Obregón protesting the expulsion. Two months later the municipality continued to operate that primary school, even after another armed expulsion.[17] Although an extreme case, this example demonstrates the high passions around education.

Throughout these conflicts, SEP authorities demonstrated more concern for asserting federal property rights than for the safety of the individuals, including primary-schoolchildren. The 1921 federalization of municipal schools and the 1926 attacks on Catholic schools have certain similarities. In 1921, municipal primary schools, although in terrible condition, were present throughout the city; as such, they challenged the SEP's ambitions to expand federal education. The schools also challenged the centralizing, state-building project of the revolution in power. Catholic schools, which represented a similar challenge, became the focus of attack in 1926, as I discuss in chapter 8.

There are also parallels between the treatment of municipal schools and the treatment of defeated revolutionary factions. Victorious revolutionary factions had taken buildings from enemies as reminders of their defeat and doled them out to supporters as gestures of good faith and to strengthen loyalties. When Vasconcelos had the police physically remove teachers from their school, he left no doubt as to which faction had won the educational struggle or how the government would deal with the losers. While the federalization of education undoubtedly had ideological motivations, the methods used were based on practical considerations as well. Even before the revolution, inexpensive rental properties had been in short supply in Mexico City. After the revolution, when the city's population swelled from 471,000, its 1910 level, to 615,000 in 1921, the housing market became even tighter. Migrants who flooded the capital helped drive up rents and make vacancies scarce. Therefore, the SEP could not afford to be generous with federal buildings if it wanted to expand its own education system.[18]

Although the SEP absorbed municipal schools and founded its own schools, it still could not educate all the children in the Federal District. Under Vasconcelos, the SEP operated in quiet cooperation with Catholic schools, admitting that they provided an invaluable public service. If those schools were closed, 20,694 children would be without education.[19] The shortage of SEP facilities was such that in 1923 the school day was halved in order to double the number of children which one school served. Francisco Morales, director of primary education, suggested that children attend either a morning session, lasting from eight until noon, or an afternoon session from two or three until five or six. One teacher was to be in charge of both sessions. According to the *Bulletin of the Pan American Union*, adopting the part-time schedule and hiring ninety-five new teachers enabled fifteen thousand more children in the Federal District to attend primary school.[20]

The schools these children attended ranged from brand-new facilities with swimming pools to rudimentary single-room schools (figs. 5.1 and 5.2). Many schools were housed in colonial-style buildings, built around a central patio. These thick-walled buildings were designed to provide refuge from the merciless sun but became chilly at Mexico City's high altitude. Decorations adorning the walls in the better-equipped schools included maps of Mexico or posters describing the dangers of alcohol. Street noises and snatches of conversation filtered in through the windows; vendors hawking their wares competed with the sounds of trams, cars, buses, and people chatting. While the hard, wooden benches provided for students would have been uncomfortable after even a short period, the children who sat on benches were lucky; many students crouched on dirt floors because their school had no benches. Many schools lacked other basic materials, such as textbooks, charts, and chalk. Doors fell off their hinges and plumbing, when installed, was quickly clogged. Hygiene conditions were so deplorable in some schools that, according to the Departamento Escolar, it would have been better for children's health not to attend school at all.[21] In taking over municipal schools, the SEP had taken over many of the schools' problems.

The SEP inherited not only the material problems of municipal schools, but also their students' bad attendance. Regular and punctual school attendance was not a priority for all parents or their children: Both had to be shown the concrete value of education. Education may have been a mandate from the revolution, but demanding greater educational opportunities is not the same thing as making a daily commitment to send one's child to primary school. A variety of factors lowered attendance. During the rainy season (June to September), when roads became difficult to traverse because of mud and flooding, absenteeism rose, particularly among students from poor neighborhoods with inadequate infrastructure. In 1923, the SEP responded to rainy-season low attendance by altering the school schedule so that children were not expected to attend school during the wettest parts of the day.[22]

The quality of education also affected attendance. Circulars suggested to teachers that if they taught well and treated their students with respect, they would attract and retain pupils. Another circular chastised teachers for being unnecessarily brusque, speaking to students harshly, and threatening them with physical force. Affection

Figure 5.1. This illustration of the number of students, schools, and teachers under the SEP in the Federal District idealizes primary education while presenting certain realistic aspects of schooling. The one-room school, complete with cracks in the plastering, is plausible, but most schools were not located in parklike surroundings, and students were not all this prosperous. The woman teacher is depicted as modern, with her short hair and skirt. (Courtesy of the Archivo Histórico de la Secretaría de Educación Pública)

was to be the ideal bond between teacher and student. Finally, a schedule that fit with local needs would also attract more children. Inspectors were told to study their communities in order to determine a viable schedule and to plan school holidays for seasons when parents needed their children's labor. Once at school, many children needed to be encouraged to participate in classroom activities. Students were reportedly timid and unsure of themselves when responding to questions. Director of Primary Education Morales believed that unless students learned to express themselves with confidence, schools would churn out weak-natured men, unprepared for life's struggles. In primary school, as in vocational school, the education of men remained the highest priority for the SEP.[23]

Tardiness also frustrated teachers and disrupted classes. Some teachers refused to admit tardy children, who then created further problems because they roamed the streets rather than returning home. Perhaps they loitered outside the school or went to the cinema, as students in municipal schools had done. To combat the twin problems of tardiness and absenteeism, in 1921 the SEP recommended that children who were absent for three consecutive days or were frequently late not be allowed to attend any SEP school. This policy would give educational priority to children who attended school regularly. It is unlikely, however, that the SEP had the means to enforce this rule: Students changed schools frequently, and communication among SEP schools was limited. Moreover, this rule would have punished the most vulnerable among the student population.[24]

At times, the SEP targeted its assistance to the most needy children. Hunger had caused attendance and attention problems since the Porfiriato. In April 1921, Roberto Medellín, head of the Departamento Escolar, reported that he had observed primary-school students exhibiting symptoms of malnutrition; in fact, some children were close to fainting from hunger. According to Medellín, children from poor families ate only once daily and could not possibly pay attention in class,

Figure 5.2. Another example of an SEP primary school, Escuela Primaria "Horacio Mann," at the corner of Avenida Chapultepec and Calle Abraham González, Colonia Juárez. This school would have been considered an ample, modern facility when it was new. (Photograph by the author)

much less learn. At approximately the same time, Mexico City news-papers published a report on the terrible health of primary-school chil-dren. There was public outrage in response to the report and Vascon-celos was forced to downplay its impact, contending that the worst problem facing primary-school children was lack of care.[25]

Later medical reports, however, contradicted him. According to an article in *Universal*, most of the school population was made up of poor students who had high rates of tuberculosis. The alarmist article went on to warn that if nothing were done, many children would be dead within a month. More believably, the article noted that hundreds were also suffering from skin and venereal diseases. In the article Dr. Gil-dardo Gómez, from the SEP hygiene service, confirmed the high rates of disease among children, noting that only the "Chinese race" showed equal rates of "degeneracy." He blamed the prevalence of disease on hereditary degeneracy, alcoholism, improper nutrition, bad hygiene, and poor living conditions. The article's conclusions were based on statistics for more than seventy thousand children taken from the medi-cal exams each child underwent before enrolling in any SEP school. In a rebuttal the next day, Vasconcelos claimed that most children just needed food and a bath, and that the medical examinations were actu-ally unreliable because they had not been specifically designed for Mex-ican children. Perhaps to avoid further embarrassment, Vasconcelos lifted the requirement that all children undergo a medical exam before enrolling in SEP schools.[26]

In response to concerns like these, Vasconcelos suggested reviving Madero's free breakfast program. While the Cámara de Diputados debated school finances, an impatient Vasconcelos asked teachers to donate part of their salaries in order to start the program immediately. When they agreed, the organizational effort began. Elena Torres, the first director of the free breakfast program, had been a delegate to the Second Feminist Congress in Yucatán in 1916, had established the first Montessori school in Yucatán, and was a founding member of the National Council of Mexican Women. The breakfast service she ran doled out three hundred grams of *café con leche* accompanied by eighty grams of wheat rolls to hungry children. Wheat was considered to have more nutritional value than corn and, moreover, wheat promised de-velopment along European lines.[27]

The breakfast program started service on 9 May 1921, feeding 608 students daily. Torres personally served many of these breakfasts, often aided by Medellín. By the end of 1921, the program was able to feed nearly three thousand students at thirty-two schools each day. In 1922, the program received federal funding and was able to increase the number of breakfasts served drastically. Gruening estimates that the program served twelve thousand breakfasts daily, while the budget allowed for more than twenty thousand. Torres wrote that Vasconcelos had given the breakfast program employees generous authority to force teachers into line. A minority of teachers, unhappy because of the deduction from their wages, told their students that they should be ashamed to eat at the expense of teachers' own children. A choral instructor at the Querétaro School for women was suspended for a month without pay because she said that it was unjust that the school staff had to reduce their salaries to feed their students. Moreover, the program added to teachers' workload because the SEP made them supervise it. The arrival and distribution of breakfast was often a chaotic time; both school materials and breakfasts went missing in the fuss.

Problems and resentment notwithstanding, the free breakfasts attracted more students, and anecdotal evidence suggests that the breakfasts improved children's ability to learn. It also improved their manners. At first, some students stole other children's bread or ate whole rolls in one bite. Students pushed and shoved each other and spilled their café con leche all over tables. Other children, shamed by their teachers' comments, claimed that they had already eaten even though by midmorning they were close to fainting from hunger. Gradually, teachers persuaded the children to accept the breakfasts and—an added benefit—to improve their manners. For example, students learned to wash up before their meal.[28]

Creating another concrete incentive to attend school, the SEP offered to buy school supplies for children from economically disadvantaged families. The program was to operate without the children's knowledge in order to avoid either embarrassment or false claims of poverty.[29] Principals were responsible for naming the students whom they perceived to be in greatest need of economic aid, so the success of the program depended upon a conscientious and efficient leader. Yet other SEP programs proved an economic burden for parents. A parent complained to the SEP that the headmistress of a girls' school had asked students to wear particular clothing for their final examinations, but a clothing requirement was impossible for poor parents to fulfill. Morales believed the matter serious enough to merit an inspector's visit. The inspector reported that the headmistress had only suggested that *if* the parents were going to buy new clothing, then these garments should be white. If the girls were not going to wear new clothing, then they should arrive dressed in their best. Eventually, Morales decided that even suggesting a color was against the "democratic practices" under which schools should operate, because many parents could not afford to purchase special clothing for examinations.[30] Concern about the financial consequences of education was common and parents protested against various programs because of the expense.[31]

Although many of the children in SEP schools were poor, classrooms did mix students from various socioeconomic backgrounds. Moreover, the prejudices and hostilities that existed in society entered classrooms along with students, teachers, and administrators. As Mary Kay Vaughan found in rural Puebla, education reinforced class distinctions present in the wider society.[32] Morales warned teachers not to curry favor with wealthy students and their families, because calling attention to economic differences made rich children feel "unhealthy feelings" and poor children feel envy and hurt. The SEP also informed teachers that it was unacceptable to select only well-groomed, elegantly dressed students for popular classroom tasks.[33] Classrooms, sites of mixed economic and social circumstances, were further complicated by the fact that changing social mores were also present. The SEP considered the dress and behavior of some young girls, particularly during school festivals, inappropriate. There were no parallel concerns for boys. In order to improve girls' behavior, principals were to speak with them and, if necessary, involve their families. Girls who did not meet the SEP's standards were not allowed to attend school festivals.[34] Educators took up the gauntlet of bringing these girls back to proper dress and comportment, but the struggle was difficult, because in all sectors of society the behavior of a new kind of female was causing concern.

The Madero School

The Escuela Industrial Francisco I. Madero stands out among SEP schools for its innovative curriculum, while also providing a concrete example of the policies and problems in education I have been discussing. Reports on this school may appear too good to be true; however, sources as diverse as Vasconcelos' memoirs, an article in *Excélsior,* and a report by Catholic priest Méndez Medina agree on the school's success. Arturo Oropeza, an artisan, had founded the school to teach working-class children practical skills, as well as literacy and basic mathematics. By providing children with skills, Oropeza — who was principal as well as founder — believed that he could break the cycle of poverty and exploitation that trapped the working class. Born in La Paz, Baja California Sur, Oropeza had no formal pedagogic training but seemed to have had a good understanding of how to motivate children. Described as simple and kind, he received visitors to his school informally, with his shirtsleeves rolled up.

Oropeza founded the new school in the Colonia de la Bolsa, a poor neighborhood filled with low, brown houses squatting along dusty, garbage-strewn streets. The elite and middle classes feared this area and would never visit because of its reputation for harboring crime. In this region, Mexico City's delinquent children found safe haven from the police. A writer for the *Boletín de la Secretaría de Educación Pública* described the children shouting and hurling stones at strangers who "invaded" their territory. While reports may exaggerate the wild behavior of these children, many had lived on the streets and had not attended school before.[35] Before the Madero School, the neighborhood had only one municipal school for two or three hundred students. (The range of capacity indicates how common it was to overcrowd primary schools.)

Oropeza began his initially single-handed campaign to educate the children of the Colonia de la Bolsa by moving to the area and offering a traveling library service to increase interest in education. Eventually residents asked the SEP for a school and were given the derelict main house of a former *hacienda* to use. Oropeza worked with local children to clean and repair the building until it was again serviceable. When the school opened in 1921, 60 children of both sexes enrolled; within eight months, enrollment had risen to 1,200. SEP reports attribute the skyrocketing enrollment to the backlog of school-age children in the area who had had limited educational opportunities.

Oropeza, believing that children would value an education they paid for, organized the school so children earned a few centavos through working and paid a few centavos for their education. At the school, children learned at their own pace, following their interests through integrated subject matter. For instance, in order to obtain a plot in the school's garden, children had to make a request in writing — encouraging them to read and write. Mathematics skills would allow them to calculate profits from their plot. Moreover, students learned traditional farming methods, such as how to create arable islands from swampy land. The *chinampas* that the children created in the school's lake earned it the name Xochimilquito (for the village of Xochimilco in the southern part of the Valley of Mexico where chinampa farming was still practiced). Children were also involved in their own and fellow students' education: Older children taught younger children carpentry or how to read while the Commission of Urbanity, made up of children, taught manners. Three girls and seven boys wrote, edited, and published a periodical entitled *El Niño Agricultor*.[36]

An emphasis on agricultural training appears repeatedly in all of these primary, municipal, SEP, and Catholic schools, suggesting that urban and rural were two extremes along a spectrum rather than oppositional poles. As I mentioned in chapter 2, the possibilities for students to garden were high even in urban Mexico City. Raquel Rubio Goldsmith's work on women's gardens in northern Mexico and Arizona during approximately the same time period suggests that the term *garden* should be understood flexibly. In nineteenth-century Mexico, the *patio* or *corral* had been the woman's sphere in which she planted herbs, fruits, and orange trees and cared for her rabbits, doves, and chickens. This space of flowering plants and singing birds was the heart of the home. For those who did not have sufficient land to plant or who had insecure land tenure, plants could be grown in movable tin cans or pots.[37] While Rubio Goldsmith examines gardening as women's work, in the Mexico City area, all students learned gardening, to make a space of productive refuge in their own homes and to be able to sustain themselves in times of hunger.

In 1922, the Madero School had twelve teachers, who were given wide discretion in creating and adapting programs to suit their students. For example, teachers believed that offering students meals would improve their attention span and energy level; as had happened in other SEP schools, regular breakfasts made the children alert and lively. When some students were reluctant to accept the free meals, the staff told them that they were not receiving charity but "justice"; it was not their fault if their parents were poor and could not provide for them. Nearly half of the students, 576 children, received breakfast daily. Eventually, the students undertook many of the organizational tasks, such as setting the tables, themselves. Once fed, students were groomed under the supervision of fellow students. Children on the Haircut Commission decided whose hair was too long and cut it. If a child did not want a trim, he or she could appeal to the Judicial Commission, whose student members were charged with arbitrating conflicts. The Madero School also had an infirmary with doctors and nurses on hand.[38]

The Madero School, like other SEP schools, was supposed to benefit the entire community. In 1921, the SEP sponsored a community beautification project in which parents cleaned the larger area and students cleaned the school's environs. Yet as Engracia Loyo notes for national cleanup campaigns later on, such a program could only be a temporary salve without improved infrastructure and social services. The Madero School also served the wider community through its library. In the evenings, the Madero School sponsored a literacy center for men and women using the teaching methods mentioned previously. Each Saturday, the Madero School sponsored a fiesta for parents and students, including lectures intended to elevate the moral and cultural levels of local families. At these events, the audience sang the national anthem, listened to piano or violin performances, and heard poetry recitations.[39] The public activities of the Madero School demonstrate the role that the SEP envisaged for its schools in leading community improvement.

While the SEP, and Vasconcelos in particular, sought credit for the school's successes, the Madero School also received donations and support from outside sources. The Ministry of Industry and Commerce donated the money to build the school's bakery. Private citizens donated farm animals and the Mexico City municipality paid for necessary construction work on the facility. Moreover, the Madero School's successes attracted international attention and national praise; Frank Tannenbaum called it the "miracle school" and John Dewey assured Oropeza that his school was among the most notable in the world. Medellín and Torres enthusiastically supported the school: Both visited regularly. On a tour of the school in 1922, the undersecretary of the Ministry of Agriculture and Development was so impressed that he donated five hundred pesos to the school's student-run bank. Méndez

Medina wrote a laudatory article on the Madero School in *La Dama Católica;* his only complaint was that the school did not offer religious instruction. Carolina Alcocer de Bonfil, a member of the UDCM, visited the Madero School and was impressed enough to hope that the UDCM would be able to win the school away from government affiliation.[40] Praise from such diverse sources indicates that the Madero School was indeed extraordinary.

Although it was never affiliated with the UDCM, the Madero School came under municipal administration in early 1925 at a time when its enrollment had declined to 550. Degradation of facilities as well as the municipality's difficulties in financing its remaining educational responsibilities were likely causes. The decline in enrollment, however, may represent the return to a more normal student population for the region; the high initial numbers may have been due to the fact that children had had only one overcrowded school available to them before the Madero School opened. The fortunes of the school were also influenced by political infighting. According to the *Boletín Municipal,* the SEP had tried to get rid of the school because it was "sectarian." "Sectarian" suggests that the SEP was no longer willing to support Oropeza's independent thinking; as early as 1922, Oropeza had reported to a member of the UDCM that he wanted more autonomy.[41] Moreover, in the mid-1920s there was a shift in the SEP's priorities toward central control and away from individual innovation. When the SEP was under Vasconcelos, who had little faith in professionals, Oropeza's unorthodox methods and lack of training were not an issue. Yet the combination of a new emphasis on professionalism and perhaps even Vasconcelos' favor itself appeared to kill SEP support for the school.

Undaunted, Oropeza continued with his innovations. By 1926, the school was organized like a confederation of unions. Each student joined a union associated with his or her chosen trade, such as shoemaker, baker, photographer, or domestic worker (notable since domestic workers were not unionized). Students were punished with fines or suspension of privileges, as if they were members of the CROM. Collected fines went to the school's central bank. When garden vegetables or student-made goods were sold, a portion of the profits also went to the bank. Overseen by students, the bank then made loans to student unions or individuals for projects.

Although the municipality planned to build a new facility that would allow the Madero School to expand, records do not indicate that the facility was actually built. By 1927, the financial and material situation of the school had deteriorated drastically. Workshops lacked even the most basic tools and the school was unable to cover its costs. Supporters of the Madero School organized the Comité Pro Escuela Francisco Madero (Pro-Madero School Committee) and staged at least one fund-raising benefit. The results of their efforts are uncertain and records do not offer any more information on the fate of the Madero School. Nonetheless, library books and swept streets alone could not improve the material conditions of families in the Colonia de la Bolsa. In 1927, when Ernest Gruening visited the area, he found most rooms housed two families, and twice as many animals as humans lived inside. The poor did not sleep on beds but on straw under a blanket that doubled as a coat during the day.[42] The work of one school could not transform the systemic problems of the Colonia de la Bolsa.

While the Madero School was exceptional, similar methods and goals were used in other SEP schools, particularly in the six model schools constructed during Vasconcelos' tenure. These model schools fostered hands-on learning in which the whole community was invited to participate. The Benito Juárez School had sixty-two classrooms, a playground, a stadium that could hold five thousand people, a swimming pool, and a library. Calles' children were among the hundreds who attended this school. The José María Morelos School had similar facilities, including eighty classrooms and a garden.

Among the model schools was the Centro Educativo "Belisario Domínguez" (Belisario Domínguez Education Center), named for the senator from Chiapas who was assassinated for publicly speaking out against the Huerta regime. The Domínguez School was built in the Colonia Santa Julia, which the SEP described as dirty, poor, and in need of help. Seventeenth-century Mexican architecture served as the inspiration for the building that was to welcome children to school. Facilities included a swimming pool, large gymnasium, showers, locker rooms, and land for gardens. Along the wide corridors, muralists had painted scenes from the Arabian Nights. The Domínguez School offered the community a four-thousand-seat amphitheater and, like the Madero School, a library. At the Domínguez School, students learned about the world around them through practical experience. They grew foodstuffs in the garden and learned to bake bread. Teachers were supposed to meet frequently, teach classes together, and exchange ideas. Like the Madero School, the Domínguez School was intended to improve local conditions. Parents were invited to hear lectures about nutrition in which they learned to eat fruits and vegetables while avoiding chile and pulque,[43] both staples and important nutritional supplements frowned upon by SEP reformers.

In 1926, five open-air schools opened in Mexico City, enrolling between eight hundred and one thousand students each. Dewey credited Puig Casauranc for these schools and praised them as clean, "well adapted to the climate," and "artistic." He also noted that their low cost would help the government accommodate all the school-age children in the Federal District in the near future.[44] The technical training offered in the open-air schools suggests that they implemented some form of action pedagogy, even though it had been officially eliminated from the SEP curriculum by that time.

Catholic Primary Schools

The problems and goals of Catholic primary schools were much the same as those just discussed for municipal and SEP primary schools. Some Catholic educators, for instance, shared the SEP's concern for practical training in primary education. The Sagrado Corazón School was founded by the parish priest of the Sagrado Corazón Church and run by the order of Salesian Sisters with donations from the UDCM. The school offered five years of primary education; between five hundred and six hundred students attended daily. The school ran a workshop with twenty sewing machines and, according to the UDCM Schools Section, many of the girls earned a living by producing goods in the workshop adjacent to their school. Most of the time, the school had more demand for its products than products to sell.[45] The students might have attended school for part of the day and worked at the machines for the other, allowing them to balance work and education.

The Sociedad Católica de la Nación Mexicana also operated free primary schools during the 1920s. As is true of municipal schools, the records of these concern material problems as frequently as pedagogic ones. For instance, while records do not indicate the number of children attending classes or how many years of education the schools offered, they do give details of missing doors and landlords' attempts at eviction. Problems with deficient buildings constantly troubled the SCNM and take up a good deal of the discussion recorded in the meeting minutes. Complaints from teachers and building owners, as well as visits by members of the society, brought dangerous conditions to the organization's attention. Even when there was evidence of serious structural damage, more often than not schools continued to function under rotting support beams and behind doorless doorways because of the difficulty of finding new sites.[46] The SCNM, like the municipalities, the SEP, and other Catholic charitable organizations, was not in a financial position to rent better, and more expensive, accommodations.

The Schools Section of the UDCM also struggled to maintain its schools, relying upon donations and fundraising activities. In times of difficulty, wealthy members of the organization would often make significant donations. For instance, when the Schools Section could not pay the rent on its Escuela del Papelero (Newsboys' School also known as the Escuela de San José, or Saint Joseph's School), a member of the section offered to cover the difference between the rent and what the Schools Section could afford to contribute. When wealthy members were not forthcoming, the UDCM staged fundraising activities aimed at the public. Public exhibitions of inoffensive films were supposed to fill the School Section's coffers but instead drained funds. Audiences were not interested in viewing such films, and eventually the Schools Section abandoned the project. Sometimes financial problems forced the section to close schools; the popular Escuela Sor Juana Inés de la Cruz, established for children of workers at the Britania [sic] shirt-making workshop, was closed in April 1924 because of financial problems. As their economic problems increased, the Schools Section considered instituting tuition at all its schools, but only for students who could afford to pay. Among the schools considered suitable for fees was the Escuela del Papelero, which began to charge tuition in April 1925. These newsboys were street children who sold dailies and lived a precarious existence. If the Schools Section was willing to institute fees at this school, their financial situation must have been desperate indeed.

Even instituting fees was not as successful as the section anticipated because the collection of tuition was often problematic. For example, after fees were introduced at the Colegio del Sagrado Corazón de Jesús in the Colonia Vallejo, attendance increased but revenues fell. Most students continued attending school, ignoring the policy change. As the Schools Section did not discuss the issue of collecting tuition, it is difficult to determine why fees remained unpaid. Perhaps school principals or teachers felt that it was not part of their duty to act as bill collectors, or perhaps they were unwilling to expel students who could not pay. Teachers and principals, in frequent contact with students, probably knew each child's situation and might not have been willing to turn away their students because of poverty.[47]

Although constantly threatened by financial uncertainty, UDCM schools continued to teach sizeable numbers of students. For example, in 1922 the Colegio Italiano had facilities adequate to accommodate the 600 children who attended primary school there. The Colegio del Sagrado Corazón de Jesús, with less space, grew from 70 students to 105, while in 1925 the Santa Lucia School had 120 students enrolled, with an average attendance of 85 students. In its annual report for 1924–1925, the Mexico City local center had four schools under its care, two of which it had founded and two which it supported.[48] A report for 1924 for the Mexico City regional center counts 5,777 students. (This figure would include students attending schools in towns around the capital that were under the umbrella of the regional center.)[49]

Not all free Catholic schools struggled for their economic survival. The Escuela Mier y Pesado, located in Coyoacán — a middle-class suburb with a convenient rail connection to the city — was supported by a generous philanthropist and operated by the order of Guadalupe. Located in a mansion, the school had ample space for the free technical training offered. Boarding students received everything they needed, from the meals they ate to the clothing they wore, as they learned to perform domestic chores. During their breaks, students could play in the gardens surrounding the mansion. Typical for a Catholic school, the Mier y Pesado School adhered to the SEP official program but also offered daily mass.[50]

While this school was unusually well funded, it was not the only Catholic school founded by a generous individual promoting a personal vision of education. Father José Castillo y Piña, a sociologist and teacher at the Seminario Conciliar, pooled his savings with donations from supporters to found the Colegio-Casa Nazaret, in order to fulfill his vision of women's education. At the "school-home" in Mixcoac, girls trained in domestic duties and small-scale crafts making. Castillo y Piña started his school in 1919, without ecclesiastical approval because at that time Mexico's Archbishop Mora y del Río was in hiding. When Mora y del Río was again openly working in Mexico, Castillo y Piña asked for his blessing, claiming that the revolution motivated him to work for the poor, especially to give poor children a Catholic education as part of the work of Catholic social action.[51]

Although Castillo y Piña said he wanted to help Mexico's poor, in 1924 the tuition charge for boarding students was thirty-five pesos per month, making this an exclusive institution. A 1922 newspaper report on the school commented that the girls came from "the most distinguished families of Mixcoac." The school's first prospectus indicates that Castillo y Piña never actually sought out the poor. According to the 1919 prospectus, the Nazaret School offered girls a modern education without neglecting their moral or feminine edification. The girls took classes in Spanish grammar, arithmetic, geometry, geography, national history, physical and natural science, civics, writing, drawing, gymnastics, and hygiene. Additionally, they studied domestic economy and handicrafts. The combination of technical and academic skills was designed to prepare the girls to be women useful at home and in society at large. Even though he promoted a domestic role for women, Castillo y Piña still believed that science was the most important aspect of his curriculum. The school also offered courses in choral singing and public speaking at an extra charge.

According to Castillo y Piña, parents were pleased with the Nazaret School, because their daughters were being trained for real life rather than a life of luxury. While his idea of "real life" had an elite bias, his emphasis on practical training was shared with the SEP. A reporter for *Excélsior*, visiting the school in 1921, found an idyllic setting complete with blooming gardens and songbirds. He observed girls cultivating silkworms from eggs donated by the government.[52] I have not found other instances of direct governmental support for Catholic schools in the Federal District; nonetheless, this example provides further evidence for my conclusion that in its early days the SEP considered Catholic schools a necessary supplement to public schools. In addition, Valentina Torres Septién notes that some Catholic technical schools received subsidies from state governments.[53]

The Nazaret School did not limit itself to practical training, but also molded the spirits of young women. Castillo y Piña wanted the teachers and headmistress at the school to work together to ensure that the girls learned good manners, tact, and culture, as well as to be models of honesty and honor. While Castillo y Piña expected the students to be able to earn a living, he still believed that it was in Mexico's best interests for women to work from their homes. Women who trained for work outside the home, according to the priest, became masculine and were in danger of thinking themselves equal to or independent from men. For him, the popular practice of training women for office work was "white-collar-worker mania." Thus, the Nazaret School did not offer languages, typing, or business courses: All the technical courses that the school offered could be practiced from women's homes.[54]

In the activities of these schools, we see that Catholics shared the SEP's concern that women's behavior was degenerating. Catholic women were just as guilty of improper dress as girls at SEP schools. The UDCM included a fashion section in its periodical in order to demonstrate proper attire for Catholic ladies (fig. 5.3). Joaquín Cardoso, a Jesuit priest, lamented that he had seen a pious señora and her two daughters mistaken for streetwalkers because of their attire. He begged Mexican mothers to become once again defenders of honorable womanhood, setting an example with their own dress and supervising what their daughters wore.[55]

Women's changing expectations, evidenced by dress the church considered scandalous, threatened established gender norms. A story in the Catholic magazine *Acción y Fe* told of two girl cousins who grew up together. Enriched by the revolution, one of the fathers, now a wealthy general, moved his family to an elegant home in the Colonia Roma. This revolutionary family believed that Catholic customs were out of date and their daughter, Julia, was educated in a Protestant school. As an adult, Julia drove her own car, wore flapper dresses, and planned to star in a film. Years later, the Catholic cousin — now a beloved wife and mother — received a note from Julia announcing her intention to commit suicide. Although rich, Julia was alone and unloved. Her lifestyle of mad parties no longer fulfilled her, but men did not marry women like her. At the end of the moralizing tale, Julia, regretting her rejection of Catholic mores, killed herself.[56] Her suicide was the ultimate rejection of Catholicism, as she died in irredeemable sin. This mini-melodrama

Figure 5.3. "La moda en París" (Fashion in Paris), showing the overcoats in fashion in Paris in the winter of 1922–23. The fashion section was included in *La Dama Católica* to guide Catholic women in their decisions about modern dress. Mexican Catholics were not the only ones concerned about the perceived provocativeness of modern dress: Fashion guidelines and condemnations were coming directly from the Vatican. (Courtesy of the Hemeroteca Nacional, Mexico City)

indicates how much young women's changing attitudes and expectations scared Catholic elements of Mexican society. Moreover, Catholics blamed women's independent behavior on changes precipitated by the revolution. The revolution enriched Julia's father materially, but his daughter's spirit was not nurtured and she died alone by her own hand. Realizing that the revolution offered women opportunities for roles beyond wife and mother, some Catholics shuddered.

In response to fears about Mexico's moral decline after the revolution, the UDCM used its schools to Christianize neighborhoods. For instance, the Colegio Italiano, under UDCM patronage and operated by the Salesian order, had a sewing workshop for women, a community chapel, and the Casa Familia (Family Home) to house the homeless. Catholic schools with chapel annexes offered Sunday mass and public classes on church doctrine. They also promoted first communions and dedicated homes and schools to Catholic saints. To celebrate the end of examinations, the UDCM often hosted and attended parties for their students. At Christmas, damas decorated a tree at the UDCM offices and distributed presents to the students in their schools. The order of Our Lady of Guadalupe and Saint Aloysius Gonzaga also arranged for a Christmas tree laden with toys, which were given to students at the Escuela de Santa Cruz de Acatlán (Holy Cross of Acatlán School) during their end-of-year party.[57]

Events at the UDCM Escuela Granja demonstrate that by reaching into communities, Catholic schools could inspire the same loyalty as public schools did. In June 1922, the UDCM founded the Escuela Granja in the Colonia Vallejo. While the colonia, located on the city's northeastern edge, had no Catholic schools at all, both Protestant and Spiritualist schools were located nearby. According to the UDCM, the local community was mostly Catholic and residents were enthusiastic about a Catholic school, particularly since the school's small chapel served the public.[58] Throngs of people attended the official opening and first mass. Community enthusiasm and participation went too far for some damas when residents began to use the school building for Sunday kermises at which there were open collection boxes.

The damas' concern about the kermises is interesting, as kermises were often sponsored by churches and held on church grounds as an annual celebration of the church's dedication. In the 1920s, the word developed a wider meaning and included street festivals for fundraising purposes sponsored by associations and neighborhoods. The damas appeared concerned that these parties were unsupervised and unauthorized, and that they might cause desecration of the site. The damas had determined to take all the furnishings, including those of the chapel, to a safe place, but when the owner of the rented building became aware of this chaos, he attempted to close the school while it was in session, and to confiscate the furnishings in order to take them with him when he filed a complaint about the disturbances. To demonstrate that he had the law behind him, the owner brought a judge with him to oversee the confiscation. In his anger, the landlord publicly insulted and threatened the school's principal. He then demanded that she accompany him to government offices in order to give a deposition. As the altercation escalated, the children attending classes began to sob in fear.

Meanwhile, news of the attack on their school and chapel brought concerned neighbors to the scene. The principal was unwilling to accompany the irate landlord, so he resorted to force. At this point the neighbors intervened, forming a human chain to block the departure of the owner, judge, unwilling principal, and confiscated goods. The barrier of bodies produced a five-hour standoff between the landlord and the (literally) surrounding community. A resident finally volunteered his house as a place to store the furniture, and with the judge's approval, the tense situation was resolved temporarily.

The next day, fifty-seven people from the neighborhood signed a letter to the Schools Section attesting to the importance of the school and pleading with the UDCM to continue its support and "protection." The residents apparently feared that the altercation would intimidate the damas, and they probably knew that the damas were unhappy with their unauthorized use of the space. The Schools Section alleviated the residents' concerns: Not only would the UDCM continue its community involvement, but damas would also look for a house large enough to accommodate the growing numbers of students. Shortly thereafter, the Escuela Granja was reopened in a bigger space. In addition, the UDCM planned to hire a priest to work full-time for the school.[59]

The residents of the Colonia Vallejo, who lived in isolation from both churches and schools, were willing to fight to maintain the presence of an organization that had given them both. Moreover, the use of the building for parties and the altercation with the landlord indicate that, once it was founded, the residents believed that the school was truly theirs, a view that alarmed both the UDCM and the landlord. The UDCM sought to reassert its authority over the neighborhood, returning residents firmly to the place of grateful supplicants. In order to retain the chapel and school, the residents accepted that rhetoric, at least in the short term.

Catholic schools, then, were a tool to educate and increase religious feeling among students and the surrounding communities, whereas SEP schools sought to promote the government's moral agenda and inspire patriotism. Both Catholics and the SEP viewed the local school as a means to indoctrinate loyalty and as a center that reached beyond the students to the entire community. Not only were educational programs similar, but church and state schools faced the same problems that defied resolution. Parents, meanwhile, had conflicting claims on primary schools, as they saw their children's education as their own affair and not solely that of church or state. These concerns were particularly evident with regard to safety.

While Article 3 of the 1917 Constitution was a constant threat to all Catholic schools, sources indicate that until 1926 these schools operated with minimal SEP interference. The SEP recognized that Catholic schools played an important educational role in the city and, at the same time, the policy set by Obregón was one of tolerance and negotiation. Without the threat of Article 3 being invoked, Catholic schools could determine their own relationship to the SEP. As discussed in chapter 2, Catholic primary schools could voluntarily incorporate under the SEP, meaning that they followed the official SEP program and were overseen by SEP inspectors. In these incorporated primary schools, students regularly took two exams: one official and witnessed by an inspector from the SEP, the other Catholic. In the pre-1926 data, I have found no indication that SEP inspectors imposed their will on Catholic schools. The UDCM Schools Section always reported that SEP inspectors were pleased with the progress of the students, which suggests that students in UDCM schools were mastering the SEP curriculum and that the inspectors had no quarrel with Catholic education. In 1926, the situation became more difficult for Catholic schools because of the enforcement of Article 3. These circumstances will be discussed in chapter 8.

6 Adults in the Classroom

Making Their Own Revolution

The experiences of students in adult education varied school by school and were the result of negotiation and conflict among teachers, students, communities, parents, inspectors, and the administration. Moreover, these schools both reflected and served the society in which they operated: Two case studies discussed here indicate how debates taking place in society were represented through adult education. Catholic adult education, in its diverse forms, continues to be a useful comparison to federal adult education, showing that Catholic educators and volunteers grappled with how to give their students a useful education and solid moral foundation. While the schools discussed here may have had similar goals and means, the students in adult education had motivations as diverse as their backgrounds. This discussion ends by addressing the students themselves: who they were and what they wanted from their schooling.

Adult Vocational Schools

In 1922 the six Mexico City vocational schools under the SEP operated both day and night schools, enrolling 10,373 men and women, who took courses in handicrafts, technical skills, languages, and physical education. The institutions ranged in size from 250 to 2,035 students. As tables 6.1 and 6.2 show, this pattern continued in 1925 in the eight SEP vocational schools. Not only did women's schools tend to be larger than men's, but schools for women outnumbered schools for men. The figures correspond broadly to the fact that young women vastly outnumbered young men in Mexico City's population, with three times as many women as men aged between twenty and twenty-four.

In each of these schools, practical experience and utility of subject matter guided the curriculum. All subject matter, including math and Spanish, was to be taught with a view to utility, and teachers were to design their classes using concrete examples.[1] Students, particularly young men, gained further practical experience through field trips and

Table 6.1. Enrollment in Men's Vocational Schools, Mexico City, 1925

School	Day Students	Night Students
Escuela de Ingenieros Mecánicos y Electristas	558	261
Instituto Técnico Industrial	213	—
Escuela Técnica Nacional de Constructores	553	664
Total	*1,324*	*925*

Source: Boletín de la Secretaría de Educación Pública 5 (March 1926): 106–9.

Table 6.2. Enrollment in Women's Vocational Schools, Mexico City, 1925

School	Day Students	Night Students
Escuela de Arte Industrial Corregidora de Querétaro	1,110	604
Escuela de Artes y Oficios para Señoritas	807	760
Escuela Nacional de Enseñanza Doméstica	754	579
Escuela Hogar Gabriela Mistral	434	615
Escuela Hogar Sor Juana Inés de la Cruz	963	—
Total	*4,068*	*2,558*

Source: Boletín de la Secretaría de Educación Pública 5 (March 1926): 106–9.

internships. For instance, the Escuela de Ingenieros sent students to visit power plants or to the mountains of Veracruz to examine the difficulties of electric rail service on rough terrain. Some students gained experience farther afield. After finishing their courses, eighteen students at the Escuela de Ingenieros undertook internships abroad, either in the United States or Germany, with their transportation paid for by the SEP and the host company paying their salaries. The SEP reported that the students' work was satisfactory to their employers, their salaries were rising quickly, and they were gaining increasing authority. Employers in Mexico also appeared satisfied with the courses and practical experience taught through the men's vocational schools. The SEP reported that students in the three men's technical schools found employment without difficulty.[2]

As part of their practical training, students manufactured goods that were sold to benefit the SEP Departamento de Enseñanza Técnica, Industria y Comercial. Because of the types of skills taught in men's schools, they had greater revenue-generating potential than did women's schools. Yet lack of adequate materials and space often scuttled orders and reduced revenue. Even with adequate supplies and facilities, the process of obtaining an order, purchasing materials, and producing the finished goods was highly bureaucratic, becoming more so during Puig Casauranc's tenure as minister of public education. Simply securing approval for the budget involved negotiations among the SEP, the client, the vocational school, and the individual teacher. Moreover, the SEP did not provide the initial investment many of these projects needed. When schools could not afford to purchase raw materials, clients became impatient and occasionally cancelled their contracts.[3]

While guidelines stated that vocational educational was to be practical and offer skills training, teachers also needed to select subject matter that addressed morality and good habits. Teachers were to train their students in social graces, protect them from bad influences, help form their character, and address their personal hygiene. Inculcating those perceived as less cultured with the desire and means to improve their morals and behavior was a fundamental goal of vocational education. Yet for many teachers simply establishing discipline over rowdy students was a challenge. Teachers had even more difficulty establishing authority over students older than themselves.[4] There were teachers who were able to embark upon a program of improvement, but their ideas of how to improve their students did not necessarily agree with the SEP's view. While the SEP viewed middle-class morality as an improvement for its poor students, students and teachers adapted vocational curriculum to their own lives and communities. Since many teachers creatively modified classes to suit the needs of their students or their own agendas, a considerable distance could emerge between SEP programs and daily practice.

Civics, Morality, and Planned Parenthood

By the 1930s, education would be identified as socialist and would be seen as a fundamental means of spreading the revolution — particularly its anticlerical elements[5] — but in the 1920s, revolutionary and conservative values coexisted within the SEP and its schools. In the first half of the 1920s, the SEP focused on expanding educational opportunities rather than promoting a revolutionary program. For the early SEP, education was a means to forge nationalism and create a concept of citizenry but, until the 1926 enforcement of Article 3, education was not a political tool for promoting a specific revolutionary ideology. Teachers, however, recognized the potential of education to mold students, and some used their classrooms to promote their own revolution.

The alleged use of Margaret Sanger's birth-control pamphlets in civics classes offers us the history of a public scandal prompted by clashing mores. Margaret Sanger (1879–1966) was a U.S. birth-control advocate. In Yucatán, Felipe Carrillo Puerto's government had distributed Sanger's pamphlets in public schools and had included sex education in Mérida's school curriculum.[6] In 1922, her pamphlets appeared in Mexico City, and reports circulated in the capital's press that SEP teachers were distributing Sanger's work; one article claimed that the pamphlet was routinely given to students in SEP girls' primary schools. In an interview with the Mexico City newspaper *La Raza*, SEP Undersecretary Francisco Figueroa responded that if the pamphlet were found to be immoral, its circulation among primary-school students would be prohibited.

While I have not found evidence that Sanger's pamphlets were distributed among primary-school children in Mexico City, at least one women's vocational school may have used Sanger's materials. The rumors about the pamphlet focused on the Gabriela Mistral School, and the story broke in the press at the same time as Mistral herself was visiting Mexico at Vasconcelos' invitation. Newspapers reported that she inaugurated the school and library named for her, and gave readings and lectures at the many parties and lunches organized in her honor. As she toured the capital, Mistral promoted her traditional vision of motherhood utterly at odds with the scandal begun at the school named for her.[7]

On 8 August 1922, the DETIC, suspecting that the Mistral School's civics teachers used Sanger's pamphlets, ordered principal Rosario Pacheco to suspend civics classes and civics lectures at school assemblies. When the principal gathered staff and students to explain the suspension, the teachers vehemently protested their innocence, condemning Sanger's pamphlet and asserting their commitment to forming virtuous young women who would sustain the domestic sphere. More than 270 teachers and students signed the meeting's minutes. The teachers also wrote to the SEP, protesting the suspension and explaining that civics courses provided a forum from which to address students' ignorance — the primary cause of errors and vice in society. The teachers did not believe that it was their role to expose their students to matters alien to their lives; nonetheless, they felt it was their duty to answer students' queries honestly. Among the signatures closing the letter were those of Dolores Castillo and René Rodríguez.[8]

The teachers' defense was carefully worded to allude to the Sanger scandal without providing evidence of misconduct that could be used against them. The teachers' rhetoric about their students' ignorance echoes that of public health reformers who feared that women had little accurate information about reproduction or sexuality and did not know what caused pregnancy. According to its critics, the church's prudish attitude toward sex was contributing to public health problems, such as high rates of syphilis. Public health reformers, those dealing with commercial sex, and these teachers all used the same rhetorical devices to discuss young women's ignorance.[9] Given the rhetoric used, other evidence I mention later, and teachers' reluctance to provide specific examples of this ignorance, I suspect that the teachers at the Mistral School were using Sanger's pamphlet, or at least discussing reproductive matters.

A week and a half later, *Universal* reported on its front page that the civics classes had been suspended because teachers were providing information about birth control and that Pacheco's protests of innocence were overshadowed by frequent complaints from parents about the civics courses. A follow-up article noted that groups of teachers and students had denied any improprieties. Nonetheless, the classes under Dolores Castillo, René Rodríguez, and another unnamed teacher taught "in accordance with certain feminist theories, which now many women teachers support," had been suspended. The article noted that after a week's suspension, classes resumed because the suspended teachers had shown the SEP that their revised course program did not address birth control. Yet the SEP, concerned that unsupervised teachers would return to their scandalous ways, appointed special inspectors to ensure that these teachers taught only the approved curriculum. Anyone caught using the Sanger pamphlet would be severely punished. The article concluded by noting that the relevant documents on the scandal were available in the SEP archive should anyone wish to consult them and that an investigation had begun into how the pamphlets were introduced into the schools.[10]

Dolores Angela Castillo Lara was born in Huayacocotla, Veracruz, in 1884. She received her normal-school degree in Puebla in 1901, after four years of schooling and a unanimous vote of support from the jury for her professional exam. She began work the same year and, between 1901 and 1911, she worked as a principal in at least four different schools in Veracruz. A letter of recommendation from 1912 described her as "competent, dedicated and of good conduct, as much inside as outside the establishment."[11] Moving to the Federal District in 1911, Castillo began work as a primary-school assistant; by 1914, she had become the principal of a primary school. Over the next several years, she was principal in various Federal District schools. In 1919, she was appointed as the stenography and typing teacher at the Escuela Nacional Preparatoria and also as the writing teacher at the women's normal school. Additionally, from 1920 on, she was the prefect for first-year students at the Preparatoria Nacional, watching over the girls so that they would not be corrupted in a coeducational setting. These students remembered her as "a lovely person who guided us and who was very devoted and conscientious about the girls."[12] There are no records to indicate when she was hired at the Mistral School, but as late as February 1921 she was working only at the Preparatoria Nacional and at the normal school. In August of that year, as a result of budgetary short-falls, she was fired from at least one of her positions, and perhaps this prompted her to seek work at the Mistral School.

Details of her life emerge as well because Castillo was one of the few women recognized as a veteran of the revolution. Martha Eva Rocha has worked extensively on these women and has found that they were generally professional women of relatively privileged background, like Castillo. Castillo supported the revolution both in Veracruz and the capital, but there are no details about her work in Veracruz. In the capital, she was part of the female revolutionary group under María Arias Bernal, also a teacher. During the Decena Trágica, Castillo engaged in anti-Huerta publicity and raised money among like-minded residents. She found a press willing to print flyers and posters, which she distributed in Tacuba, La Ronda, and Santa Julia. Her work publicizing the revolution brought her to rural areas like Santa Anita and Ixtacalco, where among the campesinos she founded small groups of revolutionary supporters who later went to fight with Zapata. She gathered weapons and recruited volunteers to send to Puebla: Her group succeeded in recruiting four or five volunteers per week. In 1915, she returned to Veracruz with the Constitutionalists when they abandoned the capital.[13] Castillo's revolutionary credentials and work in Veracruz served her well when her livelihood was threatened by the unabated scandal over the Sanger pamphlets.

Although civics classes at the Mistral School resumed a week after their suspension, the matter was not yet concluded. Concerned, and probably wondering what prompted the allegations, DETIC head Luis Massieu sent inspector Juan León to the Mistral School. It is unclear why the DETIC, which usually sent women inspectors into women's schools, selected Juan León for this assignment. Surviving records suggest that León devoted his attention almost exclusively to Castillo, reporting that she "said, among other things, that until now charge of governing society had been conferred upon the man. But the woman has a rightful place participating in this arduous labor for which she can count an infinite number of resources in the home, like [being] a wife, a daughter, a sister, or a mother. The new movement that women are forming to defend their legitimate rights is hidden from no one. The time will come when, equal to men, [women] can hold the same positions as [men do]." León found nothing scandalous in Castillo's comments, perhaps because she used women's domestic duties to justify a political role for them. At a later date, Castillo told her students why León was there, noting that there had been accusations against her in local papers but assuring students and the inspector alike that she had always stayed within the bounds of morality.

Since classroom observations had failed to produce traces of the notorious pamphlet, principal Pacheco arranged for León to interview some of Castillo's current and former students. A few of Castillo's students had already requested transfers to other civics classes under orders from parents or confessors. One student recalled that Castillo, after discussing women's emancipation, declared that three divorces were better than putting up with humiliation. Another student who had transferred reported that Castillo told the women not to let their husbands take advantage of them and that she taught "intimate things . . . which [they] were ashamed to repeat." Gossip credited Castillo with saying that it was best for married couples to have only two children and that she would tell her students how to avoid pregnancy. But the rumors could not be substantiated. In all León's investigations, he was unable to find a single witness to confirm the charge that Castillo used Sanger's pamphlet.[14] Although León had not found any evidence against Castillo, a few days after his report she and René Rodríguez were both fired, under the guise of reducing expenditures. The teachers, convinced that their termination was due to their "liberal and emancipated" behavior, not money, wrote to President Obregón in protest. Moreover, in their defense they claimed that prominent SEP officials Luis Massieu and Juan Mancera were members of the Knights of Columbus, which was against liberal ideas and free-thinking women. To prove their point about the organization, they promised to send a pamphlet. The teachers demanded an investigation into the true reasons for their sacking and offered to return to work for free, if necessary. Castillo included a letter of support from Veracruz Governor Adalberto Tejeda, attesting to her skills as a teacher and her work for the revolution. In mid-September, Obregón's office responded that the president regretted their firing and suggested that they go to the SEP to complain.[15] Although the file closes with that letter, its existence implies that both teachers were rehired. Castillo continued to work for the SEP until she retired. Shortly after Rodríguez and Castillo were fired, the DETIC questioned headmistresses in the city's other women's vocational and secondary schools about Sanger's pamphlet. The headmistresses all denied any impropriety either in private or in public. Students joined in these denials and students at the Miguel Lerdo de Tejada Commercial School, with the support of the Federación de Estudiantes de México (Mexican Students' Federation), published an outraged denial of wrongdoing and a letter of support for the school's principal, Dolores Salcedo.[16] But the press continued to allege that offensive materials were being used in classrooms, and this controversy lasted several more months. When the scandal showed no signs of abating, the SEP held a press conference at the Mistral School. Luis Massieu, SEP representative and alleged Knight of Columbus, spoke of his unwavering faith in the students irrespective of the shameful articles that had recently appeared.[17]

Lack of archival materials prevents me from completing the story of the daring civics classes at the Mistral School, but certain final points deserve mention. Probably thanks to Obregón and Tejeda, the scandal did not appear to hurt Castillo's career. In 1925, she became a teacher at the normal school, and later she became head of secondary education within the SEP. Her personnel file contains no references to the scandal or even to her employment at the Mistral School. Castillo also continued to be an active feminist, participating in the Consejo Feminista Mexicano (Mexican Feminist Council) in 1923, and on that occasion championing maternity and declaring birth control as foreign to Mexican women.[18] Principal Pacheco, however, either resigned or lost her job. While it is unclear why or when Pacheco left the school, her replacement, Luz Vera, was a prominent feminist who had been active in the anti-reelection campaigns at the end of the Porfiriato and had collaborated with the Carrancistas against Huerta. She was also a suffragist, a writer, and a political activist, and in 1934, she became the first women to earn a doctorate from the National University.[19] Considering her credentials, it seems improbable that the DETIC was ignorant of Vera's feminist views. By hiring Vera, the DETIC risked further feminist scandal at the Mistral School.

The situation at the Mistral School demonstrates a conflict between the SEP and the individuals who composed it. It also demonstrates that political, religious, and gender conflicts were embedded in postrevolutionary education. Although some of the SEP's teachers had been educated in Porfirian normal schools and continued to teach as if there had been no revolution,[20] other teachers who had been influenced by the revolution took their experiences into their classrooms. Although Castillo was educated in a Porfirian normal school, she was a dedicated revolutionary and a dedicated educator. She attributed the loss of her job to her outspoken feminist views. Perhaps Castillo never did discuss birth control but conservative students interpreted her feminism as support for reproductive rights. Or perhaps she did address reproduction but only in response to students' questions. We cannot know for certain. If, however, Castillo did support birth control, she was not unique. Elena Torres, who directed the SEP's free breakfast program, also supported birth control. She reasoned that by using birth control poor couples could have only the number of children they could afford to educate.

Moreover, feminist beliefs appear to have been common among teachers. Anna Macías contends that the majority of feminists in the 1920s were primary-school teachers.[21] Sectors of the public feared she was right, as newspaper reports on the scandal make clear. When a women's congress was held in Mexico City in April 1923, condemnation of the women and their discussions of free love, the abolition of marriage, and birth control came from both Catholic and revolutionary sectors. A member of the CROM was quoted in *Excélsior* denying any possibility that these women could be mothers, because mothers would not think such scandalous thoughts. He believed that it was better for women to be without liberties than to become disciples of "Margarita" Sanger but concluded that the ideas discussed at the congress would not influence Mexican women. The most damning part of the report was the accusation that the majority of the women who attended the congress were teachers in SEP schools.[22] The atmosphere of postrevolutionary Mexico made all teachers suspect, particularly those in women's schools, because they were in a position of authority over Mexico's future mothers.

The debate about birth control was part of a public discourse that during the 1920s increasingly addressed health concerns and sexuality. Diseases and malnutrition had taken their toll on the population, prompting public and official concern. Eugenics gained prominence in Mexican health and social debates, and much of the concern for national health centered on the bodies of women. Contemporary figures indicate that this concern for the population's health was not a moral panic. Between 1916 and 1920, syphilis was the leading cause of miscarriage in Mexico, and in one Mexico City primary school in the early 1920s, 80 percent of the schoolchildren reacted positively to a blood test for traces of the disease. The church received much of the blame for high rates of sexually transmitted diseases because it promoted secrecy regarding matters of sexuality. Young women found themselves pregnant without knowing why. In retaliation, the public health department sought to make sex a matter of public health rather than private confession. Sexual promiscuity combined with ignorance about sex created a greater health threat. Dance halls and cabarets, increasing in popularity, were known as places where sexual encounters, for money or otherwise, took place. Parks and secluded spots in the city also offered semiprivate havens for sex.[23] Thus, scandals about Sanger's pamphlet prefigured debates in the 1930s on sex education and were only one aspect of a public debate regarding sexual health and hygiene.

Cooking Up Scandal

Other courses in women's vocational schools offered opportunities for conflict between the SEP and its teachers. When teachers resisted curricular reforms, the content of women's cooking courses turned into a debate about the place of nationalism and culture in vocational education. In April 1923, Vasconcelos began criticizing the cooking curriculum because it was dominated by European foods and designed to teach "what is pompously called high cuisine." Instead, he called for teachers to concentrate on simple Mexican foods appropriate for the everyday consumption of the general population. Vasconcelos also wanted the cuisine taught in vocational schools to be a bastion of nationalism and a source of Mexican pride. The invasion of U.S. desserts further aggravated Vasconcelos, and he was determined to contain the encroaching armies of "cakes" with a gastronomic army of his own. To this end, he appointed two inspectors to revive the art of Mexican desserts.[24]

Vasconcelos' opinions were unpopular with inspectors and teachers of cooking alike. Teachers resisted the SEP's attempts to jettison foreign cuisine, justifying their curriculum on the grounds that their students were bound for employment in exclusive Mexican kitchens and needed to know how to prepare haute cuisine. In truth, teachers probably preferred to prepare dishes that allowed them to demonstrate their skills and might have considered popular cuisine beneath them. The teachers had the weight of the prerevolutionary cooking curriculum behind them in their struggle to keep their kitchens European. As Jeffrey Pilcher argues, during the nineteenth century, there had been a general condemnation of Mexican food as unsanitary and unhealthy. Mexican food was frowned upon at the Porfirian EAOM. There educators taught "modest French family cooking," preached against spicy foods, and recommended that students eat "simple English" fare. In 1908, Sierra's regulation of education made changing the diet of the poor, as well as their dress and their homes, a necessity.[25]

Teachers and inspectors still promoted this prerevolutionary view of Mexican cuisine. A few months after Vasconcelos' decree, the inspector

Figure 6.1. A class in domestic economy at the Escuela de Arte Industrial Corregidora de Querétaro. In the background hang images of an "Apache" warrior and a dancing Mexican woman with a long braid, full skirt, and large hat, reflecting the emphasis on a new folkloric idea of Mexican culture. Most of the students appear to be in their teens or twenties, but there is one gray-haired student. (Courtesy of the Instituto Mora)

of cooking and desserts requested permission to include more elaborate dishes in the curriculum. She worried that public displays of student work would disappoint the crowds of visitors who expected to be delighted and astonished by extraordinary meals. To back up her request, she reiterated the argument of the cooking teachers: Students needed to learn European cuisine if they were to earn a living in the capital's kitchens. Instead of mentioning her own preference, the *inspectora* portrayed herself as the disinterested mouthpiece of public, teacher, and student demands. Nonetheless, her boss refused the request and referred her to Vasconcelos' April circular.[26]

While circulars shuttled among administrative offices, the cooking students continued to prepare European foods. In May 1923, a second-year cooking class learned about the "history of ice cream." Throughout the following months, the women made sorbet, ice cream, canapés, and ham mousse. Another class learned to prepare German macaroni and Provence-style steak. Interestingly, Vasconcelos did not criticize the frequency with which meat appeared in the cooking curriculum. Regardless of the national origin of the cuisine, heavy reliance on meat as an ingredient made the dishes expensive for poor and working-class students.[27] The cooking-curriculum debate signals a larger question: Which models and ideals to teach students? In technical education, the SEP often encouraged teachers to use Mexican rather than foreign models. In women's vocational schools, students adorned boxes, plates, and pillowcases with styles inspired by indigenous culture. In the domestic economy class at the Querétaro School, students decorated small wall hangings with images of bare-chested men in feather headdresses or full-skirted women whose long dark braids hung below straw hats. At the same time, in porcelain painting class students decorated their vases and plates with fairy-tale birds and stylized horses (figs. 6.1 and

Figure 6.2. Batik class at the Escuela de Arte Industrial Corregidora de Querétaro. This school, inaugurated for the 1910 centennial celebrations, was a showpiece for the Porfirian regime, as the paintings on the walls indicate. (Courtesy of the Instituto Mora)

6.2). Dressmaking students were also taught how to reproduce foreign fashions. The inspectoras whom Vasconcelos appointed to oversee dressmaking classes were chosen because they "rubbed shoulders with the high classes of society and they have been able to acquire habits of refinement. . . . They will endeavor to demonstrate to the students that inexpensive materials [pobres elementos] are enough to achieve a good look."[28] Inspectoras observed both teachers and students for any signs of bad taste. Through these inspectoras, Vasconcelos tried to fashion students into cheap copies of elite women. A notorious womanizer,[29] Vasconcelos seemed to prefer the feminine figure draped in European fashions. Yet Vasconcelos discouraged traditional Mexican forms of dress at a time when the capital's fashion-conscious residents had embraced the fad of wearing huaraches and serapes.[30]

Night Life

For many Mexican workers, wearing serapes or huaraches was not a fashion statement but a matter of utility. These workers crowded into SEP night schools in order to better their educational level and economic circumstances through free primary education and technical training. There were twenty-six workers' night schools in 1923, sixteen for men and ten for women. Most were located in the center or north of the city, with several in the working-class colonias of Guerrero, San Rafael, and Morelos, and the respectable Colonia Juárez. Particularly for women, safety concerns and the schools' locations certainly influenced workers' decisions to attend night school. Students appeared to prefer attending schools in the neighborhood where they lived, rather than those near their workplace.

Material conditions were far worse in these night schools than in vocational schools. In 1923, Inspectora Consuelo Rafols observed that none of the women's night schools had bookshelves; many lacked even a single drawer in which the principal could leave her registers, so principals took the registers home each night for safekeeping.[31] As in primary schools, most students enrolled in the lower grades, and classes ranged in size from 44 to 150 students. On the whole, men's night schools had lower enrollment and attendance than women's, suggesting that they were in fact smaller. In 1923, Inspector Abraham Arellanos reported that the average total monthly attendance at men's night schools was 1,518 students, with an average per school of 101 students.

Men's and women's night schools offered artisanal or skills training in addition to literacy programs. Of the skills-training courses, "fretwork" was particularly attractive to the younger boys, those between the ages of ten and fourteen. Brass bed and radio making were also popular with the boys. Inspector Manuel Contreras reported that students younger than fourteen attended night schools either because there was not enough space for them in day schools or because they had daytime jobs. Some students attended both day and night schools, incurring Inspector Arellanos' criticism for taking places away from needy workers. Even more than in primary schools, student attendance was a concern. A teacher at a men's night school complained to Inspector Contreras that, due to the constant influx of new students with different levels of knowledge, he was unable to teach his class as one group.[32]

In addition to the Escuelas Nocturnas para Obreros, four SEP Centros Industriales Nocturnos, founded in 1923, offered training and primary education to women only. In these centers, the women students were equally divided among those who engaged in industrial and domestic work. Courses, including literacy, mathematics, and handicrafts production, were intended to give students the means to earn an "independent" living and provide for themselves. While the SEP's ideal family was a married couple with children all supported by the husband's wage, the reality was that many women were responsible for earning part or all of their family's subsistence. Thus, while the SEP extolled this ideal family, particularly through its vocational schools, its schools aimed at working-class women were designed to teach women how to manage on their own.[33] The drive for independence no doubt also reflected women's changed expectations and situation after the revolution: Families had broken apart, women had traveled throughout the country for a variety of reasons, and many had moved to the capital to work. The focus on independence suggested that women from the popular classes, although protected by men in the national myth, were likely to be supporting themselves and their children in reality. Yet training women to earn an independent living was potentially dangerous to the SEP because it allowed for new consumption patterns and a degree of independence from families and societal norms. *Chicas modernas* were independent women whose lifestyle involved fast cars, fashionable clothing, and dating.[34] Thus, a woman's financial independence led dangerously toward her personal independence, fostering an ever-present tension in SEP schools for women. Like vocational schools, workers' night schools taught women skills that neither undermined men's work nor challenged traditional feminine roles.

Irrespective of tensions in adult education, these industrial centers were a great success and had to turn away prospective students: Inspector Arellanos repeatedly noted the enthusiasm of the students who were able to enroll. These students were sufficiently excited about education to cope with small working spaces, unhygienic conditions, and lack of supplies. In 1923, the four centros industriales enrolled 530, 730, 766, and 750 students respectively, and the average monthly attendance per center was 488. The one Centro Industrial para Obreros (Industrial Center for Male Laborers) in the Federal District appears to have been founded in 1925. Enrollment varied widely; in 1925 there were 1,124 men enrolled while in 1927 there were only 551.[35] It is not clear why the SEP founded two types of workers' night schools (the centros and the escuelas) nor whether their goals were significantly different. Size was one difference: The centros industriales for men or women were much larger than the workers' night schools. Moreover by 1926, at least two of the centros industriales charged tuition while workers' night schools continued to be free.[36]

Arellanos believed that women's night schools were more successful than men's because the women learned more useful skills. Still, Arellanos was deeply disappointed that while women could improve their homes and families both "economically and morally" with their new skills, their income would only supplement a man's wage. In this aspect, he saw the schools as failing their women students. Meanwhile, Inspectora Rafols believed that women's night schools responded to "the need to give to women workers a better means of living, to open for them a larger field of action, and to give them industrial and commercial initiative without threatening their femininity, inspiring in them love and caring for their homes."[37] The differing success these inspectors attributed to night schools corresponded with their expectations. Arellanos hoped that women would learn skills that allowed them not to depend on a man, and was disappointed with the results. But Rafols, who expected the skills women learned in night schools to supplement a man's wage, was pleased with what she witnessed: The night schools did not encourage women to abandon their homes and femininity.

Initially, Arellanos was equally critical of men's night schools, observing that they taught literacy and mathematics but not the skills necessary for men to improve their standard of living. Without practical training, Arellanos did not believe that writing and spelling would help workers better their economic situations. The school's hygiene talks were also wasted, he felt, because most students lived in squalor that only improved wages could change.[38] The SEP took notice of his complaints: By the end of 1923, the situation in men's night schools had improved. The schools were more skills-oriented, and inspectors found that the workers had enthusiastically taken up the training offered.

Although workers' night schools were popular with students, easy to open, and inexpensive to run, their numbers declined after the mid-1920s. By 1928, there were only ten workers' night schools (as compared to twenty-five in 1924) and two centros industriales in the Federal District. It is not clear why the SEP limited the number of workers' night schools when demand remained high and the schools cost relatively little. The overall reduction of the education budget under President Calles might have been a factor. In 1925, the SEP budget fell because of Finance Minister Alberto J. Pani's attempts to make payments on the foreign debt. Between 1926 and 1927, the Cristero Rebellion further sapped educational funds, and the decline in oil and silver prices on the world market reduced federal revenue.[39] Yet considering the low cost of the schools, the most likely reason was a shift in SEP priorities toward emphasizing rural education.

Popular with students and frequently oversubscribed, workers' night schools nonetheless had many basic operational difficulties. Problems in these schools often arose because buildings were shared among SEP day schools and other night schools. Day-school principals became possessive of their buildings and resented the night tenants as interlopers. The more fortunate night schools had full use of their buildings, but if the day-school principal had some sort of grudge against the night school or conflict with the SEP, sections of the school would be kept locked and dark in the evening. In one extreme case, night-school students were not allowed to use the building's toilets.

Night-school students themselves created other problems for teachers and principals. At one school, some women students who arrived to find no staff present vandalized their school. In another case, four students destroyed the day school's vegetable garden, taking advantage of the fact that two teachers were absent and the harassed principal was attempting to teach both classes simultaneously. Even if students clearly caused the damage, the night-school staff was financially responsible for the destruction of property.[40] Conflicts between night schools and other SEP groups also occurred, particularly with coeducational *orfeones populares* (public choirs).

Conflicts with choral societies were common enough that when good relations existed between a night school and an orfeón, Inspector Contreras noted it. These conflicts were not gender-based; whether in men's or women's night schools, orfeones were magnets for trouble. These choruses functioned under the SEP's Departamento de Bellas Artes y Cultura Estética (Department of Fine Arts and Aesthetic Culture). In 1922, there were eight choral groups in Mexico City and ten in other municipalities. Learning to play Mexican instruments and to sing was supposed to compensate these workers "a little for the brute labors to which they are dedicated during the day."[41] From the students' point of view, however, the choral groups gave men and women a chance to interact, offering romantic and sexual opportunities. Inspector Arellanos observed, "The students enjoy a complete liberty, which leads to utter disorder. Some remain in the main entrance, others in the doorways, and finally they spend time dancing and chatting in little groups or in couples. From time to time they organize little parties like *tamaladas* [parties with tamales]. So, they prefer the disorder and little chats among buddies over attending single-sex schools where one goes to study and learn something useful."[42]

The lack of discipline in the orfeones became publicly known through the capital's press. The same newspaper that broke the Sanger scandal reported that night schools had become virtual brothels, as students in schools that hosted both women's and men's courses attended class not for learning but for "erotic sensations." Predictably, the problems were greater in centers that hosted orfeones populares.

The article reported that students enrolled in night schools in order to attend orfeones populares. When interviewed by *La Raza,* Francisco Morales explained that attendance in these choral groups was high because the atmosphere was like that in a cabaret. This licentious atmosphere, reported Morales, brought out the "idiosyncrasies" of the Mexican people. After two hours of singing and dancing, students would pair off and behave without any regard or respect for the fact that they were still in a school, although the more discreet would find a hotel in which to satisfy themselves. Morales concluded that educators in workers' night schools had to lure their students away from the orfeones with films and improved crafts training. The editorial line of *La Raza* was that the orfeones should be closed, because of their propensity for immorality and because workers needed to learn to read and write, not sing and dance.[43] Regardless of press disapproval, the orfeones remained functional, but the behavior of the singing workers appears to have calmed down. In 1928, the SEP reported that the centers were realizing their moralizing purpose of improving the leisure-time activities of the working class.[44]

When attending night school, students faced dangers not only to their morals, but also to their personal safety. The SEP founded night schools predominantly in poor and crime-ridden areas. Sometimes local louts loitered near school entrances, hurling threats or distracting the students filing past. Other students, on their way to school, threaded their way among prostitutes who would suggest an alternative activity. Robbery and assault were both very real dangers. In the autumn of 1923, shortly before the De la Huerta rebellion, male students on their way to class were targets not just for petty theft or assault, but for seizure by the infamous *leva* (forced conscription). Inspector Arellanos could verify only one incident, but rumors kept both male and female students away from school, with the men staying away longer.[45] Night-school staff tried to protect their students from these dangers. One women's night school, located south of the Zócalo, requested a guard in order "to avoid the continuous siege under which the bad elements [*mala gente*] of the neighborhood have the girls."[46]

Women, who were hailed and insulted in public at all times of day by all sorts of men, were more vulnerable to the dangers of the streets. Rape was a common crime, especially victimizing the lower classes to which night-school students belonged. Moreover, courts and juries rarely treated rape seriously.[47] Criminologists pathologized the urban lower classes, male and female alike, while simultaneously considering rape a natural male behavior. Violent male sexual proclivities were not considered out of the ordinary, either among strangers or inside marriages.[48] Mary Kay Vaughan found that in the 1930s in rural areas perceptions of violence and violence against women limited women's willingness to take advantage of educational opportunities. Even in broad daylight, women were at risk, and risks rose after dark. The ubiquitous violence against women reduced parents' willingness to send their older daughters to school, and reinforced both the suspicion of women who appeared in public and the justification for keeping women at home. Nonetheless, Vaughan finds that schools that had women teachers were more likely to enroll women students.[49] Alan Knight has also picked up on this point, noting that night schools generally tended to be male preserves because women did not want to be taught by male teachers and husbands objected to their wives' attendance.[50]

Dangers notwithstanding, women in Mexico City clamored for nighttime education and, when they and their families decided that the streets were safe enough, they attended school. Anecdotal evidence suggests that attendance fell in response to threats and rumors of violence. The capital's women certainly had more educational opportunities within easy reach than did their rural counterparts. Moreover, Mexico City's women's night schools were virtually all-female environments: Women taught classes, schools had headmistresses, and women inspectors kept an eye on activities. Thus, women created a safe public space for themselves. The popularity of women's adult education contrasts with the situation during the Porfiriato, when the Mexico City government claimed that women's night schools were frequently underenrolled. After the revolution, however, the SEP could not open enough schools to meet demand. One SEP official attributed the popularity of the centros nocturnos to women's new ideas of emancipation and desire for "advancement" for which they needed practical training.[51]

Attendance at night schools suffered not only because of dangerous streets, but also because of competing opportunities. Educational centers in the same neighborhoods vied for students. As already noted, orfeones proved tough competition for single-sex night schools. Outside events also reduced attendance. In one report, Arellanos blamed the Eucharistic Congress, a traveling carnival, and the local cinema for drawing students away. The seasons also affected attendance. As with daytime primary students, night students avoided school during the wet season, when heavy rains brought about an attendance slump.[52]

While attendance figures fluctuated, tardiness disrupted classes constantly. Teachers and principals arrived hours after classes should have begun, while many if not most students also arrived late for their classes without a valid reason. Once inside the crowded building, students meandered to their classrooms through the hubbub of fellow students and occasional dogs. Disorder was common in these schools. Inspector Contreras described scenes of undisciplined revelry, which he often blamed on an orfeón popular. Following a set schedule also proved difficult, and inspectors noted that they would arrive when classes were supposed to be in session to find the building shut and dark.

In one case of serious disorder caused by sharing space with an orfeón popular, Contreras suggested moving the school to another location, just two blocks away. The proposed location had the added benefit of being closer to the center of the neighborhood. When discussing the possibility of moving a school, neither principals nor inspectors appeared concerned about the current students. In one instance, a principal suggested moving his school to a more densely populated area in order to increase attendance, even though this would leave his current students stranded. I have not found any indications that high attendance raised wages or chances of promotion for principals; nonetheless, in both SEP and municipal schools for children and adults, principals went to great lengths — including moving schools or not releasing sick children — to maintain or increase attendance.[53]

Students selectively used tardiness and absenteeism to get the education that best suited them. While Contreras blamed dull classes and unenthusiastic teachers for problems of attendance and punctuality, some students might have deliberately missed selected courses while attending only what they felt they needed. In workers' night schools, literacy and math classes usually were held before the skills training courses. Tardy students possibly sought only technical training. Contreras reported that in a men's night school, students attended only the "subjects that they need in order to complete their knowledge."[54] To keep the students in school, the inspector recommended that the principal permit them to attend as they wished, while trying to interest them in other subjects. Ultimately, when students and the SEP clashed, the administration frequently compromised, because adults were under no obligation to attend school.

Enrollment figures were important in showing the SEP which courses students liked. Inspector Contreras reported that in men's schools courses on practical chemistry maintained high attendance rates and student interest. On the other hand, at the EAOS a group of young women dropped their cooking class upon learning that chemistry was a requirement. At the Escuela Nocturna para Obreros Número 28, older students were primarily interested in reading, writing, and arithmetic, and let the administration know what they wanted. By telling their principal which courses they valued, the men ensured that these courses would be available. Teachers also had the authority to devise new courses to suit students' needs. At the Centro Industrial Nocturno Número 2, the principal realized that the students attending the typing and stenography class lacked basic spelling skills and set aside a time for the students to work on written spelling exercises. The apparent disorganization of night schools had the unintentional benefit of allowing greater flexibility: Good night schools could adapt to the needs of their students and communities.[55]

Importantly, students cared not only about what courses were offered, but also about how they were taught. When the Escuela Nocturna para Obreros Número 21 altered its teaching system, students complained that the new "university-style" method, in which one teacher taught a single discipline in a forty-minute class, was detrimental to their learning:

> When we are just [beginning to] understand what one of the professors teaches us, [he] is substituted for the other one and, in the majority of cases, as they all teach using distinct systems, [only with] difficulty [can we] accustom ourselves to their lessons. Additionally, on various occasions, we have been extremely interested in the class which was interrupted because the time had come for the other teacher, who would continue to teach us, but as you will understand, this new teacher has no choice but to address something new because now it would not be possible to continue the class where his predecessor had left off. The result of this is that the little bit that we

were improving under the old system, we are miserably losing with the new system to which we have referred.[56]

The SEP heeded their appeal and reinstated the old system. These students understood what pedagogic method best suited them and fought to maintain it.

Catholic Centers for Adults

Day-to-day occurrences prove harder to reconstruct in Catholic adult schools than in SEP schools. Sources are scanty and, as many reports were written for public consumption, the authors are interested in proving the programs' successes and soliciting support, rather than giving objective accounts. Nonetheless, it is possible to glean enough information to assemble a picture of Catholic adult schools, which offered similar courses and operated under similar constraints as SEP schools. Because Catholic education was frequently intertwined with worker organization, I will examine the points of convergence between education and unionization. Catechism courses are discussed in this section because they became de facto adult literacy centers.

Catholic workers' night schools and Sunday schools functioned throughout the Federal District. The UDCM Academy offered fee-paying women an education while giving them "a Christian training, thus preventing them from attending those schools in which, even if they are taught, they are also perverted."[57] In 1924, there were 278 students enrolled in the Academy; 261 sat for exams and the majority of them passed.[58] These students were a mixture of industrial and white-collar workers, probably with some domestic workers as well. The UDCM founded its school for working women as an antidote to the "immorality" of secular institutions, yet the school was not open to the public but only to women involved with the UDCM. For instance, members of UDCM-affiliated unions, like women telephone operators, had the right to attend the Academy. This regulation would have served as an additional incentive for affiliating a professional or industrial union with the UDCM.[59] Although the school was not open to all women, it still publicized its courses widely to increase attendance. The UDCM periodical, *La Dama Católica*, reported on school activities each month, while publicity flyers reached out to a broader audience.

Records do not indicate what values Academy teachers tried to instill; however, based on the priorities of the UDCM I suspect that the school promoted the values of work, the importance of Catholicism, and women's maternal role. It likely taught women to defend their position and beliefs when under attack. The UDCM took threats to honor, family, and religion seriously, and women members eventually went into the streets to demand recognition of their religious rights. Catholic social action promoted a hierarchical society, within which each social class had rights and responsibilities. Working women had their rights, and probably learned about them at the Academy.

Attendance fluctuated at UDCM schools as a result of the same factors that affected SEP schools. Outside events also lowered attendance; for instance, the Academy attributed low turnout in September 1921 to the centennial festivities. The number of students enrolled varied; at the UDCM-affiliated Colegio Italiano, 214 women workers attended the sewing workshop to learn various types of embroidery. At the Sagrado Corazón School, thirty workers—probably all male—attended nighttime classes in primary education.[60] Because distance deterred students, UDCM educational centers were located within easy commutes. For example, the UDCM eventually opened a school specifically for the workers at Talleres Britania, because the Academy in the city center was too far away for the women working in the Colonia Guerrero. This night school was opened under the UDCM with both owner and management support. Even so, these students were frequently tardy; punctual students were rewarded with a film screening on Saturdays. (Records do not indicate which films were shown.) Students actually had few excuses for tardiness, since the school was in the same building as the factory.

As a further incentive for students in technical schools to perform well, the UDCM organized displays of student work and used *La Dama Católica* to promote and publicize these showings. At monthly meetings, Father Leopoldo Icaza, spiritual director of the UDCM Mexico City regional center, urged members to attend the exhibitions and donate prizes; he believed that support from damas would encourage the working women students. Family, friends, and the curious probably attended the displays as well. After student exams, the UDCM sponsored parties at the Academy and the Talleres Britania night school. The owners of the Britania workshop marked the end of the night school's academic year with a *piñata* and *posada,* a traditional Christmas caroling event, followed by a film.

Although the UDCM struggled to maintain its schools, it had one advantage that the SEP lacked: Catholic schools were affiliated with a worldwide organization. Using church connections and networks of Catholics, the UDCM was able to mobilize support to benefit its schools. Individuals, businesses, and factories donated goods and space. Typewriters and sewing machines were among the most popular items for donation. Smaller items included sweets for prizes. As mentioned previously, Talleres Britania lent the UDCM space for its school there. In addition, members and priests volunteered their time and skills to teach students. Catholic schools were also integrated into a wider program of social action, evidenced by the links between the schools, unionization projects, and moralizing entertainment. For Catholic social action proponents, schools were not an end in themselves, but rather were a means to evangelize and promote Catholic social action principles.[61]

The fact that Catholic schools operated under less bureaucracy than did SEP schools also meant that they could respond quickly to workers' demands and to new opportunities. In some cases, Catholic schools were founded in direct response to workers' requests. For example, in 1919, the order of Our Lady of Guadalupe and Saint Aloysius Gonzaga organized a series of "spiritual exercises" for workers in the Campo Florida. These spiritual exercises were a monthlong discussion series on Bible stories designed by Ignatius Loyola. Two hundred female workers from local factories attended these exercises at the Santa Brígida Church. As the end of the series neared, the workers asked for a permanent catechism center. Eager to oblige, the order of Our Lady of Guadalupe established a catechism center that eventually expanded to offer wide-ranging programs. From the point of view of the order, the catechists could be warned about lewd public dances and other immoral entertainment. Yet there were concrete benefits for the students, too. The young women of the order also founded the Patronato Tepeyac (Tepeyac Council), which offered Sunday classes, a library, and a savings program. At the Sunday school, students could attend courses in primary education, religion, and such women's handicrafts as flower making and sewing. The "well-behaved" students chose which activities they wished to attend, and the entire enterprise took place with "jubilant discipline." The Patronato also offered "suitable" entertainment for the women's leisure time. The final project of the Patronato was to unionize the women workers. According to a 1925 report, the Unión Interprofesional Católica (Interprofessional Catholic Union) was in the early stages of formation and workers had already begun to sit on a board of directors.[62]

The Catholics' use of education as a first step to forming unions was not matched in SEP education, with the exception of the Madero School discussed in the previous chapter. Because the report on the Patronato was intended to enlist public support, it probably ignored or minimized difficulties faced and may have exaggerated the workers' demand for catechism classes. Knowing the myriad problems at SEP workers' schools, I doubt that all the students were perfectly behaved. It is interesting to note, however, that the center for religious instruction expanded to provide workers with practical skills training and a place to call their own: a place to study, learn, or relax.[63]

Students at Catholic adult schools, like their counterparts at SEP schools, were able to negotiate for education on their own terms. Workers' initiative in shaping their education received public recognition and positive reinforcement at UDCM schools, recognition that the SEP did not accord its students. Sofía del Valle, secretary for the UDCM Work Section, emphasized in her reports for *La Dama Católica* the role that workers themselves played in organizing activities at the Academy. For example, the women organized a day excursion to San Angel. Additionally, a group of women workers organized and attended a pilgrimage to the Basilica of the Virgin of Guadalupe; once there workers prayed to the Guadalupana for employment in difficult times.[64] From Del Valle's report, it appears that the working women had planned and executed these activities without any help from damas, making the UDCM Academy a space within which workers could formulate and undertake their own projects.

Del Valle herself benefited from Catholic social action's promotion of women's activities. Never married, Del Valle dedicated her life to Catholic social activities, working closely with Méndez Medina at the SSM, as the secretary for feminine affairs. She organized women workers in the tobacco industry, white-collar workers, and Catholic teachers, and was involved in starting the UDCM Academy. Women's lack of formal training in Catholic social action prompted Del Valle to found the Instituto Superior de Cultura Femenina (Superior Institute of

Feminine Culture) and the Juventud Católica Femenina Mexicana (Mexican Catholic Young Women's Group), which offered women leadership training and practical opportunities to engage in social action work.[65] Thus, the framework of Catholic social action provided Del Valle, and many other damas, with a means to engage in personally fulfilling work.

Just as Catholic social action opened up unexpected opportunities for women, catechism centers also served as literacy centers. According to Jean Meyer, in the nineteenth century there was a direct link between rural literacy and the Catholic faith: The faithful learned to read in their catechism classes. My research indicates that this link existed in the 1920s in Mexico City as well. Illiteracy was dangerous, according to the Catholic magazine *Acción y Fe*, because illiterates were ignorant people who could easily be manipulated. But reading and writing were not sufficient; literacy had to include religious instruction.[66] Like Catholics, revolutionaries feared illiteracy. But although they agreed with the church that illiteracy made the masses susceptible, it was the church's influence that the revolutionaries wished to eradicate. For the revolutionaries, literacy was the means to wrest control of Mexican souls from the nefarious clergy, while for Catholics, literacy ensured that the government could not spread lies about the church.

In a 1922 report to Archbishop Mora y del Río, the UDCM counted 135 catechism centers located in churches and tenements throughout the Mexico City area. In these centers, children received religious instruction while adults learned to read and write. The damas hoped that, through basic education, they would convert non-Catholic adults to Catholics. While the damas may have helped some catechists find spiritual salvation, they taught everyone to read. The Schools Section also planned to offer free literacy training in tenements and homes. One center was to be in a tenement owned by UDCM National President Elena Lascurain de Silva. Two other members offered to open centers in their own homes. Not all centers combined religious teaching with primary education; some ignored religion altogether. The Colegio Italiano began a Sunday afternoon school where literacy, arithmetic, and sewing were taught. The oldest student was fifty-eight. Local churches also offered catechism for children, servants, and the working class.[67] These catechism classes undoubtedly included literacy training. In order to use the catechism books and read the Bible, students needed to be literate. But, once literate, students were not limited to reading religious material. Like students in SEP schools, catechism students could use their new skills for their own ends.

Other catechism centers were founded at the behest of industrialists. For example, several factory owners asked the order of Our Lady of Guadalupe and Saint Aloysius Gonzaga to found the San Alfonso María de Ligorio Catechism Center. Four young women, perhaps nuns, gave classes for women workers on Saturday afternoons. This was not an isolated case, as the San Francisco de Jerónimo Center was also created at the request of La Britania's owners. (La Britania was the same factory where the UDCM established a workers' night school and later a school for workers' children.) In January 1923, the catechism center at La Britania reported a regular attendance of 150 to 180 workers. In La Victoria factory, the order of Our Lady of Guadalupe opened a workers' school, again at the invitation of management, with separate courses for male and female workers.[68] By 1925, there were catechism centers at five factories, including La Tabacalera (cigarettes), La Victoria (cashmere), and La Britania (shirt making). Most of the students at these catechism centers were women. The catechism class at La Britania, which had grown to 280 students, was the largest. The center at La Victoria was "intended to give basic primary instruction and, above all, moralize the women workers in the factory."[69] Records do not indicate why owners wanted these centers, but their reasons probably mixed personal piety with the hope that workers inculcated with Catholic doctrine would be docile. Yet the contradictions between the goals of Catholic social action and the economic injustice of workers' situations must have created tensions that threatened harmonious relations, as a case in the next chapter shows.

Adults as Students

The students who enrolled in adult education had goals and backgrounds as diverse as the schools they attended. The male students in SEP vocational schools ranged from "comfortably off" to poor. During the Porfiriato, professionals had not wanted their sons to learn trades, but after (perhaps because of) the revolution, professionals sought out technical training for their sons. Moreover, the SEP made conscious efforts to attract men from the middle class in order to bolster that emergent sector. According to Vasconcelos, "[A]n effort is being made to create an intelligent middle class, that class which plays such an important role in any nation. Because of class prejudice, the majority of well-to-do people in the past have wished their sons to be professional men and, as a result, the country has now more of these than are needed and too few skilled mechanics." Thus, the SEP needed to create schools that would entice the upper class to enroll their sons, while helping to foster the middle class upon which national development depended. Efforts to diversify student enrollment succeeded and, in 1928, the SEP reported that, while technical schools continued to attract poor men, well-off parents also wanted their sons to have vocational training.[70]

Anecdotal evidence indicates that socioeconomic classes also mixed at women's vocational schools. The Escuela de Artes y Industrias para Mujeres (later the EAOS) was originally founded to provide poor women with skills; however, throughout the Porfiriato, enrollment was largely middle class.[71] By 1921, its student body had become more diverse. At least two young women at the EAOS considered poverty sufficient reason to ridicule their classmates; they were suspended for a month for ringleading the teasing of students who received free federal breakfasts. At other schools, students also showed the class prejudices of the elite. At the Enseñanza Doméstica School, students were supposed to help distribute these free breakfasts when the service first began, but they soon stopped because the work was "beneath them" and, according to their supervisor, they had no preparation for cooperative work. The Mistral School, site of the Sanger controversy, had the poorest students of all the women's vocational schools; the SEP reported that the majority of the young women enrolled were from the "most disadvantaged social class." The students described their school as "the most humble of the technical schools" and themselves as "the most conscious of the benefits that with paternal and prodigious hand the government gives them."[72]

The multiple options in vocational education (full-time, individual course enrollment, night courses) also encouraged students from different social classes to enroll. Day-school students tended to come from families that were able to support a child in full-time education. On the other hand, night schools, both vocational institutions and workers' night schools, were specifically designed for industrial workers, domestic employees, and retail clerks. These students worked a full day and then mustered their remaining energy for nighttime learning. They sought "increased knowledge, increased incomes, and increased pleasures." For the students at the workers' night schools neither rest nor sustenance divided the afternoon from the evening. After an insufficient meal at midday, they worked through the afternoon. In the evening, they listlessly sat through night-school classes while their stomachs rumbled. Inspectora Baños Contreras arranged for the federal breakfast service to serve these students a snack before classes began, presumably so they could benefit from increased caloric intake.[73] Night-school students' commitment to such a long day demonstrates that they valued education and also suggests that their new skills offered them concrete means to improve their economic situations.

The students' dedication and their struggle to better their personal situations is all the more notable considering the differing quality of staff between day and nighttime education. The day schools appeared to have received more experienced and better-trained teachers, while the night schools employed a lower caliber of teacher. Morales wrote of the disgraceful "differences which exist between the day and night teachers."[74] He implied that night-school teachers did not attempt to increase their pedagogic skills, as their day-school counterparts did. He did not offer an explanation for this circumstance, but it is likely that night-school teachers worked a full day before evening classes began, just as their students did. Taking into account the differences in students and teachers at the day and night schools, there was de facto stratification of education in which more resources went to the better-off students. This stratification suggests that adult education reinforced existing class differences, rather than offering students upward mobility. Night school students were expected to become better at their chosen skill, but to remain working class.

While students came from diverse socioeconomic backgrounds, they all tended to be young. In 1926, most male vocational students were between fourteen and twenty years old. Since students only had to finish primary school in order to enroll in technical education, the young age range is not surprising. While women also tended to be between fourteen and twenty years old, three times more women over twenty were enrolled than men over twenty. A contributing factor was probably the higher number of women between the ages of fifteen and twenty-four living in Mexico City. The SEP attributed the age difference solely to the different social roles of men and women. Adult men had to leave school in order to earn a living and did not have time for study. In contrast, "middle class," "comfortably off," and even poor women could continue studying after they started their own homes. Moreover, according to the SEP, a greater variety of courses was offered in women's schools, giving them more incentive to attend school. Most female vocational-school students enrolled for individual courses rather than in a degree program. For women with homes and perhaps outside employment, it was simpler to pursue a particular course for a few hours weekly than to enroll full-time for a degree. The high pass rate for individual courses (91 percent in 1926) indicates that almost all the women who continued their course to completion mastered their training. Yet many students left vocational education before the course finished and without taking their final exams.[75]

Both male and female students used vocational training for their own particular ends. They did not feel an obligation to finish their courses; rather, they sought utility from their education. In selecting courses, students preferred those with the most practical value and "immediate usefulness."[76] Because of how students used education, the DETIC minimized exams as a reliable indicator of the overall success of the adult education program. The department argued that students in technical education attended courses to attain a particular skill and improve their job prospects. Upon attaining their desired skill level, students left school; many students did not sit for exams at all. The DETIC argued that low exam attendance proved that technical schools were functioning as they should. Students who left early, however, did not benefit from the general education offered, and some of these adults remained illiterate even though they had attended school.[77]

Attrition rates varied widely from school to school, suggesting that attendance was influenced by the staff and courses as well as students' personal goals. For example, in 1924, the Querétaro School lost 33 students out of 1,081, while in 1925, a mere 4 out of 1,122 dropped out. Meanwhile, in 1924, the EAOS enrolled 1,095 students, 547 of whom left early. At the Escuela de Ingenieros Mecánicos y Electristas, 3,867 students enrolled and 897 dropped out in 1924.[78] Statistics for 1926 suggest that the SEP had yet to solve its retention problem. Among the thirteen workers' night schools, dropout rates ranged from 18 to 71 percent, with an average dropout rate of 42 percent.

For male students who completed their course, there were limited job placement services. In 1927, the Escuela de Ingenieros Mecánicos, the Instituto Técnico Industrial, and the Escuela Técnica para Maestros Constructores found positions for 148 former students in Mexico and other nations (out of 2,921 students total). The SEP also convinced the Mexico City municipality to hire graduates of the Escuela de Ingenieros Mecánicos for public works projects.[79] The SEP did not provide its women students with comparable employment services. Neither SEP vocational schools nor night schools for women workers attempted to place graduating students. The SEP even offered women training for activities where they were aware that there was no market demand, like the home economics degree available through the Enseñanza Doméstica School.[80] No evidence indicates that the SEP attempted to create a market for these women, as it could easily have done by including home economics in the primary education curriculum.

The UDCM, in contrast to the SEP, organized a job service (Bolsa de Trabajo) to find jobs for skilled women workers. The idea might have come from Méndez Medina's *Manual de formación sindical*. Méndez Medina wrote that among the activities of a Catholic labor union should be the development of workers' neighborhoods and orchards, the sale of inexpensive houses, and placement offices to provide employment services.[81] The Bolsa de Trabajo was available to women who took courses at the UDCM Academy. Connections in the Catholic community and family relations probably helped some damas find employment for Academy students. The Bolsa de Trabajo secretary also used *La Dama Católica* to seek positions. She called the job-seekers worthy women who "in order to follow the virtuous path, do not ask more than a bit of bread for them and theirs."[82] UDCM connections reached across the city and the nation, so their Bolsa de Trabajo probably provided a valuable service. Father Icaza urged damas who needed temporary — probably domestic — employees to contact the Bolsa de Trabajo. In November 1922, Sofía del Valle reported that the Bolsa de Trabajo had found eight women positions in one month, but she did not note how many others awaited work.[83] The order of Our Lady of Guadalupe and Saint Aloysius Gonzaga also placed students from its schools: Seven of the "best-behaved" students at a school established for middle-class youths were placed in "commercial establishments of the first order."[84]

While is difficult to be certain that vocational training improved students' job prospects and economic situations, the high demand for night-school training and the rise in enrollment in the day institutions indicate that courses met students' needs. At the time of the SEP's founding, the attendance at women's technical schools was already "numerous and assiduous."[85] According to the *Bulletin of the Pan American Union,* women servants enrolled for a variety of reasons: Some wanted to earn money to buy themselves luxuries, such as cinema tickets, while single mothers were able to support their children with their new skills.[86] Demands for educational opportunities from men and women further suggest the utility of skills and literacy training. Individuals and groups wrote to the municipality and the SEP asking for help to found schools in their communities. A group of workers requesting a workers' night school wrote that "the desire to educate ourselves in school is very strong [*grande*]." Their entreaty ended with two pages of signatures, which followed a reminder to the head of public education: "[Y]ou offered to help us in this sense." This letter, while respectful in tone, nonetheless closed with the assertion that the workers were simply reminding the authorities of their rights.[87]

In this chapter I have shown that a wide variety of institutions offered education to Mexico City adults. These institutions were operated by different organizations, served varied communities of students, and faced sometimes severe limitations on their work. What the educators shared was a sense that the 1920s was a decade of change and opportunity. The revolution had altered the expectations of the working class, domestic workers, white-collar workers, and even the professional classes. Education in a trade had gained respectability, so poor and rich alike enrolled in men's technical schools. Women found that in order to meet their desire for economic independence, they needed skills available in night schools and vocational schools. These schools provided opportunities not only for the students themselves, but also for their teachers and for their communities. Teachers could use their classrooms to promote their own ideals, be they a political role for women in public life or preparing the European cuisine Vasconcelos condemned. But schools were not the only means through which church and state reached into communities: Libraries, entertainment venues, and unions, addressed in the next chapter, all expanded the reach of church and state moralization projects while responding to local demands.

7 Community Education in Public Spaces

Revolutionary Entertainment and Catholic Unions

In previous chapters I have mentioned how SEP and church programs took education beyond schools. This chapter focuses on these attempts by church or state agencies to mold communities through a variety of educational and social programs. The state used festivals, film exhibitions, and live entertainment in an attempt to "moralize" and "sanitize" communities in Mexico City. The church, through Catholic social-action organizations, supported similar programs. Moreover, the church connected its educational projects to worker unionization efforts. For both church and state, community organizing was intertwined with educational programs: The same institutional actors that founded schools (e.g., the SEP or the UDCM) designed programs to reach Mexico City's poor and working-class communities. This chapter begins with an examination of projects to found neighborhood libraries, then covers public entertainment and field trips. Finally, it addresses Catholic social action in the 1920s and Catholic programs of unionization in particular.

Libraries

Libraries were central to José Vasconcelos' educational reforms and were of equal or more importance than schools, in his view. As education minister, he embarked upon a massive national campaign to found public libraries. Workers, teachers, and students responded enthusiastically to the initiative: Mutualist societies, unions, businesses, and different academic organizations petitioned the SEP for their own local libraries. Depending on a library's location, intended audience, and overall purpose, it could contain ten works or ten thousand; however, most libraries were small (fig. 7.1). The expanded SEP Editorial Section published many of the works in these libraries. Public libraries, as their name suggests, were open to all. Libraries for workers were opened in factories or union offices, while mobile libraries, which had the fewest books, traveled with rural teachers. The SEP stipulated that libraries were to have evening opening hours to accommodate workers and students, and that librarians were to be in close contact with teachers to coordinate activities. Libraries were to be opened in deprived rural or urban areas, particularly in urban "popular neighborhoods" *(barrios populares)*. In the Federal District, the SEP founded libraries in Magdalena Mixhuca and Santa Julia, while Mexico City libraries tended to be located in working-class neighborhoods. Libraries were required to sponsor at least one public event per month, such as a lecture or recital, which appears to have increased adult attendance. For younger readers, many libraries had a section devoted to children's literature. In 1923, the department opened a "model" children's library at the SEP building in the city center. To stimulate the imaginations of juvenile readers, murals and a poem by Gabriela Mistral about Little Red Riding Hood decorated the walls.[1]

When Calles became president, libraries lost their position of priority; nonetheless, even operating on a reduced budget the SEP Library Department continued to expand. Libraries were not the only section of the SEP that struggled, because the overall education budget fell from 52,363,000 pesos in 1923 to 25,593,000 in 1924 and remained at about that level throughout the Calles administration. Budgetary limits notwithstanding, in the Federal District the number of books in local libraries rose by at least 25 percent.[2] The Library Department concentrated its reduced resources on making libraries more accessible to the general population and on improving attendance by targeting its stock toward readers and by training librarians.[3] Moreover, the department publicized its services: At cinemas, stills promoted the local library, and the radio broadcast public service announcements on the importance of reading. Libraries continued to sponsor events such as parties and films, and children's libraries added a "story hour." New policies allowing readers to borrow books were reported as successful, but since libraries required a five-peso deposit, borrowing was for the wealthy while the poor could only consult materials.[4]

By 1926, the department had added several more types of libraries. Popular libraries carried many genres of books and were probably intended for the general public. School libraries stocked literature for students and reference works for teachers. Libraries in union offices included technical works; institutional libraries, in jails or barracks, carried works of "redeeming moral value"; rural libraries tailored their

Figure 7.1. The library at the Miguel Lerdo de Tejada Commercial School. Libraries like this one were popular among students, who took advantage of the reference materials and the comfortable working environment. (Courtesy of the Instituto Mora)

collections to regional needs; and children's libraries carried literature for young readers. In the Federal District, 71 libraries were founded in 1926 while 131 had their collections improved.[5] Nonetheless, in the SEP's report for the years 1924–1928 the department received strong criticism for not being active enough in expanding its work. Sending boxes of books to different schools and institutions was not enough; libraries had to tailor their collections to the needs of their local readers more effectively and to sponsor more cultural programs.[6]

The SEP's priorities for libraries approximately corresponded with those of their readers. Patrons, too, sought books on practical topics that addressed their needs; the librarian in Magdalena Mixhuca commented that he needed more books on applied sciences because workers visited his library to perfect their trades. Moreover, a library's location contributed to its popularity, as did good administration and the frequency and regularity of its opening hours. According to 1923 SEP reports, the most frequented public library, which also had the highest number of subscribers, was in the women's Corregidora de Querétaro vocational school, located in the crowded Colonia Guerrero.

As the preceding discussion suggests, in 1923, most library patrons were children or working-class adults. Workers patronized libraries located in industrial areas, while in middle-class areas, such as the Colonia Roma, readers were children and teenagers. Children continued to be heavy library users throughout the 1920s. In 1926, Juana Manrique de Lara reported in the *Bulletin of the Pan American Union* that almost 90 percent of those using local libraries were children. Public libraries were an essential resource for schoolchildren, since most primary schools did not have their own libraries and books were expensive to purchase. At the model children's library in the SEP offices, in 1926 the average daily attendance was two hundred children and, in the children's section of the Cervantes Library, the average daily attendance was four hundred children. For poor children, libraries might have offered a respite from cramped dwellings, providing a comfortable table and chair at which to work.[7]

Recognizing the moralizing potential of books, Catholics also founded libraries and stocked them with books approved by the ecclesiastical censors. In the Catholic journal *Acción y Fe,* the writers reported on the inauguration of a library next to a catechism center. To celebrate the library's opening, the founders sponsored films and a small party. The catechism teachers had purchased the library's sixty-eight books themselves, but the founders hoped that the holdings would grow and thus increase the good influences on local children. In another case, the journal noted that children from Santa Cruz de Acatlán no longer read immoral novels and, instead, read only books approved by their religion teachers. *Acción y Fe* attributed the change of interests to the nearby, recently opened library.[8]

Resolutions from the 1922 UDCM National Congress included support for public subscription libraries that would stock literature of "moral" and "social" value. The damas envisioned uplifting popular culture through improved literary taste. The UDCM valued the moralizing possibilities of books even more in areas where there was little to do, such as isolated Mexico City neighborhoods and outlying communities. In urban areas, the damas believed that moral books would counteract the cinema, which they saw as a dangerous influence. In practice, the UDCM limited its work to a partnership with the Bibliotecas Populares de Nuestra Señora del Sagrado Corazón (Popular Libraries of Our Lady of the Sacred Heart).

The first Sacred Heart library was founded in the capital in 1917 with seven books; by the end of that year there were nine libraries with 1,220 books. The Sacred Heart library regulations stipulated that libraries were to be located in the homes of Christian women of "good moral character." After paying an inscription fee of one peso, users could borrow books for five centavos each. The initial inscription fee appears costly for a working-class person, being more than one-third of the daily budget for a family of five, especially considering that SEP libraries were free for reference readers. Perhaps due to the cost, in 1924, Mexico City's Sacred Heart libraries counted only three thousand members.[9] While UDCM rhetoric promoted libraries for the poor, the high cost of membership at the Sacred Heart libraries indicates that they were not actually intended for the lower classes.

Educational Entertainment

Like the damas, Vasconcelos worried about what bored workers might get up to in their limited free time. To keep their activities licit, the SEP provided community entertainment as part of its educational mission. SEP-sponsored concerts, dances, and films were to teach Vasconcelos' version of Mexican culture to working-class audiences while entertaining them in a wholesome way. The new national culture promoted through these festivals had emerged from the revolutionary upheaval and was based on an amalgamation of multiple indigenous and regional cultures. While promoting a new cultural ideal, these moralizing festivals continued the work of Porfirian educators like Justo Sierra who had sponsored workers' choral groups and inexpensive opera performances aimed at the poor. Mutualist societies had also offered their members entertainment, such as chamber music.[10] The new feature of the SEP's cultural program, then, was its focus on national and indigenous themes.

Music, inside and outside of schools, was an essential means of moralizing, uplifting, and, simultaneously, entertaining communities. Vasconcelos, who initially found listening to school choruses a painful experience, hired specialists to teach music in schools. He reported that SEP public concerts demonstrated the good results of these specialist teachers and that these concerts — in which orchestras, bands, and choirs of thousands of children participated — were not to be surpassed. The local press reported on SEP concerts in great detail; for example, articles noted which students performed which song at which festival. In 1922, the SEP held 168 indoor concerts and founded twenty-four public orchestras. Vasconcelos also noted that the (disreputable) or-feones populares had given Sunday concerts in local cinemas and the-aters to a total of twenty thousand spectators. In 1922, the number of musical offerings held at local Mexico City cinemas rose from only three in February to twenty-nine in May. The *Boletín de la Secretaría de Educación Pública* reported that the number of people attending also rose but neglected to give figures. During the Calles presidency, various popular choruses continued to offer free concerts in venues that could accommodate between one and two thousand people.[11]

Inspired by Greek theater, Vasconcelos also brought music to the great outdoors. Open-air festivals of music and dance were supposed to educate the public while fostering their emotional faculties. In 1922, the SEP sponsored sixteen open-air festivals. The SEP's open-air con-certs and festivals at Chapultepec Park were performed in front of ten to twelve thousand audience members, sometimes including Vascon-celos and President Obregón. During the performances, students from various SEP schools sang, danced, and listened to "traditional" Mexi-can music while enjoying a day's reprieve from classes.[12] Student danc-ers wore elaborate costumes representing the region or the era of the dance they performed. Even though Vasconcelos spoke at length about the importance of Mexican models, SEP open-air performances in-cluded an eclectic mix of time periods, costumes, and themes.

The frequency of these events at Chapultepec Park appears to have declined during the Vasconcelos years and, as far as I can determine, they virtually disappeared under Puig Casauranc. Replacing the Cha-pultepec Park performances were enormous events at the newly con-structed National Stadium. Between 1924 and 1928, the SEP staged eight patriotic musical festivals: four on 15 September for indepen-dence celebrations and four on 5 May to celebrate the French defeat at Puebla. Additionally, because the inaugural festival for the national stadium was oversubscribed, the SEP staged the inauguration twice and, in honor of aviator Charles Lindbergh, it held a musical festival.[13]

In addition to live performances, the SEP sponsored films shown at locations ranging from schools to union meeting halls. Film screenings were highly popular in Mexico City. One contemporary observer reported that even the poorest could afford films, and that they would rather forgo necessities than miss the next chapter of the latest cinematic serial.[14] From the time of the first public film screening in 1896, cinema quickly became fashionable among the capital's residents, who could "see" far-flung parts of their own republic, not to mention President Díaz starring in "El General Díaz paseando por el bosque de Chapultepec." By January 1900, there were twenty-two tent cinemas set up in plazas throughout the capital. El Buen Tono cigarette company opened its own theater in its office building and, rather than charging admission in cash, the company charged a certain number of empty cigarette boxes. El Buen Tono also sponsored outdoor films on the Alameda (in 1904), just up the street from its offices. By 1907, Mexico City hosted thirty-four cinemas and an additional twenty-seven more were opened during the centennial festivities in 1910, with capacities generally between 250 and 500 seats.

These cinemas created what Anne Rubenstein calls a "new social space" in which etiquette had yet to be established; for instance, should men and women be allowed to attend the same showings? In the darkened theater, couples could engage in sexual behavior with relative privacy. The anonymity possible in cinemas partially explains the concerns that groups like the UDCM expressed regarding the moral threat of the cinema. Yet even as moralizers sought to limit the degrading influences of the cinema, they were aware that this new technology was permanently transforming entertainment. The government also recognized the propagandistic value of films and, under Obregón, the ministries of war, agriculture, and education all sponsored their own films.[15]

Besides making its own films, the SEP also sponsored free public showings of commercial films, proving itself adept at using this modern medium to attract viewers to its events. These SEP-sponsored films were sometimes the main attraction and sometimes formed part of an evening's entertainment that also included speakers and live performances. Table 7.1 shows that thousands of people attended SEP-

Table 7.1. SEP-Sponsored Films between 13 June and 30 November 1922

Location	Audience	Attendance	Number of Showings
Night schools	Workers	5,726	146
Primarias elementales/ Primarias superiores	Children	2,432	39
Cinemas	Not reported	6,500	17
Union halls	Not reported	1,346	23
Normal schools	Teachers and students	1,012	12 (Escuela Normal para Maestras)
			13 (Escuela Normal para Maestros)
Scientific societies	Not reported	348	5
Literacy centers	Workers and children	500	18
Our centers (*nuestros centros*)	Workers' families, including children	3,864	36
Total		*21,728*	*309*

Source: Boletín de la Secretaría de Educación Pública nos. 3–4 (1923): 410–11.

sponsored films in a six-month period in 1922. More than half of the approximately twenty-two thousand attendees saw films either in cinemas or in workers' night schools. These figures indicate how popular cinema-going was: 22,000 people represent more than 3 percent of the total population (615,367 in 1921) of Mexico City. Of course, some could have been repeat attendees.[16]

Because most Mexico City residents did not work on Sundays, the SEP frequently sponsored Sunday events that included a film showing. The SEP also invited noted professors or teachers to speak about issues concerning contemporary Mexico during these events.[17] Program leaflets from the Cultural Festivals organized jointly by the SEP Departamento de Bellas Artes and the Workers' Cultural Center—probably one of the SEP workers' night schools—indicate the variety of SEP-sponsored entertainment available at the Cine Montecarlo, one of the city's high-class cinemas. Programs, starting at ten in the morning,

included poetry recitations, plays, lectures, films, and dances performed by members of the workers' center or invited guests. During the
films, the literate read the subtitles to their illiterate companions in a
whisper. Films shown at the Cine Montecarlo included *Use of Bamboo
in Indochina, Panama Canal,* and *The Circus.* The lectures to which the
audience listened included "The Proletariat in Mexico and the Commu-
nist Revolution" or the "Easy Theme 'The Woman.'" On another occasion, the workers' center headmaster offered one lecture about work
and another entitled "What Should Be Understood by Wealth: Its Distribution." For five straight weeks, the invited speakers included "one
of the members of the Socialist Block of the Law School."[18] Because
lectures frequently had no title, it is difficult to determine how often the
audience heard themes relating to work. Moreover, without the text of
the lectures, it is impossible to know whether speakers on the specified
topics called for radical redistribution of wealth or acceptance of the
status quo. Without knowing the content of the talks, we cannot as-
sume a particular perspective, although the presence of the Socialist
Block suggests at least some left-leaning talks.

The prominence of cultural events was a hallmark of Vasconcelos'
tenure at the SEP. Under Puig Casauranc, the number of films screened
declined from 3,514 in 1924 to 1,662 in 1928, and conferences declined from 821 in 1924 to 210 in 1928. Entertainment could have
been less frequent because the SEP budget fell between 1924 and
1928.[19] Still, entertainment, like libraries, appears to have been a lower
priority for this SEP administration, which did not emphasize cultural
activities and moral uplift, but rather focused on practical, easily quan-
tified skills and results.

The Unión de Damas Católicas Mexicanas also recognized that films
were a powerful ideological tool, a tool that members believed could
either moralize or contaminate young minds. The UDCM used films as
rewards for good behavior in its schools. For example, punctual students at the UDCM Academy were invited to Saturday matinees. As
mentioned in chapter 5, the UDCM also attempted to open its own
cinema to raise money for the Schools Section, but the venture was
never profitable.[20] The public preferred the immoral (or at least less
moralistic) films shown in other establishments to the films the damas
selected.

Because the public flocked to films, some revolutionaries shared UDCM concerns. The Mexico City regional center of the UDCM wrote to Vasconcelos about their desire to establish a commission that would rate and approve films. In response, Vasconcelos informed the damas that he agreed with them about the menace of immoral films. He added that Obregón was also concerned about the cinema's influence on children and that the UDCM "could count on the president's support for their noble work."[21] This correspondence further indicates that representatives of the Catholic Church and the state shared concerns regarding the morals and leisure pastimes of the common people. In this case, when the state, represented by Obregón and Vasconcelos, supported the work of the church, represented by the UDCM, the damas proudly published the correspondence. The UDCM appeared to view Vasconcelos as a worthy collaborator and had earlier sought his support for their plan to open a boarding school for indigenous children in the Colonia del Valle. There are no indications that the school ever progressed beyond the planning stage, but the UDCM attempt to gain SEP support still indicates common sentiments on educational and moral concerns.[22]

Other Catholics shared these worries about immoral films: Joaquín Cardoso, a Jesuit contributor to *El Mensajero del Sagrado Corazón de Jesús de México*, lamented that immoral films could cause permanent damage to viewers and lead to increases in crime. Cardoso advised his readers to obtain projectors, so that instead of attending public films, which were always a risk, readers could watch suitable films at home. The films Cardoso recommended, however, did not necessarily promote the moral standards a modern reader might expect. One film was described as the story of a drunken police officer whose state of inebriation caused humorous incidents. This genre of film was a direct descendent of the comedy popular among Mexico's lower classes and originating in the *carpa* theater: In these ill-reputed revues, drunks or foolish authority figures delighted the crowd.[23] Moreover, Cardoso's suggestion that readers purchase a projector indicates that either he consciously addressed a wealthy readership or he was unaware of the economic realities of most Mexicans.

In a city where residents were constantly seeking things to do, public exhibitions were another means to moralize and entertain. As noted in the previous chapter, the UDCM sponsored expositions of students' crafts at its academy for working women located in the UDCM headquarters at Avenida Guatemala 24. UDCM spiritual director Leopoldo Icaza requested that damas attend the expositions, in order to encourage the women workers in their labors. Icaza also suggested that the damas donate small items to give as prizes for students who had distinguished themselves in their work.[24] I have not, however, found large-scale public displays of work sponsored by Catholic institutions. Budgetary constraints likely account for this absence.

In contrast, the SEP's public displays of vocational school handicrafts attracted thousands of visitors and merited articles in *Demócrata, Universal,* and *Heraldo de México.* Journalists reported in meticulous detail which students created the most elegant hats or best-crafted tables. According to these journalists, the public enthusiastically attended the exhibitions, viewed the products, and sampled the food. The women's schools put on fashion shows and displays of handmade goods: Products ranged from stylish dresses to tooth powder. Large numbers of city residents attended these popular exhibitions: An exhibition at the Querétaro School in 1923 attracted 66,649 people in just ten days.[25] High attendance at SEP exhibitions suggests that the public took advantage of free entertainment; if reports can be believed, most exhibitions that the SEP or Catholic agencies sponsored attracted flocks of people.

In 1926, the DETIC announced plans to open a store for the permanent exhibition and sale of vocational-school products. The store, called E.T.I.C., would allow students to gain experience in selling their products while earning a fraction of the proceeds. The DETIC hoped that the store would commercialize the vocational schools' products by bringing them to the public's attention. Moreover, through the E.T.I.C. store, both teachers and students learned to calculate costs and profits, thus completing the business aspect of their training. According to the SEP, technical-school teachers themselves had been ignorant of the market and finally learned, through the E.T.I.C. store, to produce goods that were in demand. The SEP, however, did not have the funds to sustain the store, and it lasted only two years.[26]

The existence of the E.T.I.C. store indicates that artisanal crafts and Mexican popular arts manufactured in vocational schools were being sold to a local population, and the high attendance at the various exhibitions suggests interest in these products. So the Apache and *china poblana* wall hangings that women in vocational schools learned to manufacture may well have decorated the rooms of a Mexico City resident. While Vasconcelos was inventing a homogenized indigenous culture through the SEP's entertainment program, a commodification of that new folkloric culture was taking place, and its appeal extended to those with disposable income. Yet women's handicraft production was not limited to items inspired by indigenous themes. In vocational schools, women also learned to produce and care for high-value luxury items that would have fit within the homes of the most demanding Porfirian family. For example, in the display dining room created by Mistral School students, atop an Oriental carpet sat a linen-covered table. Polished silver awaited the guests, whose meal would be illuminated by a Tiffany-style lamp. Thus the various vocational schools sold a mixture of folkloric, luxury, and practical items at the E.T.I.C. store, from pottery and wicker furniture to pharmaceutical products and table runners.[27] In SEP schools, poor women learned how to participate in modernity by making items for their own use and by making products that would satisfy consumer demands.

Field Trips

While entertainment or exhibitions offered occasional diversions from the school routine, educators expected excursions to form a regular part of the students' formal education. Beyond the school walls, students would see examples of phenomena that, in school, they had learned as abstract concepts. Excursions appear to have become more frequent during the 1920s, perhaps as the countryside was pacified. In 1920, the municipality authorized more than 150 field trips. Trams hired at a 50 percent discount transported children to destinations outside Mexico City. Tram routes, leaving from the Zócalo, connected Mexico City with suburbs such as San Angel, Coyoacán, and Tlalpan, all of which would have offered sites of interest. Beyond discussion of tram discounts, I have found no records addressing the cost of field trips. When the headmistress of one school hired a tram, she was responsible for the cost of the rental, a cost she probably passed along to parents.[28]

Programs survive from two field trips for students at a girls' municipal school. Students and staff were to go to Guadalupe Hidalgo, a town of ten thousand that wore "a perpetual air of joyousness." At 8:30, students were supposed to leave their school to catch the train; during the trip students were expected to sing and listen to explanations of what they were about to see. In Guadalupe Hidalgo, students were to visit the municipal offices, as well as schools and monuments. Notably missing from the sites chosen is the Basilica of the Virgin of Guadalupe. From the highest point of a nearby hill, the headmistress planned to discuss the products of the Valley of Mexico. In addition, each grade was to stage a mountaintop performance for the other years: First and second graders planned to perform a gymnastic game, the third and fourth graders were to sing a song about spring, and the fourth graders were also to recite "The National Flag." The headmistress was realistic enough to note that when the students descended the hill, they would be in high spirits. She planned that her students would eat their simple lunches after the mountaintop performances. At 3:30, the students were to gather at the base of the statue of Hidalgo to listen to a fourth-year student tell the story of his life. Afterward, the plans called for students to sing a "hymn to Hidalgo." At 4:30, everyone would return to Mexico City.

Third-year students from the same municipal girls' school took a field trip to the National History Museum. According to the schedule, the students left school at 9:30, making their way to the museum on foot. At the museum, the students visited the ancient history rooms, paying special attention to the Cholula pyramids. After looking at the exhibits, the students listened to a lecture on surviving pre-Colombian monuments. At the end of the day, pending permission, the girls would sing a song as a farewell to the museum and its staff. Both of these trips were well planned and used nearby resources, thus reducing expenditures.[29]

Like the municipality, the SEP emphasized the importance of field trips and was determined that excursions should have educational value. A 1921 circular advised inspectors and principals that schools needed to send their students on monthly outings related to the curriculum. Yet these field trips were planned without regard to the economic burden they placed on parents: It was unrealistic to expect parents to pay for transportation each month. Moreover, SEP educators had a narrow idea of what constituted a field trip. For example, students could have visited local sites that were accessible by foot, as municipal students had done, thus avoiding high transportation costs. By 1927, while still underlining the educational value of excursions, the SEP admitted that outings were expensive for families and not always feasible.[30]

The SEP Departamento de Dibujo y Trabajo Manual (Department of Drawing and Manual Labor) mitigated the high transportation costs of its excursions by trading advertising space in the department's magazine, *Pulgarcito,* for discounts or free passes on trams. In 1926, the department hired individual train cars, sometimes marked "special" (to the delight of the children) to take students on adventures. The trips sponsored by *Pulgarcito* occurred on weekends and during the long Christmas vacation and were to inspire the children's artistry and writing. The volcanoes in Puebla were a popular destination for these trips. Once at their destination, students played with local children, visited the sites, drew pictures of their surroundings, and explored. *Pulgarcito* also sponsored trips to local factories. For example, one group went to visit the Larín chocolate factory. Although warned not to ask for sweets during their tour, the children were lucky enough to receive sample chocolates. Eduardo Soto graciously shared his chocolates with his mother and younger siblings upon returning home.

Some of the children's essays and illustrations from these trips were later published in the magazine. One boy wrote that, the night before his field trip, having fallen asleep thinking about it, he jumped out of bed early, rushed to the deserted Ministry of Public Education, and was convinced he had been left behind only to discover that in his excitement he had arrived hours early. For other children, SEP-sponsored trips offered their first experience outside of the city. As Benjamín Castañeda expressed it, "[T]he excursion had the objective of giving us the means to admire places that many of us still don't know because of not having traveled yet and having few opportunities to go to the countryside." In contrast, parents — like Benjamín's mother, who wanted reassurance that students were not visiting a dangerous area — might have been nervous about allowing their children to travel. Most of the writers published in *Pulgarcito* were boys, and all expressed gratitude for the opportunity to visit a new place. Nonetheless, among *Pulgarcito*'s pages are also admonitions to children to attend the field trips for which they had registered. On one occasion, although approximately twenty students had signed up, only six or seven actually went on the trip. Even though *Pulgarcito*'s contributors expressed boundless excitement at the prospect of outings, field trips were apparently not as popular as might be expected. While financial considerations could have reduced the number of participants, there are no indications that *Pulgarcito* charged students. Moreover, transportation, the most expensive part of a trip, was often free.[31]

As mentioned in chapter 6, students in vocational schools went on trips related to their degree programs, usually to factories or commercial establishments. The Dr. Mora Commercial School excelled in field trip organization, sending students on twenty-eight trips around the Federal District for the benefit of their moral, intellectual, and physical development. At least two of the trips were overnight hiking excursions, intended to take students away from the city, to give them fresh air to breathe and hills to climb. One hundred fifty students spent two days in the pine-covered mountains known as the Desierto de los Leones. They climbed San Miguel Peak and spent the night amid the ruins of the old monastery there. A similar number of students went to the Ajusco Peaks, leaving from Tlalpan and spending the night in Ajusco village. There were no major problems reported on any of these twenty-eight trips. Principals, teachers, and students from other schools accompanied staff and students from the commercial school. The school's principal, Federico Cervantes, also founded a *cuerpo de exploradores* (explorers' division) for the boys at his school, to teach them a love of nature. The first trip planned was to Chapultepec Heights.[32]

While the students on all of these trips were young men, whose activities were described in militaristic language such as "to quarter" and "bivouac," exercise was important for both male and female students. Physical exercise, on the school grounds or during trips away from school, was considered an integral component of the curriculum (fig. 7.2). Educators recognized that students had to be physically healthy in order to receive the full benefits of schooling. Moreover, these urban educators viewed the city, with its cinemas, gambling, and lively street life, as inherently corrupting, while they believed that the countryside was wholesome and would strengthen mind and spirit.

My research indicates that Catholic schools did not organize outings with the same frequency as public schools did. I suspect, however, that

Figure 7.2. Physical education for young men emphasized virility and strength. The contrast between this image and that in figure 3.3 is not only in how the students exercised but where. While the young women exercised outside in a sunny patio, these young men were flexing their muscles in the gymnasium, with its medicine ball and climbing rope. This class was photographed at the Escuela de Ingenieros Mecánicos y Electristas. (Courtesy of the Instituto Mora)

this perception is due to my sources rather than an actual Catholic disregard for days out. I have found at least one instance of the UDCM Academy sending students on a day trip to San Angel, and the prospectus for the Colegio-Casa Nazaret mentions periodic excursions as beneficial to body and soul. Founder Castillo y Piña criticized other women's schools for not following the most recent theories on using trips, recreation, and physical education as part of an overall program of "hygiene." An article published in *Acción y Fe* condemned the popularity of films, even among the poorest families, and promoted family trips to the countryside as a healthy, honest, and invigorating alternative. Furthermore, students in Catholic schools visited shrines or attended important masses. For instance, in 1922, the Archdiocese of Mexico reported that more than four thousand children had made a pilgrimage to the Basilica of the Virgin of Guadalupe. In 1926, the UDCM Schools Section reported on field trips made by students in one of their schools to Chapultepec and to a plant nursery.[33]

Yet simply being outdoors could not guarantee moral improvement, particularly in unsupervised situations. Concern for public immorality reached a new height when the municipality sought to teach park-goers what they should and should not do. In 1926, the municipality built the Parque México in the Colonia Condesa on the site of a defunct race-track. Paths meandered around the park and, as the young trees were then only waist-high, visitors could look toward Chapultepec Park to see the castle perched upon its hill, while northward the Angel of Independence guarded the wide Paseo de la Reforma. Along these winding paths, now overhung by trees, are still signs that date from the park's construction, exhorting temperate behavior from visitors. These signs command attention and plead with park-goers to "make proper use of the benches." The play areas of children are restricted: "In this park there is a special place for children's play. Don't permit your child to play outside it." Signs advise against littering ("Throwing litter or fruit rinds detracts from the culture and urbanity of any person."), prohibit eating within the park, and require that dogs be on a leash.[34] The profuse entreaties to behave in a strictly proscribed manner are surprising in a park constructed in a middle-class neighborhood. Either the middle class needed more moralization than generally thought, or the park was a popular attraction for people from less "moral" areas of the city.

Catholic Social Action

The social and educational work of the federal government reached into the most private spaces and moments of its citizens. The Catholic Church, too, linked private and public through social action, expanding its purview beyond private devotion. For the church, leaving the private realm of belief to enter the public sphere risked conflict with the state. The social action programs that the Catholic Church promoted in the 1920s demonstrate that the church's community work evolved in response to the political and social situation of postrevolutionary Mexico. The church, like the state, sought to improve working-class morality and gain workers' loyalty. But, unlike the state, the loyalty the church promoted was to the church and the morality code was based on Catholic teachings. Education was simply one aspect of the Catholic social action program that touched the working class and, as such, it is necessary to examine Catholic social action more generally.

Catholic social action organizations demonstrated impressive growth in the first half of the 1920s, a growth that bears similarities to the resurgence of the church during the Porfiriato. During both eras, Catholics were aware that their social and political programs had little or no legal basis and that they depended upon the goodwill of government leaders. In the 1920s, however, the situation was simultaneously more dire and yet more hopeful than it had been for earlier generations of Catholics. Although the 1917 Constitution denied the juridical existence of the church and strictly limited the church's sphere of influence, Catholics were more mobilized, both to protect their religion and to promote Catholic social programs, than they had been during the Porfiriato.

The engine for social action that oversaw Catholic programs in the 1920s was the Secretariado Social Mexicano. The SSM was founded in October 1920 at the initiative of the Mexican episcopate, to organize, coordinate, and support Catholic social work. Alfredo Méndez Medina, already the informal head of Catholic social action, was appointed director. His background and education, which amply prepared him for social work, were discussed in chapter 4. Méndez Medina was careful not to encroach upon the territory or limit the autonomy of existing organizations, which continued their independent growth. During his five years as SSM director, Méndez Medina devoted most of his attention to workers' organizations, a long-standing priority of Catholic social action. Ceballos Ramírez writes that the majority of the members of the Catholic workers' circles, which had prospered in the first decade of the century, joined SSM-coordinated workers' unions during the 1920s. Méndez Medina's work to promote unions was also supported by the Catholic hierarchy. In a 1923 letter to Obregón, several bishops and archbishops, including Mora y del Río and Archbishop of Guadalajara Francisco Orozco y Jiménez, described unions as an effective means to combat individualism and its harmful repercussions. Unions would improve workers' skills, morals, intellect, and financial situation. Nonetheless, the bishops sanctioned strike action only when arbitration had failed. The church also asserted that unions were effective only if each class had an organization to represent its interests; for example, organized workers should meet with organized owners.[35]

Catholic unions grew out of the nineteenth-century mutualist society movement, which was given a new impetus, justification, and broader orientation through social action that promoted the participation of laypeople in organizing Catholic groups. The unions reached beyond working life into every aspect of their members' existence, offering religious orientation, educational opportunities, cooperatives, and entertainment. Robert Curley notes that these unions were organized by and for people for whom existence was a struggle and for whom the unions meant aid when ill and condolence in times of mourning. The unions were based on a corporatist ideal that did not separate the spheres of public and private. For example, Catholic unions considered low pay and dangerous conditions to be detrimental to the family as a whole and, therefore, conditions that needed to be combated.[36]

In 1922, at a conference in Guadalajara, independent Catholic unions affiliated under the Confederación Nacional Católica del Trabajo (National Catholic Confederation of Work, or CNCT), based in that city. Although the conference hosted more than 1,300 delegates from thirteen, mostly central, states, fully 60 percent of the participants were from Jalisco. Women were involved in the organization of the CNCT because UDCM-affiliated women's unions had sent representatives to Guadalajara. The CNCT's subsequent growth is notable. At the time of its founding in 1922, the CNCT counted 67 affiliated unions representing 7,540 workers; by 1925, the CNCT had 384 affiliated unions with 19,500 members. In 1926 the CNCT had more than 22,000 members.[37]

While the confederation officially professed Catholicism, not all member unions were Catholic. Curley has suggested that Méndez Medina supported CNCT openness to workers who were not affiliated with a Catholic union: Free workers from Monterrey, Puebla, Saltillo, Orizaba, the Federal District, Toluca, and Querétaro all affiliated with the CNCT. The fact that non-Catholic unions joined the CNCT indicates that the confederation met workers' needs — Catholic or not. It also demonstrates the confederation's independence. SSM Director Méndez Medina promoted union independence in general; the CNCT remained autonomous and independent of the church hierarchy. Méndez Medina appeared to see his role as one of facilitator rather than leader: Only on questions of morals and doctrine would he consult ecclesiastical authorities. Méndez Medina consistently stood up to the episcopate regarding CNCT autonomy, and the CNCT unanimously expressed its commitment to independence at the 1922 Guadalajara congress. Nonetheless, tension over leadership of lay organizations existed throughout the 1920s and was partially responsible for the hierarchy subordinating lay organizations after the Cristero Rebellion.[38]

Although Catholic union membership continued to increase during the 1920s, the legal standing of these unions was uncertain. Meanwhile, the CROM had the support first of Obregón and later of Calles. Under Calles, CROM leader Luis Morones became a member of the cabinet, as the Minister of Industry, Commerce, and Labor. In this atmosphere, all independent unions were threatened, with Catholic unions being particularly singled out. In the Federal District, the enforcement of constitutional Article 123, at the end of 1925, prohibited unions with a religious affiliation. Nonetheless, by then the CNCT had received recognition from, among others, the National Chamber of Commerce and the Confederation of Industrial Chambers.[39]

Whereas CROM apologist Marjorie Clark dismisses Catholic labor unions as ineffectual because they never called a strike, their role in organized labor before the escalation of the church-state conflict deserves further investigation. Curley's work on the Catholic Union of Free Workers in El Salto, Jalisco, indicates a lively, popular, and combative union that sponsored a band, religious and secular study, and successful negotiations with management. Curley also suggests that the Catholic labor unions were as much a part of the mass organizations and mass politics that emerged in Mexico in the postrevolutionary period as any left-wing groups. By the 1930s, restrictions on the lay activities of the church had removed Catholic unions from the arena of organized labor; yet, between 1920 and 1925, Curley argues, Catholic unions were dangerous competition for both official and leftist syndicalism. As Curley rightly points out, the hostility of lay unions toward Catholic unions by itself indicates their importance.[40]

The tobacco workers' union at El Buen Tono cigarette factory is an example of another Catholic union that was strong enough to threaten management. In the 1920s, El Buen Tono operated the largest factory in Mexico City: The mostly women workers numbered up to two

thousand. Moreover, the factory was considered progressive in its policies toward workers. For instance, workers' baths, opened in 1901,
were so unusual that the Superior Council of Health commended El
Buen Tono. El Buen Tono had enjoyed a strong relationship with Catholic organizations for years. The factory had a chapel that was consecrated to the Sacred Heart in 1914. In the early 1920s, the factory
served pulque at noon and strongly encouraged male workers to affiliate with the Knights of Columbus. The company also donated sixty
pesos monthly to the Asociación de Damas Católicas/UDCM from
1913 to 1924, the bulk of which the damas used for their projects
oriented toward workers. The relationship between Catholic organizations and El Buen Tono appears to have disintegrated by the mid-
1920s, due to the dismissal of Catholic workers. The CROM might
have been behind these layoffs: Ernest Gruening notes that El Buen
Tono was among the earliest factories to affiliate with the CROM. If we
consider that El Buen Tono also had a Catholic union, tension between
the two would have been inevitable. Eventually, El Buen Tono was
named on pamphlets as one of the targets of the economic boycott
organized by Catholics (discussed in chapter 8).[41]

Even in this paternalist, religiously oriented factory, a Catholic union
stood up to management when necessary. In 1923, the president and
secretary of the Unión Profesional de Tabaqueras de México (Professional Union of Women Tobacco Workers of Mexico) wrote to El Buen
Tono board member Roberto Núñez complaining of unjust treatment.
The oldest and most "worn out" women employees were threatened
with dismissal; moreover, management was not even following the
correct dismissal procedure. The union representatives, presenting their
demands in a paternalist discourse in which the factory owners owed
them protection in exchange for loyalty, wrote that El Buen Tono had
been like a home to them and they had devoted themselves to the company's good. The union officials asked Núñez to influence the board to
stop the dismissals that they believed would both shame the factory and
cause sorrow among good families. Concluding their letter with a veiled
threat, they noted that they were in contact with numerous Catholic
organizations around the country that were carefully watching the outcome of this situation.[42]

This threat shows the confident action of a strong union. It also
shows that the paternalism and strong class structures on which Cath-

olic social activities were initially based had been broken down by the revolution, and this letter uses both discourses. Although the letter begins by claiming rights based on a moral pact between workers and their boss, it ends with a threat of action only possible due to the national strength of Catholic unions. Catholics and non-Catholics alike exhibited a strong militancy and awareness of their rights in the 1920s, and were not hesitant to demand that these rights be respected.

In the early 1920s, the Catholic Church promoted unions not just for industrial and agricultural workers, but for all segments of society. After the first CNCT congress in Guadalajara, the SSM called on professionals, teachers, and white-collar workers, among others, to form their own unions. Only teachers and white-collar workers, however, formed unions that affiliated with the CNCT. The second national CNCT congress, which took place at the SSM offices in Mexico City, established a subcommittee entrusted with organizing the Liga Nacional de la Clase Media (National League of the Middle Class). Nonetheless, Ceballos Ramírez concludes that middle-class unionization concerned the CNCT very little in comparison to unionizing the working class and campesinos.[43]

In the mid-1920s, Méndez Medina realized that the "ruling classes," like large-scale land and factory owners, had little need for collective action and were reluctant to organize under the church's tutelage. The apathy and reluctance of the ruling classes toward Catholic social action aroused the ire of some clerics, including Méndez Medina and Archbishop Orozco y Jiménez. Méndez Medina eventually devoted his attention almost exclusively to workers, leaving the wealthy classes to fend for themselves. Moreover, the lack of interest that the ruling classes, particularly wealthy agriculturists, had for Catholic social action prompted Méndez Medina to modify his programs. His land reform program had originally depended upon generous landowners who, motivated by Christian charity, would sell or lease their lands at minimal cost. Faced with uncooperative landowners, however, Méndez Medina's views radicalized. By 1925, the Jesuit supported the government's forced land expropriation policy, even though it violated church principles regarding the sanctity of private property.[44] While his views were on the left of the Catholic social action movement, his continued popularity among the bishops, discussed in chapter 8, indicates that he had not yet gone too far in his search for what we would now call social justice.

Although Méndez Medina concentrated on organizing workers, as SSM director he was involved in other Catholic social action projects. For example, Archbishop Mora y del Río appointed him ecclesiastical advisor for the first national congress of the UDCM in 1922. No doubt his role in the congress reflected his position as the leader of Catholic social action, but there are no indications that he imposed his own opinions on the congress.[45] He described his role as one of orienting the damas toward social work, while expecting the women to do the rest with both ingenuity and good grace. Writing for *Acción y Fe,* Méndez Medina praised the damas for their work at the congress. He responded to anticipated ridicule from male readers by writing that there would certainly be some "who just reading the title of this article, turning the page, say scornfully: *congress of women . . . what smugness! what jubilation!*" Méndez Medina exhorted men who were not "superficial" to continue reading about the women's successful combination of delicacy and strength.[46] He also worked with the UDCM on their unionization projects, periodically giving talks to workers to spark their interest in collective action.

During the 1920s, with or without Méndez Medina's influence, the UDCM expanded its activities to include support for working women and promotion of Catholic unions. The UDCM acted in partnership with various factories to increase the education and Christianization of their workforce. Both La Moderna (candles) and Larín (chocolates) factories were dedicated to the Sacred Heart during a ceremony that the UDCM organized. The ceremony at La Moderna began with a priest blessing the institution and then hanging a sacred image. Five women workers at the factory, after their first communion, were treated to flowers and a breakfast prepared by damas. The UDCM reported that the ceremony at Larín was a bigger success than the ceremony at La Moderna. At Larín, the young women who worked behind the counter in the chocolate sales section were enthusiastic and encouraged other employees to take part in the ceremony. Because of their efforts, thirty-four workers took communion. Moreover, Mr. Larín promised the UDCM that he would build a chapel inside the factory for his workers.

In 1923, four factories were consecrated and dedicated to the Sacred Heart through UDCM efforts.[47]

The UDCM also increased its involvement in socioeconomic activities during the course of the 1920s. As their work became more oriented toward the problems of the working class, their approach became less obviously condescending. For example, the UDCM helped promote a "chair law" for women shop clerks so that they did not have to remain on their feet all day but could sit down when no customers were present. Interestingly, Puig Casauranc, when he was a congressional representative from Veracruz, prepared a bill regarding women's health in industry and domestic service that included a similar stipulation. Moreover, the chair law had already been proposed at the Second Mexican Child Welfare Congress.[48] Again, the goals of revolutionaries and the social action wing of the church overlapped.

Working in partnership with the Knights of Columbus and the SSM, the UDCM sponsored a housing program for the Unión Profesional de Empleados (Professional Union of White-Collar Employees), composed of separate male and female unions. These small homes were built in San Pedro de los Pinos, south of Tacubaya. According to *La Dama Católica*, it was a wonderful site: both hygienic and within easy commuting distance of Mexico City. Their description notwithstanding, the photograph accompanying the article shows a flat area with few trees and fewer homes. The housing program offered four styles of homes for sale, costing between 1,800 and 5,200 pesos. Purchasers had three years to pay off their loan at 8 percent interest. Within two months, fifty-one members of the union had already purchased lots, seven homes were finished, and thirty more were under construction. While the writer for *La Dama Católica* called this program beneficial for the humble, the humble could not afford to pay several thousand pesos for a home.[49] Considering the housing prices and loan terms, these union members must have been financially comfortable.

The UDCM also organized unions throughout the country. While Guadalajara was the national center of these union activities, the UDCM was involved with or planned to found unions from Monterrey to Mérida.[50] The UDCM even organized a union at Talleres Britania in spite of managers' objections. When management denied damas permission to talk to the women workers about the benefits of unionization, the damas waited outside to recruit women who streamed out of the factory at the end of the day. The UDCM also intertwined vocational training with the organization of workers into Catholic unions. For instance, the UDCM Academy, discussed in the previous chapter, offered students suggestions on how to organize a union. The UDCM reported that it had founded the Unión Profesional de Empleadas Católicas (Professional Union of Catholic Women White-Collar Employees) and the Sindicato de la Aguja (Union of the Needle). Preparatory talks were under way for the foundation of the Unión Profesional de Maestras (Professional Union of Women Teachers), with the support of the SSM. The UDCM was also affiliated with the Unión Profesional de Empleadas y Operadoras en el Ramo de Teléfonos (Professional Union of Women White-Collar Workers and Operators in the Telephone Division) and the Unión Profesional de Tabaqueras (Professional Union of Women Tobacco Workers)—the previously mentioned El Buen Tono union. The SSM supported the UDCM's work, giving talks and organizing workshops on how to found unions. The UDCM, in turn, supported the CNCT, both "morally" and through its work of directly founding unions.[51]

The CNCT did not pose a threat to organizations like the CROM and the government because of its failures and unpopularity, but rather the reverse. In 1926, the CNCT had more than 22,000 members organized in 301 affiliated unions, 14 regional confederations, and 17 local federations. While Catholic unions are still under-investigated, the numbers do suggest that thousands of workers believed that confessional syndicates best served them professionally and spiritually. Although the unions did not believe in "class conflict," that does not mean that they were unable to represent the interests of their members to management and owners. For instance, Curley has found examples of Catholic unions in Jalisco successfully negotiating better terms of employment for their members.[52] Considering that *Rerum Novarum* promoted both the education and the unionization of the working class, combining these goals was a logical step. The social work of the Catholic Church, however, brought it into the realm of the state, as the next chapter discusses, and set the scene for church-state conflict.

Church and state agreed that education was one of the most effective tools for gaining loyalty from the public while simultaneously moralizing children and adults, yet schools reached only a small segment of the population. Thus, both organizations used a variety of cultural and social programs to entertain, uplift, educate, or organize the working class. While reports on entertainment available in Mexico City suggest that these programs were popular with their intended audience, their popularity does not necessarily mean that the audience believed the moralistic message in the package. As was the case with education, the public used the services and entertainment offered by both church and state for their own goals, which ranged from hopes for better employment to an afternoon's entertainment. The loyalty that both church and state sought to inspire through these events and institutions became crucial when the institutions began to clash during the presidency of Calles. Both church and state turned to the patrons of libraries, students in adult education, and members of their unions for displays of public support. The common goals and common ground of church and state did not serve as mitigating factors when the political situation became tense. In fact, the successful social action programs of the church probably brought it into greater conflict with the state.

8 Church-State Tensions Turn into Conflict

From Catholic Social Action to the Cristiada

Examination of SEP educational programs and the work of Catholic social action in the previous chapters has demonstrated how church and state programs complemented each other and intersected ideologically, even as the political relationship between the institutions was becoming more troubled. This disintegrating political relationship, including the role organizations such as the UDCM, the CNCT, and the government-allied CROM played in it, are treated in the present discussion, which traces the reasons for the escalation of tension both on a national level and in Mexico City. This tension came to a head with the 1926 enforcement of the constitution, in particular the clause prohibiting religious primary education. After the government threw down the gauntlet, Catholic social action organizations were instrumental in leading public protests against the new policy, while working behind the scenes to ensure that restrictions on religious education did not spell the end of religious instruction.

Background to the Conflict

As discussed in chapter 1, the 1917 Constitution offered the Catholic Church only minimal protection and great restriction, including a prohibition on church involvement in primary education, nationalization of all church property, and denial of juridical status to the church. Between 1917 and 1924, any enforcement of the constitution was left to the discretion of local authorities. On a national level, President Carranza pursued a policy of conciliation that allowed exiled clergy to return home and restored some confiscated church properties. During the presidency of Alvaro Obregón, official pragmatism toward the church hierarchy was called into doubt by bombings and street fighting that increased tension between Catholics and the government. On the one hand, Obregón did not implement the religious restrictions in the constitution and had cordial relations with the new apostolic delegate Ernesto Filippi. Nonetheless, he responded quickly to challenges from the church, feeding Catholic mistrust of him that originated from his anticlericalism while a revolutionary general. Rumors that implicated him in two 1921 bomb attacks against the church in the Federal District were likely due as much to his reputation as to hard evidence. In response to both bombings, the government suggested that Catholics themselves had planted the devices to prompt public outrage; neither crime was ever solved.[1]

Another incident that increased tension was the gathering to dedicate Mexico to Christ the King, on 11 January 1923. Forty thousand pilgrims, led by Filippi and members of the episcopate, gathered on a hilltop in Guanajuato to place the first stone for a monument to Cristo Rey. Given that the gathering violated the constitutional prohibition on outdoor religious demonstrations, Obregón responded by ordering the expulsion of the Vatican representative. Catholics predictably protested. Although the church had broken the law, Obregón did not seize the opportunity to enforce other constitutional restrictions on religious practice. Rather, he sought conciliation with the bishops, telling them that the government's social program "is essentially Christian and is a complement to the fundamental program of the Catholic Church." He believed that with goodwill on both sides, harmony was possible. If programs of the church and state were to be successful "happiness and well-being would remain definitively conquered for all in this and in the other life."[2]

The bishops responded that they were impressed with the "general tone" of Obregón's letter and were grateful for the "spirit of harmony" it represented. They wrote, "[W]e congratulate ourselves upon seeing that from your letter emerges recognition of the church's personality." The church's program was "perfectly defined by you as an important element in the solution of the social problem." Nonetheless, even though both programs responded to many of the same difficulties in society, they had conflicting origins. Socialism (which the hierarchy believed the government promoted) attributed class conflict to private property, family relations, and religion while, according to the bishops, Catholics attributed the same problems to religious ignorance and the abuse of property. Nonetheless, the bishops noted that in Belgium and Germany, Catholics and socialists had been able to collaborate, notwithstanding their divergent opinions on the causes of social problems. The bishops also hoped that the government would soon lose its "prejudice that the liberals always had" against Catholics and paranoia that Catholics wanted to take over the government, both of which were interfering with their programs of social work.[3] Although the president and the bishops did not completely agree, their correspondence demonstrates that the two powers sought accommodation and common ground. In contrast, Calles, Obregón's successor, appeared intentionally to seek confrontation with Catholics and their hierarchy.

With Calles' public support, CROM attacks on Catholics grew, including the dramatic seizure of a church in Mexico City. In February 1925, schismatics took La Soledad Church, located in a working-class neighborhood, and founded a national "Catholic" church. The head of the movement was José Joaquín Pérez, a former Catholic priest and soldier in the Porfirian army; Pérez's career already included marriage, membership in a Masonic lodge, and one break then reconcilement with the church. While the origins of the schism are unclear,[4] the hand of the CROM was evident in the entire event: *Cromistas* guarded the hostage church and attended schismatic masses. Although Pérez said mass in Spanish, not Latin, and distributed gifts in poor neighborhoods, his church was unpopular. According to Gutiérrez Casillas, residents were so furious that they attempted to lynch one of the schismatic priests. Describing themselves as artisans, shopkeepers, industrialists, clerks, white-collar, and industrial workers, 2,700 residents of the neighborhood wrote to Calles protesting the seizure and invoking their constitutional right to the free exercise of religion. Decline in mass attendance also had a damaging economic impact on local businesses.[5]

Neither the community's anger nor their economic and legal arguments swayed Calles; schismatics held the church for a month before the president intervened. Ultimately La Soledad became a public library. As a consolation prize, Calles gave the dissidents a church on the Alameda. Although they had a talent for causing trouble, the religious dissidents attracted few followers and their church did not survive. Pérez eventually repented (again) of his break with Rome, and died, reconciled to the church, in 1931. The seizure of La Soledad demonstrated that the CROM, its leader Morones, and Calles were willing to challenge the church not only in factories, where the CROM and the CNCT had been rivals, but also in sacred spaces. The watershed year in church-state relations was 1925. From that year onward, the unwritten policy of conciliation that had given Catholics a margin for social action was replaced by a policy of confrontation.

Strengthened by the support of Calles, CROM attacks on Catholics increased in the workplace. While evidence indicates that cromistas used their influence to pressure companies into dismissing Catholic workers, the scale of the dismissals remains unclear. State legislatures and governments joined with the CROM in this offensive. Officials harassed Catholic unions, which had questionable legal status, and jailed Catholic employees. Various state legislatures and the federal Cámara de Diputados all discussed making closed shops mandatory. Positions in government were denied to Catholics who professed their religious beliefs or refused to join pro-government unions.[6] Yet even within the CROM there was dissent. During the Obregón presidency, the CROM had attempted to attract Catholic members. At a time when the CROM annoyed rather than attacked Catholics, workers might not have worried about becoming cromistas, affiliating out of professional necessity or political sympathy. Roberto de la Cerda Silva concludes that Catholic workers chose to affiliate with the CROM because its unions were more attractive than Catholic ones, and it offered greater hope for rapid improvement of their working conditions.[7] Catholic cromistas might have felt protected by CROM statutes that prohibited union involvement in religious and political matters. As late as 1926, the CROM secretary-general still paid lip service to nonintervention in these arenas, and flyers signed by Catholic cromistas called upon the leadership to respect those statutes.[8]

A Resignation amid Escalation

Against the background of the deteriorating relationship between church and state and increasing hostility toward Catholics, in May 1925, Méndez Medina resigned as director of the Secretariado Social Mexicano. The Jesuit leadership, not Méndez Medina himself, notified Archbishop Mora y del Río that Méndez Medina was to resign and could not be replaced by another Jesuit. The Mexican bishops, realizing Méndez Medina's crucial role in organizing Catholic social work, proposed an appeal, which they apparently did not pursue. Reasons for the resignation remain unclear; however, Méndez Medina's radicalization, including his support for forced land redistribution, might have been a factor, at least among the Jesuits. The fact that the vast majority of the Mexican hierarchy wanted Méndez Medina to stay in his post, even as his ideas became more radical, suggests that his radicalism was neither threatening to them nor viewed as an impediment to his position. It also suggests their support for Méndez Medina's decentralized approach, one that promoted the autonomy of lay organizations.

Méndez Medina's replacement was Miguel Darío Miranda, a young, inexperienced priest who was not a member of a religious order. Miranda's work in the Catholic social action movement had occurred under the tutelage of Méndez Medina and from classes taken during summer vacations. As a secular priest, he was more dependent upon the ecclesiastical hierarchy than his Jesuit predecessor had been; moreover, Miranda did not stand up to the bishops. For example, whereas Méndez Medina had staunchly supported the independence of lay Catholic organizations, in particular the CNCT, Miranda asked Mora y del Río's opinion regarding union autonomy from the church hierarchy.

Rather than continue with Méndez Medina's programs — expansion of Catholic social action and personal attention to regional projects — Miranda consolidated existing projects and began training an "elite" to direct social action organizations. Under different circumstances, his ideas might have served the movement well, but not in Mexico in the mid-1920s. Miranda turned the SSM, which had been a national organization with ties to local problems and activities, into an organization largely oriented toward Mexico City.[9] Moreover, considering the government's hostility to Catholics, the SSM needed a director with a flair for grabbing the public's imagination and answering anti-Catholic propaganda with tangible projects. Méndez Medina had those skills, Miranda did not.

The loss of Méndez Medina weakened the social action movement at a critical juncture. President Calles, state builder and avowed anticlerical, seemed intent on eliminating the Catholic Church's influence in Mexico. Calles' anticlerical views, however, tapped into generalized anticlericalism among the revolution's winners, while being popular with labor groups that competed with Catholic labor unions. Since the church needed its strongest leaders in the mid-1920s, Méndez Medina's resignation was unfortunate. Nonetheless, as Calles seemed intent on provoking a confrontation with the church, it would be naive to suggest that Méndez Medina alone could have averted the crisis to come.

In February 1926, Mexico City's *Universal* published remarks by Archbishop Mora y del Río calling for a campaign against the constitution. The archbishop denied that an episcopal campaign to undermine the constitution existed, and *Universal* admitted that, possibly, the reporter had been in error. The remarks were actually the republication of a protest made nine years earlier. Nonetheless, Calles seized upon any excuse to begin enforcing the constitution, even starting sedition proceedings against the elderly archbishop. Under the rubric of the constitutional prohibition on foreign clergy, the government began closures of religious orders and deportations.[10] Further provoking Catholics, in February 1926, Minister of Public Education Puig Casauranc announced that all primary schools would be inspected to ensure their compliance with government regulations banning religious affiliation. As the academic year began in February, the SEP could not have chosen a worse time to enforce regulations about curriculum, staff, and building requirements.

Letters between Mora y del Río and Calles indicate that the president had found his excuse to confront the church. The president wrote to Mora y del Río:

> No road is more wrong than the one that you are following. I want you to understand, once and for all, that not even the agitation that you try to provoke in the interior, in the exterior, nor any other step that you take . . . will be capable of changing the firm intention of the Federal Government to ensure that what the Supreme Law of the Republic commands is strictly enforced.
>
> There is no other road that allows you to avoid difficulties . . . and I declare to you, also once and for all, that any act of rebellion in complying with the legal precepts or [any] lack of respect for the authorities charged with enforcing them will be punished without consideration of any kind.[11]

Mora y del Río responded that "we the Bishops . . . are lovers of peace, tranquility, and national well-being and we would never march" against "our brothers" to spill blood; yet, during the spring of 1926, the

hierarchy was divided. The hawkish faction—including Pascual Díaz
(Tabasco), José de Jesús Manríquez y Zárate (Huejutla), and Leopoldo
Lara y Torres (Tacámbaro)—favored strong resistance but stopped
short of calling for armed rebellion, while the moderates—like Leopoldo Ruiz y Flores (Morelia) and Miguel de la Mora (San Luis Potosí)—favored using legal means to repeal the restrictive measures of
the constitution. Mora y del Río stood between those promoting accommodation and the hawkish faction.[12]

The promulgation of the so-called Calles Law on 14 June codified
the anticlerical articles of the constitution, legalized the seizures and
expulsions that had already occurred, and gave the government the
right to appoint and dismiss clergy and regulate the number of priests in
a region. Furthermore, the Calles Law prohibited the teaching of religion in primary schools, forbade clergy or members of religious orders
from teaching in primary schools, prohibited foreigners from acting in
a religious capacity, banned religious orders, instituted penalties for
political action by clergy, and confiscated all church property in the
Federal District and territories. In immediate protest, the Liga Nacional
para la Defensa de la Libertad Religiosa (National League for the Defense of Religious Liberty—a lay organization dedicated to protecting
Catholic political rights), planned an economic boycott to begin on
14 July. The Liga called on Catholics to abstain from using public
transportation, attending theaters, buying luxury goods, or sending
their children to government schools. Prompted by the Calles Law
going into effect on 31 July 1926 and in support of the Liga's boycott,
the Vatican and bishops agreed to close churches and cease masses. On
1 August 1926, for the first time since the conquest, Mexico's church
bells remained silent and barred doors shut out the faithful. With si-
lence from the pulpits, the laity assumed de facto leadership of the
church. Demonstrations in Mexico City met with violent government
repression, and uprisings during the summer initiated the three-year
Cristero Rebellion.[13]

Seeking conciliation with the government, the episcopate submitted
a proposal to the Cámara de Diputados calling for amendments to the
constitutional articles that limited religious freedom. A letter supporting the proposal had two million signatures. Catholic organizations,
including the Liga and the UDCM, had probably mobilized members
to circulate and sign the petition. Ironically, the petition promoted the

rights of former enemies — the Protestants. The government expropriation of churches was "absurd" because foreign communities should own the churches that they had built and foreigners would be "deprived of the benefits of the liberty of religion, if they do not have priests [who speak] their language." The world had truly turned upside down when Catholics promoted the rights of Protestants. Attempting to address long-standing liberal fears of clerical privilege, the petition declared, "[W]e are not striving for special legal status [*fueros*] nor privileges of any sort. We only want religious freedom, which is the conquest of all modern people."[14] The petition was rejected on 24 September. Meanwhile, the laity continued their boycott and the cristeros their rebellion.

The UDCM in the Conflict

The Liga, which was founded specifically to protect the rights of Catholics, was accompanied in its struggle by other lay Catholic organizations, such as the UDCM. Originally founded as an organization without political affiliations, the UDCM had quickly become politicized as a result of church-state tension during the revolutionary period. Damas had appealed, without success, to President Madero to halt the public speech of a woman socialist. In 1914, they asked then General Obregón to return a church that had been confiscated by the Constitutionalist faction and given to a labor organization; Obregón refused. Damas also met with Pancho Villa, (again) unsuccessfully asking him to rescind his order expelling foreign clergy. Although many damas were uneasy about their political role, they continued to become more active during the 1920s, especially as Catholic education, their territory, came under attack. In 1926, the pope provided further justification for political action, reminding them that if politicians meddled in religion, Catholics had a duty to enter the political arena. UDCM rhetoric still expressed reluctance regarding a directly political role for women, but women were encouraged to participate in politics indirectly using their "moral influence."[15]

The church-state conflict was not only about politics and beliefs, but also about gender. Put crudely, anticlericalism was a program developed by men and aimed at women and children. In seeking to regulate the public spaces of the Catholic Church, the state also limited the public spaces of Catholic women. The prohibition of Catholic education and unions curtailed women's public activity while challenging their position as arbiters of morality. Because children's education was a task assigned to women, be it in homes or in primary schools, any attack on education was also an attack on women's right to rear and teach children as they saw fit. These attacks against their most basic beliefs, their religion, and the responsibilities of their gender united Catholic women from all classes in protest against threats to their home, community, church, and children. In their political activism, the damas redefined the only role that both state and church had allowed them — motherhood — in order to undermine the actions of the state. Accepting the role into which they were cast, these women also subverted it by declaring that they had raised men who would be Catholic warriors against the government.[16]

Besides boycotts and petitions, street demonstrations provided an impromptu venue for Catholic anger and frustration. Women, including members of the UDCM, often comprised the ranks of street demonstrators. The closure of the Sagrada Familia Church, in the middle-class Colonia Roma in February 1926, brought thousands of angry protestors into the streets.[17] According to Minister of the Interior (Gobernación) Adalberto Tejeda, the church was closed because its clergy had not solicited permission to remain open by the government's deadline. When female domestic workers arrived at the church for their weekly Lenten exercises, they found the building bolted shut. Assuming that the exercises were running late, they waited for ten minutes. When the church doors remained firmly closed, the servants ran to alert their señoras. The news quickly spread around the neighborhood, and protestors, many of them high-society women, came to the church by foot and car.

An hour after the alarm had been raised, three thousand people crowded the streets around the Sagrada Familia. Protestors included the wife of the director of *Universal* and the wife of the Belgian consul in San Luis Potosí. Although the protest united elite women and their servants, reports of the protestors' behavior still emphasized class differences. The ladies sought calm, as they assured *Universal*, while their servants were violently furious. *Universal* reported that when the police commissary of the tenth district arrived alone to try to calm the crowd, servants attacked him with sticks; it was only the intervention of the ladies that saved him.

The society ladies then took their demands to the Ministry of the Interior, while in front of the church the fire department turned its hoses on the remaining protestors. These women responded by hurling rocks at government forces and were not dispersed until the mounted police arrived. Tejeda is reported to have said, "[I]f there is another demonstration of this sort, I will disperse it with fire hoses if it is women and with tanks if it is men."[18] While their servants were being dispersed with fire hoses, the señoras, no doubt aided by their social position, entered the government building to present their demands. Over the next few days, the government tried to play down the incidents, saying that all those who had been detained were released the next day and denying that anyone had been killed or wounded. The UDCM central committee sought to publicize the clash, asking Catholics to express their outrage at the incident by draping their homes and places of work in black sashes.

These protests suggest that women of all classes, including damas, were using the mass movement tactics of the revolution. During the revolution, workers had demonstrated and paraded throughout the capital. Residents witnessed women publicly denouncing hoarding of food by merchants, forcing their idea of a just exchange in bakeries and markets, and occupying government buildings to demand services and food.[19] Although these women were typically not from the upper class, some middle-class damas might have participated in the mobilizations. Moreover, Catholic women, perhaps damas, did protest in the streets when Obregón jailed 180 clergy in Mexico City in 1915. The women were dispersed by Obregón's troops, but the next day further clashes resulted in two deaths.[20] Even if no damas participated in any of these demonstrations, they would certainly have been aware of their effectiveness.

The Battle for the Children

As the church-state conflict inflamed the committed on both sides, education became a pivotal issue. Whereas Robert Quirk suggests that the church fought for a Catholic educational system over which it had complete control,[21] in the 1920s, I believe that Catholics had generally accepted that the state had a role to play in education. Catholic groups, such as the Unión Nacional de Padres de Familia (National Union of Parents) and the UDCM, however, continued to support "freedom of education" and an amendment to Article 3 that would allow for religious education in private primary schools.[22] Catholics demanded the option of teaching religion and religious history in private schools, which was denied to them by the constitution. Some professed hope that in a far-off future, Catholicism could be taught in local public schools if the majority of parents wanted it. Quirk exaggerates when he posits a Catholic conspiracy to take over the educational system, and I would argue that, while many Catholics promoted religious education as a brake on perceived immorality,[23] most were realistic enough to realize that in the current anticlerical climate, the Catholic faith could not officially be taught in public schools. They may have dreamed of regaining that right, but they knew it would be a challenge.

The February 1926 SEP regulation and the June Calles Law meant that primary schools could not have a religious affiliation, designate a room for prayer, or decorate the building with religious images. Schools could not be in contact with churches or religious groups, school principals could not be members of religious orders or secular clergy, and members of religious orders were prohibited from teaching.[24] According to Valentina Torres Septién, the church responded to the 1926 primary school regulation by founding the Secretariado Arquidiocesano de Educación (Archdiocesan Secretariat of Education), under the Jesuit Joaquín Cordero. She describes the Secretariado as a multifaceted organization, designed to coordinate, organize, and improve Catholic pedagogic quality; its primary goal was to protect the interests of Catholic schools, by confronting civil authorities if necessary.[25] The function and organization of this body, whose effects are unknown, are reminiscent of the SSM. In the same year, Pascual Díaz, the exiled bishop of Tabasco, brought together representatives from more than one hundred Mexico City Catholic schools. The Unión de Colegios Católicos Mexicanos (Union of Mexican Catholic Schools) was founded at this meeting, with the mandate to lobby congress to amend Article 3. Like the other lay organizations of social action, this lobbying group accepted advice from the hierarchy without being directly under the bishops or becoming a puppet organization. The leadership of the Unión de Colegios Católicos Mexicanos was composed of women: Puig wrote letters to and received letters from Señoritas Concepción Peredo, Jerónima Orozco, Dolores Echeverría, and Marina Astorga, all Catholic school principals.

In April 1926, Catholic-school principals protested the enactment of Article 3 and supported instead an amendment originally proposed by Carranza in 1918, which would have allowed for the teaching of religion in private schools. While acknowledging that public schools should be lay because the state "does not recognize any protection of religion," the principals believed that parents had the right to decide their children's education. Furthermore, the church should be allowed a role in the education of Catholic youth. Puig Casauranc retorted that, if education was primarily the right of parents, then the home was the proper place for religious education. He then threatened to suspend schools that did not comply with the regulation; in their place he would open public schools for children whose parents realized that religious instruction belonged in church or at home but not in school. Puig implied that education would be denied to those whose parents disagreed with him. The Unión de Colegios responded that they were willing to comply with Article 3 while Congress considered their amendment.

Both because the Unión de Colegios had agreed to abide by Article 3 and as a gesture of good faith, the SEP created a commission under Puig to study the implementation of Article 3. Three members of the commission were named by the SEP, two by the Catholic school union, and one by a private non-Catholic school. Although the Unión de Colegios had women in leadership roles who had been lobbying Puig, at this important meeting the interests of the Catholic schools were represented by three men. The one woman present during the discussions was the secretary, Esperanza Castillo. Not surprisingly, the panel did not recommend alterations to Article 3, but instead emphasized that religious affiliation was prohibited only in primary schools.[26]

Historians tend to agree with the contemporary press that these regulations and the atmosphere of anticlericalism were disastrous for Catholic and public schools. School attendance declined due both to closures and to the boycott of government schools. A report that in Guadalajara 900 primary-school teachers were fired for being Catholic and 22,000 of the 25,000 school-age children ceased attending public school is typical.[27] One report estimated that 2,000,000 students nationally were without a school because of closures, while the government estimated the number at 1,211,937. Antonio Ruís Facius believed that immediately after the enforcement of Article 3 in February, ninety-three convents and schools were closed in the Federal District.[28] These figures represent a huge blow to the educational effort of the postrevolutionary governments. *Universal* reported that some schools closed voluntarily, rather than await official closure. Stories even circulated that children who had been in Catholic schools were not permitted to enroll in public facilities.[29]

Meanwhile, the SEP tried to downplay the repercussions of its regulation. Puig claimed that Article 3 had little effect on Catholic schools and, due to the SEP's fairness, "almost all the Catholic primary schools" continued to operate in compliance with the law.[30] A report on closures in the archives of the Ministry of the Interior lists only the Colegio Teresiano, the Colegio del Pilar, and the Escuela Santa Teresa de Jesús as having closed in Mexico City and the surrounding towns. Another list reports fifty-six chapels annexed to primary schools, but no schools themselves, as being closed.[31]

Detailed local investigation is needed before any firm conclusion can be drawn, but in Mexico City, in the initial period after the enforcement of Article 3, the majority of Catholic schools appear to have superficially adapted to the new restrictions while offering covert Catholic education. Without teaching religion and sacred history, without mass and displays of the crucified Christ, Catholic education had no reason for existing, and so some principals and staff opted for clandestine education. School principals had already warned the SEP that unless Article 3 was amended, they would defend their rights and continue to teach religion in accordance with the wishes of Catholic parents and the dictates of their faith.[32] As a report from the mid-1920s on the impact of the enactment of Article 3 noted, most subjects could be taught without regard to religion. So most of the curriculum at Catholic schools could conform to SEP demands. The subject of history certainly could be controversial, but the report noted that even in this subject there was a certain level of agreement in historical interpretation. Teaching colonial history did not present a problem because the nation as a whole agreed with historians as to how to interpret that time period, and public opinion was generally against the Spanish.

From the time of independence onward, however, the report noted that interpretations of history were influenced by personal politics. Similar problems arose in civics courses as well, because institutions and government policies imposed an anticlerical perspective.[33] Thus, while schools superficially conformed to SEP regulations, classes in religion and sacred history were taught without textbooks, outside of school hours, and children were instructed not to bring religious articles to school. School chapels were closed or disguised, but masses did not cease. Schools were rechristened, religion classes moved, and new principals appointed, all to fool the SEP.

The UDCM worked with Catholic schools to circumvent SEP regulations, as letters to UDCM national president Elena Lascurain de Silva indicate. On 6 March 1926, the Escuela Gratuita para Niños Pobres San Felipe de Jesús (St. Philip of Jesus Free School for Poor Boys), located next to the Santa Inés Church, received notification that it was not in compliance with SEP regulations and would face sanctions. The school had previously been incorporated into the SEP and affiliated with the UDCM. A copy of the letter was sent to the local SEP inspector, to inform him of the school's infractions. Four days later, the school board, composed of damas, met principal Raúl Sylve — a priest. The board noted that, due to the new SEP regulations, religion classes had been cancelled, but students now received instruction in the adjoining church. By 1 May 1926, Lascurain de Silva appears on documents as the principal of the Felipe de Jesús School, thus bringing the school into compliance with SEP regulations. Lascurain de Silva, however, was only a nominal principal and trusted custodian. Sylve informed her of the school's progress, while clearly remaining in charge. Nonetheless, as far as the SEP was concerned, Lascurain de Silva was the principal and her signature appeared on official documents. SEP officials must have known Lascurain de Silva was the president of the UDCM, an organization frequently making headline news, and realized that her position was a hoax. Yet, members of the UDCM were invited to preside over the school's final exams joined, "as usual," by a representative of the SEP. As late as November, then, the SEP and members of the UDCM jointly observed the students' final examinations. In this case, the SEP was clearly willing to look the other way as long as its regulations were observed on paper.[34]

This case was not unique. The Colegio Franco-Mexicano (Franco-Mexican School), in the prosperous Colonia Roma, was closed in February 1926; the school was covered with official seals to keep out staff and students. Although principal Dolores Lozano requested permission to reopen, within a month it was too late.[35] Students had waited throughout February, when the school year began, for classes to resume, but by March they had enrolled elsewhere. The teachers had found other positions and the school's furnishings were gone — perhaps confiscated by federal authorities. The closure of the Franco-Mexican School echoes the municipal school closures, described in chapter 5. In both cases the SEP represented interests of the centralizing revolution, not those of students or teachers.

By August 1926, the Franco-Mexican School was functioning under a new principal, Adela Echeverría. The school was incorporated into the SEP and classes were taught in Spanish instead of French — a nod to patriotism. (Fee-paying Catholic schools had typically taught at least a few classes in French.) It is not clear how many of the students and faculty remained from the school's previous incarnation, but the school continued to be Catholic. In the autumn of 1926, the Franco-Mexican School received notification of an impending SEP inspection. When the inspector arrived, he found a crucifix hanging on the wall, a legitimate reason to close the school. Rather than closing the school, however, the SEP administrator warned the principal not to repeat the violation, reminding her that she had had prior notification of the visit.

Violations of Article 3 appear to have been endemic. A group of teachers wrote to Calles in August 1926 complaining that religious communities, including foreigners, directed more than one hundred schools in the Federal District without being subjected to inspections, either by the SEP or the Secretaría de Gobernación. The letter included a list of schools, with addresses and the names of the religious communities involved. A few weeks later, Calles received another letter from angry teachers responding to a report they had heard that fifty schools had been closed for violating Article 3. They doubted the accuracy of the report, rather claiming that 130 Catholic schools continued to function in the Federal District operated by members of religious orders or their trusted confidants.[36]

These Catholic schools continued to operate due to lack of staff to enforce the regulations, SEP tolerance and deliberate blindness at the grassroots level, and tolerance within the SEP structure. The protesting teachers complained to Calles that neither the SEP nor Gobernación had any interest in inspecting private schools. Lack of communication among government ministries appears to have been part of the problem. Gobernación waited to be notified of infractions by the SEP, while the SEP apparently told inspectors to ignore Catholic schools. So inspectors either did not visit, informed schools of inspections beforehand, or turned a blind eye during visits. These teachers also suggested that corruption impeded the implementation of the regulations.[37] Part of the SEP's trouble was that there were not enough inspectors of private primary schools. Teachers complained to Calles that private schools had not been inspected in four or five months. In 1928, there were five inspectors in the Federal District for the 248 private schools that required SEP oversight. Thus, each inspector was responsible for ensuring that approximately 50 schools were in compliance with Article 3. In comparison, the seventeen inspectors of the 200 Federal District public urban primary schools were responsible for about 12 schools each. The burden on SEP inspectors indicates that it would have been easy for "former" Catholic schools to hide religious activities even had inspectors sought out violations.

In addition to being too overburdened to conduct frequent inspections, inspectors often ignored infractions when they did visit Catholic schools. Reasons for allowing the schools to continue to function were personal and diverse. SEP employees might have covertly assisted schools that employed family members, friends, or professional colleagues. Because SEP inspectors were assigned to a particular region and, numbers permitting, were required to conduct monthly visits, they would have become acquainted with teachers, students, and principals. Thus, personal relationships may have influenced decisions to ignore clandestine religious education and inspectors might have protected "their" schools from the harsh impact of SEP regulation. Inspectors also worried that closing Catholic schools would force children out of primary education and adopted the attitude that Vasconcelos himself had: Better Catholic education than no education. As already noted, teachers had complained to Calles that corruption influenced the way former Catholic schools were treated. Finally, inspectors who were not in agreement with the restrictions might have ignored infractions.[38]

Disregard for rule-breaking occurred at higher levels of the SEP administration too. While Calles and Puig rhetorically attacked the church and its schools, in practice the SEP appeared to have a policy of ignoring violations of Article 3. Raúl Sylve, hidden principal of the Felipe de Jesús School advised Lascurain de Silva of a perplexing letter he had received from the SEP. In the letter, the SEP's *oficial mayor,* who was in charge of the ministry's administrative operations, reminded him that religion classes were prohibited during regular school hours because an inspector might be lurking. After school hours, however, the SEP would tolerate classes in religious doctrine. Sylve assured Lascurain de Silva that he had not replied to the communication nor had he mentioned it to anyone else, implying that it might be a trap. Yet due to the oficial mayor's assurances, Sylve had removed the crucifixes from hiding and resumed catechism and sacred history classes in the school building, albeit outside school hours.[39]

In the documents relating to Catholic schools under SEP regulation, inspectors noted public displays of crucifixes as an infraction. Nonetheless, even the question of crucifixes in classrooms elicited multiple answers, and the confusion regarding this aspect of the regulation is symbolic of the SEP's half-hearted attempts to police Catholic schools. In early 1926, the Unión Nacional de Padres de Familia had negotiated with the SEP for permission to hang crucifixes in former Catholic schools. In August, Calles had approved an exemption to Article 3 allowing the display of crucifixes, but the exemption was never implemented. Puig Casauranc said that the exemption had not been applied because of the "attitude" of clerical figures who had turned the "noble figure" of the crucified Christ into a "flag of rebellion."[40]

According to Valentina Torres Septién, in October, the government altered its rules yet again; crucifixes had to be removed or schools would lose their incorporated status. The SEP's brusque order annoyed the papal nuncio, who responded — from exile in Rome — that Catholics should defy their persecutors' orders and crucifixes should remain in place.[41] Either Torres' source is incorrect, or the SEP reversed its policy once more. On 29 September 1926, the Unión de Colegios wrote to Puig Casauranc, asking him about the legality of crucifixes in schools and reminding him of the earlier exemption. Puig Casauranc responded that the crucifix was not solely a symbol of religious belief, nor even tied to a particular religion; rather, the crucifix should be considered as something larger than the religions that used it: "as a philosophical expression of redemptive moral values." As such, it was not subject to the regulation of religious symbols in schools. Puig Casauranc's reply seems expedient rather than honest. Moreover, Puig Casauranc was actually parroting an argument Catholics had made in support of crucifixes. He closed the letter, saying, "[U]ntil things become normal, I do not believe it is opportune to present . . . to the consideration of the President of the Republic the favorable interpretation of the petition."[42] Puig's letter to the Unión de Colegios provides further evidence that, at various levels, SEP forces initially mitigated the effects of Article 3.

While turning a blind eye to Catholic rule-breaking, the SEP also promoted its schools as a "moral" educational alternative. As discussed in chapter 2, in 1925, the federal authorities had introduced a morality code. In 1926, Puig Casauranc, seeking Catholics' support for public schools, reminded them about the code and its requirement for monthly confession. Using revolutionary rhetoric in support of Christianity, Puig Casauranc wrote that the morality code followed the laws of Moses and would form "healthy, useful, moral, good children who could have lived the life of Christ or of a Christian in the early days of the church." Puig challenged the church hierarchy to find "one line or word" that "any true disciple of Christ" would fault. His challenge was swiftly answered. Appalled by Puig's remarks, an angry Catholic authored a rebuttal, writing "THE LIFE OF CHRIST ONLY CHRIST COULD HAVE LIVED." For Catholics, morals could not be detached from a religious context.[43]

The SEP, however, could not detach its schools from a culturally Catholic society. Children brought religious values and images to school. Some also treated religious themes in their schoolwork, subsequently published in *Pulgarcito*. In February, *Pulgarcito* published thirteen-year-old Josefina Saldaña's illustration of a sleeping girl, watched over by the Virgin of Guadalupe and a cross. In May, an illustration accompanying the article "The Duties of a Girl," depicted a little girl kneeling at prayer in her bedroom with an image of the Virgin Mary hanging on the wall (fig. 8.1). In December 1926, Matilde Gómez's illustration, showing her family on the way to her brother's baptism, was published (fig. 8.2). So, even if teaching religion in primary schools was forbidden, it appears that students were allowed to include

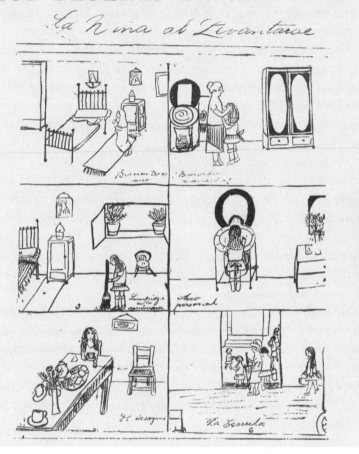

Figure 8.1. "Los deberes de una niña. La niña al levantarse" (The duties of a girl. The girl upon getting up). The girl's duties include thanking God, saying good morning to her mother, cleaning her room, washing and personal hygiene, eating breakfast, and going to school. In her bedroom, this girl has the image of a saint on the wall. The editorial comment for this drawing held the author up as a model both as a girl and as a student. This illustration shows that SEP publications printed drawings with religious content despite the Article 3 ban on religion in education. (Courtesy of the Bancroft Library, University of California, Berkeley)

EL BAUTIZO DE MI HERMANITO

DIBUJO HECHO POR LA ALUMNA MATILDE GOMEZ

Figure 8.2. "El bautizo de mi hermanito" (my little brother's baptism), a drawing by schoolgirl Matilde Gómez, another depiction of religious belief and practice published despite the Article 3 ban. (Courtesy of the Bancroft Library, University of California, Berkeley)

religious themes in their schoolwork and, more remarkably, that an official SEP publication was willing to exhibit that work.[44]

An Official Ending

My research does not stretch into the years of the Cristero Rebellion, and more study is necessary to demonstrate to what extent Catholic schools hid their religious activities, closed, or received surreptitious SEP protection in the late 1920s. The year 1929 marked the official end of the Cristero Rebellion under the terms of the Arreglos (Accords). To the government, the Arreglos with the church symbolized the church's surrender while, to the cristeros, the Arreglos meant betrayal by their leaders. In signing the historic accords, however, members of the ecclesiastical hierarchy believed that they were protecting the future of the church. They had also been convinced of the need to take back the leadership of lay organizations. In 1929, the ecclesiastical authorities created Acción Católica Mexicana (Mexican Catholic Action) to coordinate lay social activities. Mexican Catholic Action intended to discipline and control the independent lay organizations that had been radicalized by the church-state conflict. According to Manuel Ceballos Ramírez, the success of Catholic social action ultimately led to its demise. In the 1930s, the government was no longer willing to tolerate Catholic involvement in social work, while the episcopate and the SSM would no longer tolerate a brand of lay Catholicism dedicated to social action. Mexican Catholic Action replaced Catholic social action and, as had been the case with Méndez Medina and Miranda, the replacement paled in comparison to the original. The philosophy of Mexican Catholic Action placed individual duties before social duties, returned the laity to the pews, and the clergy to the pulpits as their leaders. Yet the laity would not relinquish its social work easily, and on a grassroots level lay groups maintained the living church during the resurgence of anticlericalism in the 1930s.[45]

While the Calles era did not snuff out Catholicism or witness mass defections to atheism, Calles' church-state conflict wounded Catholic social action and ultimately limited the church's public role. Furthermore, the church returned to an uncompromising position on education; Pius XI's 1929 papal encyclical *Divini illius magistri* affirmed that education could not be complete without Catholic principles.[46] In attempting to eradicate the Catholic Church, Calles destroyed the branch of the church that had the most in common with revolutionary ideals. In doing so, he also silenced one of the most powerful critics and instruments for social change the revolution-in-power would face.

Epilogue

"On the Subject of Politics, Morality, and Bras"

Nineteenth-century liberal attacks against the established church were part of a process of centralization and secularization that continued throughout the Porfiriato and into the revolutionary period. This centralizing project included an ideological component seeking to eliminate alternative nationalisms and loyalties. The postrevolutionary state cast itself as the "supreme arbiter and sole embodiment of the national interest" and continued to centralize power, reducing the independence of municipal governments that until then had often made space for Catholic political opposition. The expansion of federal education was one part of this centralizing project, a project that sought to weaken municipal, church, and state schools, while creating a national system promoting the revolutionary government's definition of Mexican. Attacks on the church under both Juárez and Calles, although motivated in part by the desire to eliminate competition for the hearts and minds of Mexicans, failed to rid Mexico of the institutionalized church. After the presidency of Lázaro Cárdenas (1934–1940) and particularly after the Second World War, successive governments began to relax their enforcement of legal restrictions on the church, and anticlerical legislation was gradually amended in the church's favor.[1]

Since the 1940s, political Catholics have gradually increased their public role and sought to renegotiate the terms of being a public Catholic. Under President Manuel Avila Camacho (1940–1946), for the first time since Díaz was in office, Mexico had a "believer" as its leader.[2] With greater freedom of activity, the church sought to reclaim its role as arbiter of public morality. The hierarchy campaigned for social justice, public morality, and freedom of religion, while campaigns by Catholic lay groups in the 1950s condemned provocative films, scandalous publications, and the menace from the new dance, the mambo. Alfonso Junco, who had been the editor of *La Dama Católica* in the 1920s, was named official censor of pornographic publications.[3]

Even as relations between church and state grew more cordial, the two institutions vied for public loyalties, particularly in the area of culture and morals. Anne Rubenstein convincingly argues that, while the government never restricted the modern entertainment that offended staunch Catholics, it positioned itself as the mediator between the burgeoning industry and concerned citizens. For instance, the Comisión Calificadora de Publicaciones y Revistas Ilustradas (Ratings Commission for Illustrated Publications and Magazines) provided a forum in which conservatives could express their distaste for depictions of other religions, sex, and divorce in print material. The Comisión Calificadora was an official government body that could find against publishers. Yet it had no power to enforce its decisions against publishers or distributors: Publishers still churned out stories of women jailbirds, while films left less and less to the imagination.[4]

Throughout the church-state tug-of-war for loyalty, women have continued to be important activists and objects of institutional censure or approval. Mexican women finally received the municipal vote in 1946 and the presidential vote in 1953. Women's expanding educational and employment opportunities have continued to challenge societal expectations and gender definitions. Many contemporary debates about the position and freedoms of women echo debates from the 1920s: How should women dress? How should they entertain themselves? What rights do they have in terms of reproduction and marriage? Women's decisions, even in terms of what to wear to work, have political and moral dimensions as the current equivalent of the chica moderna continues to threaten the establishment. In 1995, miniskirt-wearing secretaries in a Guadalajara city department were taken to task by their boss. While the miniskirts were not actually banned, then mayor César Coll enjoined the city's employees (male and female alike) not to be "exaggerated" or "sexually provocative" in their clothing. Anti-miniskirt comments from local government officials around Mexico have turned the daring clothing into a political weapon. For example, women demonstrators protesting globalization at the United Nations International Conference on Financing for Development in Monterrey in January 2002 wore miniskirts.[5]

For the daring chica moderna, the Wonderbra is the obvious accessory. In the mid-1990s, on billboards along prominent thoroughfares, blonde model Eva Herzigova sultrily gazed down at drivers accompanied by the caption, "I'm sorry, I can't hide it." What the model could not hide was her larger-than-life cleavage, courtesy of a

Wonderbra. Hundreds of complaint letters from Monterrey and Guadalajara arrived at parent company Playtex, while the Puebla municipal government took down the advertisements on the grounds that they
lacked the requisite permissions. A Playtex spokesperson, noting that
no complaints had been received in the United States or Europe when
the same ads ran, commented that the letters were from "women who
said we were corrupting the minds of younger people and being immoral." Playtex compromised by hiding the model's shoulders and
midriff under a suit that still showed her dramatic décolletage.

Many of the complaints came from cities under the political leadership of the conservative, Catholic-associated Partido Acción Nacional
(National Action Party, or PAN). The PAN leadership, in an open letter
"on the subject of politics, morality, and bras," disassociated itself from
the complaints and accused Playtex of using the scandal for free advertising. These complaints and the subsequent media furor indicate that
public mores, eroded by the revolution, continue to be challenged by
urbanization, modernization, the changing position of women, and
international influences.[6] They also show that some women still consider themselves champions of public morality.

While unable to halt public "immorality," the church has ultimately
fared better in the area of education. Pope Pius XI's 1929 encyclical
Divini illius magistri argued that the purpose of education was to save
children's souls and that it could not be complete without a Catholic
component. The encyclical reiterated the church's position that parents
had the right to determine the education of their children, a right given
to them by God, while it condemned sex education and coeducation.
Yet that uncompromising position gradually relaxed. Influenced by the
Second Vatican Council, a new approach to education emerged in the
1960s; Catholic schools were conceived of as part of a broader service
to humanity, in collaboration with public education, and Christian
education was viewed as taking place in the home and in catechism
classes, rather than strictly in Catholic schools. This new approach
gradually gained greater acceptance and in 1977 the Vatican's *The
Catholic School* depicted education as a task not only for the church
but also for other agencies, including governments. The church also
accepted criticisms that Catholic claims to educational universality
were anachronistic when national governments had long since taken on

the responsibility of mass education. The Catholic hierarchy in Mexico, responding both to domestic criticisms and changing times, declared that it would make its education more pertinent to concrete problems and would work officially with state agencies. It also admitted that its policy of favoring religious orders in education and refusing to allow laypeople to participate in Catholic education had to change.[7]

As the international and domestic church relaxed its rigid approach to education, so did the Mexican state. Under President Carlos Salinas de Gortari (1988–1994) many of the anticlerical restrictions of the 1917 Constitution were rescinded: Reforms restored the church's juridical status, allowed clergy the right to vote, gave churches the right to own property, and most controversially established the right to religious primary schools. Salinas also restored diplomatic relations with the Vatican. In practice, the church had still greater freedoms, as restrictions on public religious expression were routinely ignored. When Pope John Paul II visited Mexico in January 1979 and again in May 1990, he held mass in outdoor stadiums, acted as a foreign priest, and wore his papal dress in public. These actions were permitted despite the fact that all violated either the constitution or the Federal District penal code. Public tolerance points to a private agreement for mutual support. For instance, the papal nuncio appointed after Salinas restored relations with the Vatican began to purge Mexico's clergy and hierarchy of those sympathetic to or actively promoting liberation theology.[8] Good relations notwithstanding, the Vatican remains sensitive to Mexico's history of church-state conflict, and the importance of relations with Mexico have been highlighted by Pope John Paul II's frequent visits to the country.

While the church hierarchy and recently ousted ruling party, the Partido Revolucionario Institucional (Party of the Institutionalized Revolution, or PRI), found it in their mutual interest to agree, Catholic teachings are open to alternative interpretations. The Vatican's nineteenth-century condemnations of liberalism and modernity have given way to condemnations of neoliberalism and unfettered capitalism. Whereas the nineteenth-century antimodern strain originated in the Vatican, the church's stance on neoliberalism emerged from Latin America. Well before John Paul II's 1998 visit to Cuba, when he warned of "the resurgence of a certain capitalist neo-liberalism which subordinates the human person to blind market forces," Latin

American bishops at the 1992 Santo Domingo conference had blamed neoliberalism for growing poverty rates in their countries.[9] The central role that Bishop Samuel Ruiz of San Cristóbal de las Casas played in negotiations with the Zapatista rebels in the 1990s shows how those within the church can still use their position to demand social justice.[10] Pope John Paul himself noted in 1999 that "without recognition that the indigenous people were the first owners of the land" there would be no solution to the problems in Chiapas.[11]

Today after a century and a half of church and state separation, the festival of the Virgin of Guadalupe still makes front-page news, as do photographs of the PAN's Vicente Fox draping himself in a flag emblazoned with the Guadalupana. President Fox's 2000 electoral triumph and personal behavior have again brought up the question of the church's role in politics. In a presidential campaign that was more about change and personalities than about policies, one of the hotly debated questions was the future role of the church in politics.[12] The PAN, founded in 1939 by political Catholics, espouses a program of Catholic morality and neoliberal economic policies, but it has never affiliated with the church or been under the hierarchy. Legally, political parties cannot have a religious affiliation, and thus officially Catholics still have to separate their religious and political lives.[13] Yet in practice this separation is not always clear-cut, and centrists in the PAN have struggled to distance themselves from the party's conservative Catholics. Fox, however, has intentionally courted the support of political Catholics. He started his presidential campaign wearing the flag of the Virgin and, as president-elect, began his presidency praying "privately" at her basilica — accompanied by newspaper and television reporters, as well as his military guard. Photographs show Fox surrounded by the press while taking the Eucharist.[14] Hours later, during his televised inaugural speech, Fox's daughter, Pauline, gave him a Christ figure, which he propped on the podium as he addressed an audience that included Archbishop of Yucatán Emilio Berlie and Bishop of Ecatepec Onésimo Cepeda.[15] During his address, members of the PRI tried to shout down the president with cries of "Juárez, Juárez, Juárez."[16] The controversies surrounding Fox's use of Catholic symbols and the opposition's political, selective uses of history to counter them indicate how porous is the separation between religion and politics and how alive history remains.

Moreover, Fox's closeness with the church has emboldened conservatives in the PAN.[17] Since his election, the PAN-controlled legislature of the state of Guanajuato has sought to increase the penalty for abortion, in all cases, to time in prison. Left-controlled legislatures in Mexico City and in Morelos responded by preparing to liberalize their abortion laws. As a result of protests, Guanajuato's new governor vetoed the reform, but unrepentant state deputies responded that they would try again. For Mexican feminists, the proposed restriction on the already limited right to legal abortion (essentially permitted only in cases of rape) at least brought the issue to public debate.[18] The attacks on women's rights moved to Mexico City, where the PAN failed in its challenge to a law allowing the district attorney to authorize abortions for women who had been raped. Moreover, the Supreme Court upheld the law that allowed for abortions in cases of birth defects, danger to the mother's life, and "involuntary artificial insemination," while reducing the prison term for having or performing an abortion.[19]

The actors discussed in this book would find these debates on morality and the position of the church in public life familiar. The question now, as it was in the 1920s, is whether a state has to be openly anticlerical to be lay. The fact that the vast majority of Mexicans are nominally Catholic indicates the failures of the anticlerical policies pursued in both the nineteenth and twentieth centuries. Whereas anticlerical policies have consistently failed, educational programs in the postrevolutionary period succeeded in offering children, women, and men technical training, literacy skills, and intellectual challenges, often in a place that became part of the local community. Working in parallel and sometimes in cooperation, church and state provided Mexico City residents and their children with the means to "better themselves" as they saw fit and to realize some of the goals of the revolution in their lives.

Notes

Abbreviations Used in the Notes

AGN O/C	Archivo General de la Nación, Presidentes Obregón and Plutarco Elías Calles
AHCM IP	Archivo Histórico de la Cuidad de México, Instrucción Pública
AHSEP DE	Archivo Histórico de la Secretaría de Educación Pública, Departamento Escolar
AHSEP DEPN	Archivo Histórico de la Secretaría de Educación Pública, Departamento de Enseñanza Primaria y Normal
AHSEP DETIC	Archivo Histórico de la Secretaría de Educación Pública, Departamento de Enseñanza Técnica, Industria y Comercial
AHUFCM	Archivo Histórico de la Unión Femenina Católica Mexicana
AHAM	Archivo Histórico del Arzobispado de México
ASSM	Archivo Histórico del Secretariado Social Mexicano
AyF	Acción y Fe
BM	Boletín Municipal
BPAU	Bulletin of the Pan American Union
BSEP	Boletín de la Secretaría de Educación Pública
CESU LNDLR	Centro de Estudios Sobre la Universidad, Liga Nacional Defensora de la Libertad Religiosa
CNCT	Confederación Nacional Católica del Trabajo
DEPN	Departamento de Enseñanza Primaria y Normal
DETIC	Departamento de Enseñanza Técnica, Industria y Comercial
LDC	La Dama Católica
MSCJM	El Mensajero del Sagrado Corazón de Jesús de México
SEP	Secretaría de Educación Pública
UDCM	Unión de Damas Católicas Mexicanas

Introduction

1. *AyF* 3 (1 Sept. 1924): 395–97.

2. *BSEP* (Oct. 1925): 101–9. See also Torres Septién, *Educación privada,* 110.

3. See Vaughan, *Cultural Politics in Revolution;* and Rockwell, "Schools of the Revolution," as examples. Vaughan's earlier work, *State, Education, and Social Class,* focused on curricula.

4. See Fell, *José Vasconcelos,* 110–11; Meneses Morales, *Tendencias educativas, 1911–1934,* 239–45; Vaughan, *State, Education, and Social Class,* 122–24.

5. Torres Septién, *Educación privada.*

6. See Purnell, *Popular Movements and State Formation;* Butler, "The 'Liberal' Cristero."

7. Adame Goddard, *Pensamiento político y social;* Ceballos Ramírez, "Encíclica 'Rerum Novarum,'" "Sindicalismo católico en México," *Catolicismo social.* For examples of works focusing on the conflict, see Bailey, *¡Viva Cristo Rey!;* Quirk, *Mexican Revolution and the Catholic Church.*

8. See, for example, Soto, *Emergence of the Modern Mexican Woman,* 113–18.

9. Kaplan, "Female Consciousness and Collective Action," 551, 566; see also chap. 5 in *Red City, Blue Period.*

10. Dore and Molyneux, *Hidden Histories of Gender and the State;* French and James, *Gendered Worlds of Latin American Women Workers.* On Mexico see Fowler-Salamini and Vaughan, *Women of the Mexican Countryside,* and Stern, *Secret History of Gender.*

11. See, for example, Bliss, *Compromised Positions,* "Guided by an Imperious Moral Need," and "Science of Redemption"; Piccato, *City of Suspects;* Wood, *Revolution in the Streets.*

Chapter 1. Church Politics and Educating Mexicans

1. See Ceballos Ramírez, "Encíclica 'Rerum Novarum,'" 7, and "Vida de los vencidos," 374–75; Gutiérrez Casillas, *Historia de la iglesia en México,* 354; Lynch, "Catholic Church in Latin America," 532–33; and Torres Septién, *Educación privada,* 55–56, for statistics on the growth of the Catholic Church during the Porfiriato.

2. See Ceballos Ramírez, *Catolicismo social,* for a detailed history of Catholic social action in Mexico.

3. Ibid., 48–49. *Rerum Novarum* is reprinted in George, *Condition of Labour.*

4. See Meneses Morales, *Tendencias educativas, 1821–1911,* 269; Staples, "Panorama educativo"; Vaughan, *State, Education, and Social Class,* chap. 1; Thompson, "Children and Schooling in Guanajuato," 26–27; and González y González, Cosío Villegas, and Monroy, *República restaurada,* on early education efforts.

5. González y González, Cosío Villegas, and Monroy, *República restaurada,* 692.

6. On municipal education see Tanck de Estrada, "Tensión en la torre de marfil," 64; Meneses Morales, *Tendencias educativas, 1821–1911,* 269, 351; González y González, Cosío Villegas, and Monroy, *República restaurada,* 677–78; González Navarro, *Porfiriato,* 571–72; Rodríguez Kuri, *Experiencia olvidada,* 141–42; Díaz Zermeño, "Escuela nacional primaria," 62–63.

7. On teachers see Arnaut, *Historia de una profesión,* 21; Bravo Ugarte, *Educación en México,* 142, 154; Calderón Ita and Deloya Domínguez, *Maestros de primeras letras,* 50, 61.

8. Galván de Terrazas, *Educación superior de la mujer,* 16; Meneses Morales, *Tendencias educativas, 1821–1911,* 336, 655.

9. Galván de Terrazas, *Educación superior de la mujer,* 23; and *Maestros y la educación pública,* 176.

10. On the law see Vaughan, *State, Education, and Social Class,* 21–22. On violations of the 1888 law see Schmitt, "Díaz Conciliation Policy," 519.

11. Vaughan, *State, Education, and Social Class,* 57, 59; Meneses Morales, *Tendencias educativas, 1821–1911,* 424.

12. Bazant, *Historia de la educación,* 42–43; Meneses Morales, *Tendencias educativas, 1821–1911,* 546.

13. Meneses Morales, *Tendencias educativas, 1821–1911*, 516, 519, 550; Bazant, *Historia de la educación*, 36, 42.

14. Bazant, *Historia de la educación*, 36–37; González Navarro, *Porfiriato*, 537.

15. Vaughan, *State, Education, and Social Class*, 60–61. For statistics on primary schooling see Bazant, *Historia de la educación*, 41, 92–95; Dirección General de Estadística, *Estadísticas sociales del Porfiriato*, 43; Meneses Morales, *Tendencias educativas, 1821–1911*, graph facing 464.

16. Bazant, *Historia de la educación*, 106–7, 123.

17. Ibid., 118–21; Vaughan, *State, Education, and Social Class*, 69–70, for more details on these schools.

18. Hanson, "Day of Ideals," 90–91; González Navarro, *Porfiriato*, 272. See also Ceballos Ramírez, *Catolicismo social,* and Ceballos Ramírez and Garza Rangel, *Catolicismo social en México,* for detailed analyses of Catholic social action.

19. Meyer, *Cristiada,* 2:52. By 1910, there were twenty-five Catholic workers' circles with approximately nine thousand members nationally.

20. Hanson, "Day of Ideals," 161.

21. Ceballos Ramírez, *Catolicismo social,* 160. In 1900, Catholic primary schools comprised 4 percent of primary schools, increasing to 5 percent by 1907. Nationally, the number of Catholic primary schools grew from 493 in 1900 to 586 in 1907 (González Navarro, *Porfiriato,* 600). Because of legal restrictions on Catholic education, some schools might have hidden their religious character; thus, these figures probably under-represent Catholic primary schools.

22. Nationally, public-school enrollment fell by 5.5 percent between 1900 and 1907, while private-school enrollment rose by 19 percent. In the Federal District, private primary schools accounted for 30 percent of all primary schools, and private-school attendance rose 21 percent between 1900 and 1907 (Vaughan, *State, Education, and Social Class,* 53–54).

23. Torres Septién, *Educación privada,* 57–59, 65, 71.

24. Ibid., 72, for a discussion of curriculum. See Vaughan, "Primary Education and Literacy," 45, on Catholic school goals and programs.

25. Ceballos Ramírez, *Catolicismo social,* 161; Torres Septién, *Educación privada,* 67–69.

26. Adame Goddard, *Pensamiento político y social,* 170–71; Correa, *Partido Católico Nacional,* 196.

27. Lear, "Workers, *Vecinos,* and Citizens," 185; Meyer, prologue to *Partido Católico Nacional,* 14; Adame Goddard, *Pensamiento político y social,* 174–75; Ceballos Ramírez, *Catolicismo social,* 414. See also Knight, *Mexican Revolution,* 1:402–4.

28. Knight, *Mexican Revolution,* 2:1–2. See Correa, *Partido Católico Nacional,* for a description of PCN involvement with Huerta; also see Ceballos Ramírez, "Democracia cristiana," 215.

29. Curley, "Laicos," 163; Meyer, prologue to *Partido Católico Nacional,* 15.

30. Adame Goddard, *Pensamiento político y social,* 247–58.

31. Reich, *Mexico's Hidden Revolution,* 12.

32. Knight uses the term "nominal Catholic," which he opposes to being "politically Catholic." Knight, "Revolutionary Project, Recalcitrant People," 233.

33. Purnell, *Popular Movements and State Formation,* 21.

34. SEP, *Educación pública,* 168. During the Porfiriato, the school year had been modeled on the U.S. school calendar, with a long vacation over the summer.

35. See Meneses Morales, *Tendencias educativas, 1911–1934;* SEP, *Educación pública;* and Torres Septién, *Educación privada,* 85–89, for a discussion of education in this period.

36. Knight, *Mexican Revolution,* 1:482–90, 2:78, 87, 172, 180–81. On building confiscation see Lear, "Workers, *Vecinos,* and Citizens," 281–82. On the class divisions of the city see Piccato, *City of Suspects,* 35–40.

37. Torres Septién, *Educación privada,* 98.

38. Knight, *Mexican Revolution* 1:143; 2:309, 314–16, 416, 419–21; Lear, "Workers, *Vecinos,* and Citizens," 326. Also see Piccato, *City of Suspects,* 136–44, on robbery during the revolution.

39. On education in this period see SEP, *Educación pública,* 186–87, 192; Meneses Morales, *Tendencias educativas, 1911–1934,* 145–48, 184; Vaughan, *State, Education, and Social Class,* 123.

40. On workers' demands for education see Anderson, *Outcasts in Their Own Land,* 68–69, 196; Morgan, "Industry and Society in the Mexico City Area," 168–70, 209. On peasant demands see Vaughan, *State, Education, and Social Class,* 85.

41. Vaughan, *State, Education, and Social Class,* 134–36.

42. Ibid., 136.

43. Fell, *José Vasconcelos,* 668.

44. Vaughan, *State, Education, and Social Class,* 138–39.

45. Loyo, "Lecturas para el pueblo," 319 n. 46.

46. Vaughan, *State, Education, and Social Class,* 149.

Chapter 2. Primary Education

1. Meneses Morales, *Tendencias educativas, 1911–1934,* 193, 196, 199, 260.

2. Summarized from María Portugal, Vda. de Guerra, 1er año grupo C, Dec. 1917; Ana de la Fuente, 2do año grupo A, 30 April, 30 March, 31 May 1917, AHCM IP 2560 "Programas de reconocimiento mensuales 1917"; Dolores Rossell, "Temas para el 2do Reconocimiento Trimestral del 1er año Grupo B," 11 Nov. 1918, AHCM IP 2538/5 "Exámenes y premios, 1916–1918."

3. Guadalupe Jiménez, "Temas para el reconocimiento del primer trimestre del año escolar de 1918," 1918; and "Temas para reconocimiento final de las alumnas del tercer año en el año escolar de 1918," 13 Nov. 1918, AHCM IP 2538/5, "Exámenes y premios 1916–1918."

4. María Portugal, Vda. de Guerra, 1er año grupo C, Dec. 1917; Ana de la Fuente, 2do año grupo A, Dec. 1917; Felisa Torix, 3er año, 18 Dec. 1917; all in AHCM IP 2560 "Programas de reconocimiento mensuales 1917." Also Guadalupe Jiménez, "Temas para reconocimiento final de las alumnas del tercer año en el año escolar de 1918," 13 Nov. 1918, AHCM IP 2538/5 "Exámenes y premios 1916–1918."

5. On population and migration see Knight, *Mexican Revolution,* 2:523; Lear, "Mexico City," 464. On Catholic support for agricultural education see, for example, Carolina Alcocer de Bonfil, "Escuelas granjas," prepared for 1922 UDCM National Congress, 1922, AHUFCM 6/34.

6. Ana de la Fuente, 2do año grupo A, 31 May, 31 July 1917; Felisa Torix, 3er año, 31 July, 1917, no day 1917, 14 Dec. 1917; all in AHCM IP 2560, "Programas de reconocimiento mensuales 1917."

7. Pulque, fermented juice of the maguey cactus, was the alcohol of the rural and

urban poor. Gruening, *Mexico and Its Heritage,* 537–39; Vaughan, "Rural Women's Literacy and Education," 114.

8. Inspector to teachers, Feb. 1919, AHCM IP 2555/1; Guadalupe Jiménez, "Temas para reconocimiento final de las alumnas del tercer año en el año escolar de 1918," 13 Nov. 1918, AHCM IP 2538/5 "Exámenes y premios 1916–1918."

9. SEP, *Educación pública,* 185, 192.

10. Jesús Ganz to headmaster of school number 39, 22 March 1917, AHCM IP 2555/1; Comisión de Instrucción Pública, 20 Jan. 1921, AHCM IP 2664/4 1917–1921, "Circulares, disposiciones"; María Portugal, Vda. de Guerra, 1er año grupo C, Dec. 1917; Ana de la Fuente, 2do año grupo A, n.d; both in AHCM IP 2560, "Programas de reconocimiento mensuales 1917."

11. Ana María Correa, fourth-grade program, 13 Dec. 1917, AHCM IP 2560, "Programas de reconocimiento mensuales 1917"; Dolores Rossell, "Temas para el 2do reconocimiento trimestral del 1er año Grupo B," 11 Nov. 1918, AHCM IP 2538/5, "Exámenes y premios 1916–1918."

12. Guadalupe Jiménez, "Temas para reconocimiento final de las alumnas del tercer año en el año escolar de 1918," 13 Nov. 1918, AHCM IP 2538/5, "Exámenes y premios 1916–1918"; Felisa Torix, third-grade programs, 31 May, 30 June 1917, 31 Aug. 1927, 18 Dec. 1917, AHCM IP 2560, "Programas de reconocimiento mensuales 1917"; María Araiza, "Temas para el reconocimiento final de las materiales correspondientes al cuarto curso de educación primaria elemental en el año escolar de 1918," 14 Nov. 1918, AHCM IP 2538/5, "Exámenes y premios 1916–1918."

13. Anderson, *Imagined Communities.*

14. Tenorio-Trillo, "1910 Mexico City," 91.

15. "Proyecto de horarios escolares," n.d. (in 1921 file), AHSEP DE 39/17/18–23. My research in the SEP archive took place in the 1995–96 academic year, in Sept.–Oct. 1997, and in April 2002. The references were accurate when I did this research. Some of these may now be out of date, as the archive is in the process of reorganization.

16. SEP, *Esfuerzo educativo,* 1:160.

17. Fell, *José Vasconcelos,* 104–5, 122, 150–82, 189.

18. Vaughan, *State, Education, and Social Class,* 165–66, 173.

19. Dewey, *Experience and Education,* 35–36.

20. Dworkin, *Dewey on Education,* 22, 26; quotations on pp. 39 and 42, respectively.

21. Vasconcelos, "Bases conformes a las cuales deberán organizar la educación pública federal," 12 Feb. 1923, AHSEP DE 44/59/1–3.

22. Massieu to director of primary education, 27 April 1923, AHSEP DE 46/50/82–83.

23. Massieu, Circular 30, 15 Feb. 1923, AHSEP DE 46/50/32–34.

24. Statistics compiled from SEP, *Noticia estadística, 1925,* 62–63; SEP, *Esfuerzo educativo,* 1:174–75; Meneses Morales, *Tendencias educativas, 1911–1934,* 463–64. On the required subjects in primary education see Vasconcelos, "Bases conformes a las cuales deberán organizar la educación pública federal," 12 Feb. 1923, AHSEP DE 44/59/1–3.

25. On funding and teachers see Vaughan, *State, Education, and Social Class,* 174; SEP, *Esfuerzo educativo,* 1:191.

26. On education in this period see Arce Gurza, "En busca de una educación revolucionaria," 150–53; Vaughan, *State, Education, and Social Class,* 138, 174–75. On pledges and school celebrations, see *BPAU* 59 (Nov. 1925), 1169; Comisión Organiza-

dora de las Fiestas del Centenario, to principals, various schools, 25 Aug. 1921, AHSEP DE 39/17/165. On the morality code see Loyo, "Lecturas para el pueblo," 320–21; Vaughan, Ibid., 175–76; *BSEP* 10 (Oct. 1925): 103–10.

27. *BSEP* 60 (May 1926): 73–76.

28. Head of DE to Vasconcelos, 31 May 1923, AHSEP DE 63/5/69.

29. Torres Septién, *Educación privada,* 101.

30. The regulations are in Libro de Actas, Sección de Escuelas 1920–1926, Feb. 1922, 8, AHUFCM. Conclusions drawn from an overview of minutes of the Sección de Escuelas.

31. Libro de Actas, Sección de Escuelas 1920–1926, 7 July 1920, 1, Dec. 1921, 5, Jan. 1922, and Dec. 1923, 19, AHUFCM.

32. Ibid., Jan. 1924, 20.

33. Ibid., Jan. 1922, 6.

34. Ibid., May 1922, 9.

35. "Conclusiones aprobadas, bibliotecas populares de Nuestra Señora del Sagrado Corazón," Primer Congreso Nacional, 1922, AHUFCM 6/33/68.

36. Miguel Miranda, "Seis años de actividades del Secretariado Social Mexicano, 1925–1931," 7, ASSM.

37. Fernández-Aceves, "Political Mobilization of Women," 299–304.

38. Libro de Actas, Sección de Escuelas 1920–1926, May 1922, 9, and Aug. 1922, 11, AHUFCM.

39. Prospectus, Feb. 1919, AHAM 155, "Censuras de libro," "Nazaret."

40. Morales to inspectors, 7 March 1923, AHSEP DE 46/50/53.

41. Morales to inspectors, 19 May 1923, AHSEP DE 46/50/91.

42. See Fernández-Aceves, "Political Mobilization of Women," 155, 266, for discussion of this situation in Guadalajara.

43. Libro de Actas, Sección de Escuelas 1920–1926, Jan. 1922, 7, and Dec. 1923, 19, AHUFCM.

Chapter 3. Vocational Education

1. Statistics in *BM* 3 (29 Nov. 1918): 1059. Comments on texts in Bazant, *Historia de la educación,* 109. Night-school inventories from night school number 2, 30 June 1917, AHCM IP 2570/3/195; night school number 5, Sept. 1917, AHCM IP 2570/3/261; night school number 36, Sept. 1917, AHCM IP 2571/259; night school number 33, 15 Sept. 1917, AHCM IP 2571/251; night school number 3, Ibid., 1917.

2. Meneses Morales, *Tendencias educativas, 1911–1934,* 492–93. He also includes a list of textbooks used in primary schools between 1918 and 1928.

3. For a description of typical school conditions see Bravo to Comisión de Instrucción Pública, 4 July 1918, AHCM IP 2570/3/230. For the school decorations and cooperation between principals see Comisiones de Instrucción Pública, report, 11 June 1918; Téllez Escalante to municipal president, 19 Aug. 1918; municipal president, authorization, 29 June 1918; all in AHCM IP 2570/3/193.

4. A reference to the work of Martínez Assad, *Laboratorio de la revolución.*

5. Galván de Terrazas, *Maestros y la educación pública,* 69.

6. Fell, *José Vasconcelos,* 196–98; report of director of DETIC, 17 June 1922, AHSEP DETIC 72/51/47; Vaughan, *State, Education, and Social Class,* 202; SEP, *Noticia estadística, 1926,* 286–87.

7. *BSEP* 5 (Feb. 1926): 107, 114; Fell, *José Vasconcelos*, 202. For Obregón's letter on tuition see Obregón, 22 July 1924, AGN O/C 121-E-E-2 1073.

8. Inspector to director of DETIC, 26 July 1923, AHSEP DETIC 68/34/6–9.

9. Vaughan, *State, Education, and Social Class*, 192–94.

10. Meneses Morales, *Tendencias educativas, 1911–1934*, 96–97; SEP, *Esfuerzo educativo*, 1:498–99. The SEP also sought to found a textile school to train men, again sidelining the large numbers of women in the industry. This school was never opened due to lack of funds (Fell, *José Vasconcelos*, 197–98).

11. On reasons for founding the school see Fell, *José Vasconcelos*, 197; *BPAU* 56 (April 1922): 414–15. On the politics around the school see Vaughan, *State, Education, and Social Class*, 195–96; Carr, *Movimiento obrero*, 168–69, 196; Fell, *José Vasconcelos*, 198–200. On its financial problems see Agustín Arenas to Obregón, 8 Nov. 1922; and response from Fernando Torreblanca to Arenas, 28 Nov. 1922, AGN O/C 711-F-18.

12. "Plan de estudios y datos que interesan a los que pretendan ingresar a la Escuela Técnica N. de Constructores," 1928, AHSEP DETIC 74/17/14; "Escuela Nacional de Constructores plan de estudios y otros datos interesantes," n.d. (filed with 1925–1928), AHSEP DETIC 74/17/1–5.

13. "Informe relativo a los cuatro centros de educación cultural femeniles," 24 Dec. 1923, AHSEP DETIC 68/29/13–14.

14. Meneses Morales, *Tendencias educativas, 1911–1934*, 381–82.

15. Luque Alcaide, *Educación en Nueva España*, chap. 5. On the modernized patriarchy see Vaughan, "Modernizing Patriarchy."

16. Meneses Morales, *Tendencias educativas 1911–1934*, 381.

17. Course listing for EAOS, 1926, AHSEP DETIC 74/3/13.

18. Pamphlet for Querétaro School, Jan. 1927, AHSEP DETIC 74/3/24; report of director of DETIC, 17 June 1922, AHSEP DETIC 72/51/48. On the founding of the Querétaro School see Sierra, *Educación nacional*, 431.

19. See Rosario Pacheco, founding charter of Mistral school, 22 July 1922, AHSEP DETIC 72/4/1; *BSEP* 3–4 (1923): 249; Elodia Chirón y Gómez, "Finalidades de la escuela," 21 Nov. 1928, AHSEP DETIC 74/18/4. A prominent writer and social activist, Gabriela Mistral endorsed a traditional domestic ideal of the housebound women and promoted motherhood as women's highest calling. She also believed that domestic responsibilities gave women the right to a political role. On Mistral and her writing see *MSCJM*, Aug. 1924, 509–13; Franco, *Plotting Women*, 103; Vaughan, *State, Education, and Social Class*, 207–8. See the introduction to Mistral's *Lecturas para mujeres* for a summary of her work in Mexico and the hostility to her collaboration in the revolutionary project that prompted her to leave.

20. On Mexican puericulture in practice see headmistress to director of DETIC, 25 Aug. 1922, AHSEP DETIC 72/7/36; *BSEP* 5 (Feb. 1926): 125. For a discussion of maternalist discourse see Lavrin, *Women, Feminism, and Social Change*. Quotation in Stepan, *"Hour of Eugenics,"* 77–78. Stepan addresses the French origins of puericulture and its evolution in Latin America.

21. *BSEP* 1 (Sept. 1922): 94; headmistress of Escuela de Enseñanza Doméstica, "Informe de la exposición," 29 Nov. 1923, AHSEP DETIC 68/70/17.

22. Pamphlet for Escuela Hogar Sor Juana Inés de la Cruz, 1926, AHSEP DETIC 74/15/19–20.

23. Galván de Terrazas, *Educación superior de la mujer*, 45; Lear, "Workers, *Vecinos*,

and Citizens," 356; Macías, *Against All Odds*, chap. 5. For example, on women after World War II in Britain see Beddoe, *Back to Home and Duty*.

24. Inspector to director of DETIC, 26 July 1923, AHSEP DETIC 68/29/3.

25. Fell, *José Vasconcelos*, 202–3; Meneses Morales, *Tendencias educativas, 1911–1934*, 382; SEP, *Esfuerzo educativo*, 1:180–81, 506–7.

26. SEP, *Esfuerzo educativo*, 1:340–41, 343.

27. Soto, *Emergence of the Modern Mexican Women*, 100. On population see Blum, "Public Welfare and Child Circulation," 256–57 n. 130 and Piccato, *City of Suspects*, 22.

28. *LDC* 3 (May 1923): 31.

29. Information on the UDCM Academy is in *LDC* 1 (Sept. 1921): 18–19; 3 (May 1923): 34; and 4 (Dec 1924): 18. On ideal cooking classes see Soledad del Moral Vda. de Iturbide, "Establecimiento de escuelas," 4 Nov. 1922, AHUFCM 6/34.

30. "La moralización de las sirvientas y obreras," prepared for 1922 UDCM National Congress, Nov. 1922, AHUFCM 6/34. Use of charitable and welfare institutions to train domestic servants had been common during the nineteenth century too (see Blum, "Conspicuous Benevolence," 21).

31. On leniency toward rape see Macías, *Against All Odds*, 110, 118–19; and Ramos Escandón, "Señoritas porfirianas," 153. See Rocha, *Porfiriato y la revolución*, 123–29, for the 1917 constitutional convention debate. See Bliss, *Compromised Positions*, 28–29, 40, 83, 103–6, 123–33, and "Science of Redemption" for discussions of sexual behavior and the double standard. For a broader discussion of violence against women see Piccato, *City of Suspects*, chap. 5.

32. UDCM Central Committee, n.d. (filed in 1926 folder), AHUFCM 2/11/611.

33. Vaughan, *State, Education, and Social Class*, 211.

34. Torres notes that after the revolution, nuns were no longer referred to as "sister" but as "madam" or "miss" (Torres Septién, *Educación privada*, 98).

35. *AyF* 1 (March 1922): 212; and 4 (April 1925), 68.

36. *AyF* 2 (Oct. 1923): 618–19. On Tlalpan see Pilcher, *¡Qué Vivan los Tamales!*, 52, 64; Terry, *Terry's Mexico*, 406.

37. *AyF* 3 (Feb. 1924): 96–100; and 3 (June 1924): 282–83.

38. Méndez Medina, *Manual de formación sindical*, 64.

39. *AyF* 3 (Dec. 1922): 840.

Chapter 4. Urban Missionaries

1. On Porfirian teachers see Galván de Terrazas, *Soledad compartida*, 152–63; and González Navarro, *Porfiriato*, 536.

2. Summarized from Cockcroft, "Maestro de primaria," 565–68; Rockwell, "Schools of the Revolution," 178; Galván de Terrazas, *Maestros y la educación pública*, 187, and *Educación superior de la mujer*, 29–31. See Cleland, *Mexican Year Book, 1920–1921*, 371, for a contemporary account of teachers in the revolution.

3. Fell, *José Vasconcelos*, 110; Meneses Morales, *Tendencias educativas, 1911–1934*, 204. In January 1921, the municipality of Mexico City employed 118 male and 591 female primary teachers. None of the men were employed in girls' schools. ("Informe mensual de instrucción pública municipal, correspondiente al mes de enero de 1921" (tables with figures for girls' and boys' schools), *BM* 6 (3 June 1921).

4. See teachers to municipal president, 27 June 1918, AHCM IP 2526/113, "Escuela

Elemental 272," for an example of the accounting department seeking to extort money from teachers claiming their paychecks.

5. See parents from Colonia Santa María la Ribera to municipal president, 15 Oct. 1918, AHCM IP 2468/31, "Varios Regina E. de Sevilla . . ."; and Meneses Morales, *Tendencias educativas, 1911–1934*, 240, for public support for teachers.

6. Secretary of public instruction to inspector, circular number 3, 2 May 1918, AHCM IP 2443/2. See Rockwell, "Schools of the Revolution," 194, for teachers working multiple jobs.

7. Galván de Terrazas, *Maestros y la educación pública*, 57–58.

8. Ibid., 192–93; Meneses Morales, *Tendencias educativas, 1911–1934*, 189, 240–43; Carr, *Movimiento obrero*, 93. See De la Huerta to Obregón, 22 Aug. 1922, AGN O/C 121-H-E-13, on delinquent salaries.

9. Galván de Terrazas, *Maestros y la educación pública*, 221; Meneses Morales, *Tendencias educativas, 1911–1934*, 437.

10. On municipal regulation and duties of inspectors see general director of public instruction to municipal president, 27 Aug. 1917, AHCM IP 2527/117, "Escuela Elemental 308"; inspectors' regulation, 1 April 1921, AHCM IP 2664/4 "circulares, disposiciones 1921." On the history of inspection see Bazant, *Historia de la educación*, 47. For resentment of inspectors see *BM* 4 (22 April 1921): 342.

11. "La Dirección General de Educación Pública del Distrito Federal ha consultado a este H. Ayuntamiento ceses de profesores," 26 March 1918, AHCM IP 2514/3189.

12. Rafael Santamarina, médico escolar, "Estudio sobre el proyecto de reglamento para la admisión de las profesoras casadas en el servicio escolar," Aug. 1922, AHSEP DE 49/22/162.

13. *BPAU* 56 (March 1923): 233, 235; Head of DE to inspectors, 23 July 1922, AHSEP DE 39/28/41; Fell, *José Vasconcelos*, 119.

14. Galván de Terrazas, *Maestros y la educación pública*, 229.

15. In 1925, most Federal District teachers were between twenty and forty years old, although there were teachers as young as sixteen and as old as seventy-five. In 1925, there were 1,579 SEP primary-school teachers in the Federal District. Of these, 227 had finished primary school, 161 had finished primary school as well as attended three years of normal school, 103 had attended four years of normal school, and 946 had completed five years of normal school to receive their degree. In the Federal District's primary schools in 1926, there were 117 headmasters and 151 headmistresses. SEP, *Noticia estadística, 1925*, 73–74; SEP, *Noticia estadística, 1926*, 96–97, 110–11, 300–1.

16. DEPN rules for married teachers, 29 May 1922, AHSEP DE 49/22/147–48.

17. Rafael Santamarina, "Estudio sobre el proyecto de reglamento para la admisión de las profesoras casadas en el servicio escolar, presentado por el Sr. director general de educación primaria y normal," Aug. 1922, AHSEP DE 49/22/156–62; "Dictamen que presenta el C. Dr. Alberto Román, médico escolar, con motivo del proyecto de reglamento para utilizar los servicios de las profesoras casadas, que presenta la Dirección General de Educación Primaria y Normal a la Secretaría de Educación Pública," 8 July 1922, AHSEP DE 49/22/163–69. See SEP, *Esfuerzo educativo*, 2:7–14; Meneses Morales, *Tendencias educativas, 1911–1934*, 497, for background on Santamarina.

18. Jonás García et al., 20 March 1923, AHSEP DE 49/22/153–54.

19. On sanitary booklets see oficial mayor to head of DETIC, 22 March 1926, AHSEP DETIC 74/16/18. See oficial mayor, "Resumen de las disposiciones dictadas por esta

Secretaría relativas a la asistencia de personal de sus dependencias en el Distrito Federal," Jan. 1928, AHSEP DETIC 74/16/54, for regulations.

20. Gutiérrez to head of DE, 27 Oct. 1924, AHSEP DE 49/34/49. See Meneses Morales, *Tendencias educativas, 1911–1934*, 437–39, on press coverage of teachers' working conditions.

21. For further education see Massieu to director of DEPN, 21 April 1923, AHSEP DETIC 72/50/12; Morales to school principals, 15 June 1921, AHSEP DE 39/17/136. See also Gutiérrez to head of DE, 27 Oct. 1924, AHSEP DE 49/34/50; Morales to inspector Antonio Pons, 11 Oct. 1922, AHSEP DE 39/18/184; *BSEP* 5–6 (1924): 463.

22. On teachers' subsidies for further education see headmistress of Querétaro School to director of DETIC, 14 March 1924, AHSEP DETIC 72/15/25; Arellanos to director of DETIC, 26 July 1923, AHSEP DETIC 68/29/5. For a lucky few, further education offered the opportunity for state-sponsored study in Europe or the United States. See SEP, *Esfuerzo educativo*, 1:489–91.

23. Circulars from 1921 chastising teachers and giving them guidance are in AHSEP DE 39/17. See also Bernard to headmistress of Querétaro School, circular no. 13, 16 Feb. 1925, AHSEP DE 74/16/5. Quotation from Morales to inspectors/principals, circular no. 43, 18 Feb. 1921, AHSEP DE 39/17/51.

24. Becker, *Setting the Virgin on Fire*, 90.

25. "Proyecto de promociones al personal de las escuelas primarias, presentado a la consideración de la 'Asociación Nacional de Maestros Normalistas,'" 2, 20 Oct. 1923, AHSEP DE 49/23/9.

26. See Sáenz to Vasconcelos, 26 May 1923, AHSEP DE 41/3/8, 10; "Manifesto" by teachers at Escuela Superior Morelos to Calles, 22 Dec. 1922, 3; AGN O/C 121-E-M-35, for particularly descriptive complaints.

27. *BSEP* 3–4 (1923): 220–22; Dewey, *Impressions of Soviet Russia*, 152.

28. On home visitors see *BSEP* 4 (Dec. 1925): 210–12, and 5 (May 1926), 61–64; Dewey, *Impressions of Soviet Russia*, 169.

29. Letter lacking signature or addressee, 13 July 1915, and José Cervantes Milanés to vicario general, 24 July 1915, both in AHAM 73, "Escuelas," "Formación de Comité," "Informes 1911–1916."

30. "Memorandum sobre el problema de la educación," n.d, 3; AHAM 73, "Escuelas."

31. "Anteproyecto para la fundación de una escuela normal católica para profesoras," prepared for the 1923 UDCM General Assembly, AHUFCM 4/22; Clara G. Arce, "Informe de la Secretaría," prepared for the 1924 UDCM General Assembly, AHUFCM 4/23; "La organización nacional de los maestros católicos," prepared by the Yucatán regional center for the 1922 UDCM National Congress, AHUFCM 6/33. See also Torres Septién, *Educación privada*, 293–94.

32. Summarized from "Libro de Actas de la Sociedad Católica de la Nación Mexicana," 15 March 1922–7 Feb. 1923, AHAM 4 L4C/4. In the same year, the SEP gave students in technical schools subsistence grants ranging from 25 to 100 pesos per month, with 50 pesos being the most common amount (see students with grants, 1923, AHSEP DE 41/12/97–98). Housing prices in "Cuadro que manifiesta el precio de artículos de primera necesidad a que se cotizaron durante el mes de julio de 1924," *BM* 7 (20 Dec. 1924).

33. See, for example, Quirk, *Mexican Revolution and the Catholic Church*, 127.

34. "Libro de Actas número 43 Actas 14/05/1913–06/03/1923," 20 Aug. 1918, 33, AHUFCM. Quotation in UDCM statutes, n.d., Condumex Cristeros 1/84 1/46 2.

35. *LDC* 1 (Sept. 1920): 2. See Bastian, "Modelos de mujer protestante," 176, for criticisms of Catholic attitudes toward women.

36. Kaplan, "Female Consciousness and Collective Action," 551.

37. *LDC* 4 (July 1924): 40; and 2 (June 1922): 20. For statistics on the UDCM see *Acción Femenina, "Después de Veinte Años de Trabajo,"* 1 Jan. 1933, 46.

38. Article 10a from "Testimonio del Acta de protocolización de los Estatutos de la UNDCM," 4 Dec. 1922, AHUFCM 1/2; "Libro de Actas número 43 Actas 14/05/1913–06/03/1923," Dec. 1921, 63–64, AHUFCM; "Libro de Actas número 7, Comité Central 1926–1928," 19 July 1926, Acta 120, AHUFCM.

39. "Extensión de la Unión de Damas Católicas," n.d., prepared for 1925 UDCM National Congress, AHUFCM 6/34.

40. Libro de Actas, "Sección de Escuelas 1920–1926, Feb. 1922, 8, AHUFCM. List of members' addresses is at the back of the Sección de Escuelas 1920–1926. Quotations from Terry, *Terry's Mexico*, 263–64; *LDC* 2 (Oct. 1922): 9; 3 (Jan. 1923): 21.

41. Overview of *LDC* 1921–1924. Quotations from *LDC* 1 (July 1921): 11; and 2 (Sept. 1922): 21.

42. On the marginal city see Piccato, *City of Suspects*, 35–40.

43. History of the early years in Hanson, "Day of Ideals," 183–86, 190–92. Memories of dama hospital volunteer in *LDC* 1 (June 1921): 4.

44. Adame Goddard, *Pensamiento político y social*, 185.

45. Valverde Téllez, *Bio-bibliografía eclesiástica mexicana*, 3:87–88.

46. O'Dogherty, "Restaurarlo todo en Cristo," 140.

47. Libro de Actas, Sección de Escuelas 1920–1926, AHUFCM.

48. Hanson, "Day of Ideals," 347–49.

49. *LDC* 1 (1 Dec. 1922): 3–4.

Chapter 5. Daily Life in Primary Schools

1. On municipal school conditions see teachers to municipal president, 27 June 1918, AHCM IP 2526/113, "Escuela Elemental 272"; Junta Escolar, 25 July 1928, AHCM IP 2541/6; *BM* 4 (29 Aug. 1919): 572–73; *BM* 4 (1 Aug. 1919): 488–93.

2. On the school police see principal to inspector, 9 Jan. 1918, AHCM IP 2559 "Comunicaciones mandadas." Truancy figures are in Meneses Morales, *Tendencias educativas, 1911–1934*, 199, but he does not specify whether these figures are for 1916 or 1917. Enrollment decline is discussed in Vaughan, *State, Education, and Social Class*, 123. SEP, *Educación pública*, 201, presents the closures as justification for the federalization of municipal schools.

3. For health issues related to municipal schools see Manuel del Valle to municipal president, n.d.; inspector to director public instruction, 16 Nov. 1918, both in AHCM IP 2527, "Varios"; inspector to headmaster, 16 March 1918, AHCM IP 2559, "Comunicaciones mandadas"; president of commission on public instruction, 31 Aug. 1918, AHCM IP 2443/42, "Circular 44." Details of epidemics are from Knight, *Mexican Revolution*, 2:420–22. Although there is no documentary evidence linking attendance to funding or promotions, there must have been a strong incentive to retain sick pupils.

4. María Guerrero to inspector, 12 Nov. 1917, AHCM IP 2559, "Comunicaciones mandadas"; dirección general educación pública, 26 Nov. 1917, AHCM IP 1312, "Circulares".

5. Terry, *Terry's Mexico*, 262.

6. Letters on threats to morality are in director of public education to municipal president, 3 Sept. 1917 and 13 Dec. 1917, AHCM IP 2525/94; municipal president's secretary to Julio Alberto, 8 Aug. 1918, AHCM IP 2525/94. The complaint about the pulquería is from "Unos vecinos que no quieren pulquerías," 28 Sept. 1922, *Universal*, sec. 2. On prohibition experiments in Yucatán see Fallaw, "Dry Law, Wet Politics," 37–64.

7. Secretario gobierno to municipal president, 19 June 1917; and reply from director of public education to secretario gobierno, 8 Aug. 1917, AHCM IP 2468/21. On prostitution see Rivera-Garza, "Masters of the Streets," 227, and Bliss, *Compromised Positions*. On the zonas de tolerancia see Bliss, Ibid., 66–67, 156–61, 181; chap. 2 discusses changes to the sex trade in the postrevolutionary era.

8. Social changes are discussed in Knight, *Mexican Revolution*, 2: 522–24; Adler Lomnitz and Pérez Lizaur, *Una familia de la élite mexicana*, 55; Piccato, *City of Suspects*, 2, 99–102. See Schell, "Honorable Avocation for Ladies," for Catholic morality concerns. Examples of Porfirian school conditions are in Gamboa, *Santa*, 17, and "Discurso del c. doctor Manuel Domínguez, presidente del ayuntamiento de 1893," 30, quoted in Díaz Zermeño, "Escuela nacional primaria," 79. On the question of public versus private activities, see Piccato, *City of Suspects*, 20–21, 116. The AHCM IP includes school enrollment registers for the postrevolutionary period, listing students' names, ages, addresses, parents' names, and parents' occupations. These registers offer an invaluable resource for further detailed study of where children lived and house by house investigation of Mexico City.

9. Andrés Osuna to director of public education, 3 Aug. 1917, AHCM IP 2526/112; J. L. Ramírez to municipal president, 10 July 1918, AHCM IP 2526/104; Comisión de Instrucción Pública notice, 15 July 1918, AHCM IP 2514/3201. On the city's crime rate after the revolution see Knight, *Mexican Revolution*, 2:403–4. On the role of the porter in protecting a neighborhood see Piccato, *City of Suspects*, 150.

10. See Luis Flores Merino et al. to secretary of public instruction, 17 Sept. 1918, and reply, 25 Sept. 1918, AHCM IP 2468/30, for an example of concerned parents. On the crime rate and the new nature of crime see Piccato, *City of Suspects*, 2, 99–102.

11. *AyF* 2 (March 1923): 184–88. On the increase in guns see Piccato, *City of Suspects*, 99.

12. Letter forwarded and transcribed by technical department head to municipal president and reply to department of public education from municipal president's secretary, 5 June and 30 July 1918, AHCM IP 2525/93. On coeducation see SEP, *Esfuerzo educativo*, 1:187.

13. "Inspección de la 7a. ZONA ESCOLAR URBANA. Recitación para el 1er. año escolar," 1918, AHCM IP 2541/6.

14. "Temas para las asambleas generales," 1917, AHCM IP 2542/5.

15. President of commission on public instruction to teachers, 9 July 1918, AHCM IP 2443/16; Eloy Morales to municipal president, 27 July 1918, AHCM IP 2443 "Acuse recibo de la circular 18." The emphasis placed on local government could have been a result of the strong *municipio libre* (municipal rule) ethos of the revolution.

16. "Dos mil nombramientos de maestros, firmados," *Universal*, 11 Jan. 1922.

17. On the federalization of municipal schools see Vasconcelos, *Ulises Crillo*, 952; *BSEP* 1 (1 March 1922): 506–8 (from *Excélsior*, 24 Dec. 1921); Vasconcelos to unknown addressee (probably Obregón), 24 Nov. 1921; and González to Obregón, 24 Nov. 1921, González to Obregón, 14 Dec. 1921; all in AGN O/C 241-E-E-6.

18. Symbolism of building donations in Lear, "Workers, *Vecinos*, and Citizens,"282, 369; Population statistics in *BSEP* 1 (1 March 1922): 508 (from *Excélsior* 24 Dec. 1921). On building donations see also Aguirre, "Promoción de un fraccionamiento," 218–19.

19. Head of DE to Vasconcelos, 31 May 1923, AHSEP DE 63/5/69.

20. Ibid.; Morales to inspectors, 2 April 1923, AHSEP DE 46/50/61; *BPAU* 57 (July 1923): 84.

21. Request for materials from Escuela Número 31 para Niños, 9 July 1923, AHSEP DE 44/2/11; Andrés Castro to head of DE, 14 July 1924, AHSEP DE 44/11/25; Morales to head of DE, 8 Aug. 1923, AHSEP DE 44/19/8; Consejo Técnico report to head of DE, 28 Sept. 1922, AHSEP DE 49/35/8. See Cleland, *Mexican Year Book, 1920–1921*, 369, for a foreigner's opinion of the schools. On the city's atmosphere in the 1920s see Piccato, *City of Suspects*, 26–40.

22. Morales' secretary to inspectors, 26 June 1923, AHSEP DE 46/50/112. See Terry, *Terry's Mexico*, xxiv, on Mexico City's climate.

23. Circular number 125, Morales to inspectors/principals, 24 June 1921, AHSEP DE 39/17/138; head of DE to SEP delegates, 12 July 1922, 39/24/1–2.

24. Morales to inspectors/principals, 20 Jan. 1921, AHSEP DE 39/17/24; circular number 113, Morales' secretary to inspectors/principals, 27 May 1921, AHSEP DE 39/17/125; Morales to inspectors, 16 Aug. 1923, AHSEP DE 46/50/129.

25. Fell, *José Vasconcelos*, 170; Meneses Morales, *Tendencias educativas, 1911–1934*, 318. On Porfirian conditions see Díaz Zermeño, "Escuela nacional primaria," 70.

26. "La tuberculosis ha invadido las escuelas," *Universal*, 24 February 1922; " 'Tienen mucha hambre los niños,' dice el Lic. Vasconcelos," *Universal*, 25 February 1922.

27. Meneses Morales, *Tendencias educativas, 1911–1934*, 318–19. Biographical information on Torres in Macías, *Against All Odds*, 106–7. Torres' papers are held in an archive at the Universidad Iberoamericana, Mexico City. On wheat versus corn see Pilcher, *¡Qué Vivan los Tamales!*, chap. 4.

28. On the breakfast program see *BSEP* 1 (1 March 1922): 112–14; *BPAU* 58 (March 1924): 321; Gruening, *Mexico and Its Heritage*, 518. On teacher and student responses see Morales to principals, 23 May 1921, AHSEP DETIC 39/17/123; head of DE to SEP delegates, 12 July 1922, AHSEP DE 39/24/36; Morales' secretary to inspectors, 17 Sept. 1923, AHSEP DE 46/50/137; circular number 125, Morales to inspectors/principals, 24 June 1921, AHSEP DE 39/17/138.

29. Requests for materials from Escuela Número 31 para Niños, 28 Feb., 9 July, 23 Aug. 1923, and 8 April 1924, AHSEP DE 44/2/2, 7, 10, 11.

30. On examination clothing see J. J. Sierra to secretary of public education, 1 Nov. 1923, AHSEP DE 56/6/4; Morales to head of DE, 19 Nov. 1923, 6 Dec. 1923, AHSEP DE 56/6/6, 8.

31. Vaughan, *State, Education, and Social Class*, 176–78.

32. Vaughan, "Women Schoolteachers in the Mexican Revolution," 149.

33. The circular on not currying favor with rich children appears in *BSEP* 1 (1 March 1922): 182–83, and in the Mexico City newspaper *La Raza* ("Una energética circular del Director de Educación Primaria," 2 June 1922, sec. 2).

34. Morales' secretary to inspectors/principals, circular number 95, 3 May 1921, AHSEP DE 39/17/106.

35. *BM* 14 (31 Dec. 1926): 22; "La escuela agricultora establecida en la Colonia de la Bolsa debe servir de noble ejemplo para toda la República," *Excélsior,* 5 Oct. 1922; *BSEP* 1 (1 March 1922): 102. On the conditions in the Colonia de la Bolsa see also Tannen-

baum, "Miracle School," 500; Piccato, *City of Suspects,* 37; and Terry, *Terry's Mexico,* 257. For Vasconcelos' opinion on the school see Vasconcelos, *Desastre,* 54. Arturo Oropeza's surname is also spelled "Orpeza"; however, I use the more standard "Oropeza."

36. *BSEP* 1 (1 March 1922): 102; municipal president to Obregón, n.d.; and reply, 7 July 1925, both in AGN O/C 242-C7-E-5; Tannenbaum, "Miracle School," 502–3; *LDC* 3 (1 May 1923): 4–7; "La escuela agricultora establecida en la Colonia de la Bolsa," *Excélsior,* 5 Oct. 1922. I have not been able to find copies of *El Niño Agricultor.*

37. Rubio Goldsmith, "Seasons, Seeds, and Souls," 142–46.

38. Meneses Morales, *Tendencias educativas, 1911–1934,* 316; *BSEP* 1 (1 March 1922): 101–2, 114; Tannenbaum, "Miracle School," 504; *LDC* 3 (1 May 1923): 7.

39. *BSEP* 1 (1 Sept. 1922): 102–3, 210; Tannenbaum, "Miracle School," 506; *BM* 13 (16 March 1925): 28. On the hygiene campaign see Loyo, "Medios extraescolares de educación," 942.

40. *BSEP* 5–6 (1924): 436; Tannenbaum, "Miracle School"; "La escuela agricultora establecida en la Colonia de la Bolsa," *Excélsior,* 5 Oct. 1922; *LDC* 3 (1 May 1923): 8; Carolina Alcocer de Bonfil, "Escuelas granjas" prepared for 1922 UDCM National Congress, AHUFCM 6/34; Dewey's letter reproduced in "Una visita a la Escuela 'Francisco I. Madero,'" *BM* 14 (31 Dec. 1926): 28. See Meneses Morales, *Tendencias educativas, 1911–1934,* 316, on the visits of Medellín and Torres.

41. *BM* 14 (31 Dec. 1926): 29; Alcocer de Bonfil, "Escuelas granjas," 1922, AHUFCM 6/34. On the decline in facilities see municipal president to Obregón, n.d.; reply, 7 July 1925, AGN O/C 242-C7-E-5.

42. *BM* 14 (31 Dec. 1926): 27; Rosa Navarez to Torreblanca, 7 July, and reply 14 July 1927, AGN O/C 205-E-67; Gruening, *Mexico and Its Heritage,* 534–35.

43. Vasconcelos, *Desastre,* 172; *BPAU* 58 (Dec. 1924): 1277; Vásquez to secretary general of Padres de Familia Juárez School, 25 July 1927, AGN O/C 241-E-E-63; *BSEP* 3–4 (1923): 11–13; *BSEP* 5–6 (1924): 627–28. See Knight, *Mexican Revolution,* 2:66–67, on Domínguez's anti-Huerta stance and assassination.

44. Dewey, *Impressions of Soviet Russia,* 151–52. SEP, *Esfuerzo educativo,* 1:179, has a list of the open-air schools operating during the Calles presidency, with their addresses, number of students, and cost.

45. Libro de Actas, Sección de Escuelas, 1920–1926, 7 July 1920, 1, AHUFCM.

46. "Libro de Actas de la 'Sociedad Católica de la Nación Mexicana,'" Nov.–Dec. 1922, 4 Nov. 1925, AHAM 4 L4C/4.

47. The previous section is based on reports in the Libro de Actas, Sección de Escuelas 1920–1926, between 1924 and 1925.

48. *AyF* 1 (Apr. 1922): 293–94; Libro de Actas, "Sección de Escuelas, 1920–1926," 16 Feb. 1925, 30, AHUFCM; *LDC* 6 (1 Jan. 1926): 16.

49. Paz Gómez, "Informe que rinde el Centro Regional de México ante la Asamblea General en el año de 1924," AHUFCM 4/23.

50. *AyF* 1 (Jan. 1922): 42–44; and 1 (April 1922): 293–94. See Terry, *Terry's Mexico,* 408, for a description of Coyoacán.

51. Castillo y Piña to Mora y del Río, 7 Feb. 1919, AHAM 155, "Censuras del Libro," 1919; Castillo y Piña, *Cuestiones Sociales,* 173–74.

52. *LDC* 4 (1 March 1924): 19; Prospectus, Feb. 1919, AHAM155, "Censuras del Libro" "Nazaret"; *AyF* 2 (Aug. 1923): 494. Quotation from "Fiesta escolar celebrada en un colegio católico," 28 Aug. 1922, *Excélsior,* sec. 2.

53. Torres Septién, *Educación privada,* 100–1.

54. Prospectus, Feb. 1919, AHAM 155, "Censuras del Libro," "Nazaret"; *AyF* 2 (Aug. 1923): 494–95; and 1 (April 1922): 290–91. Castillo y Piña phrased his concern as *empleomanía*.

55. *LDC* 4 (1 Aug. 1924): 23; *MSCJM,* May 1920, 261–67.

56. *AyF* 1 (Dec. 1922): 861–64.

57. Libro de Actas, Sección de Escuelas 1920–1926, Jan. 1922, 7 AHUFCM; *LDC* 1 (31 Dec. 1921): 16; *AyF* 1 (Feb. 1922): 157.

58. *LDC* 2 (1 Sept. 1922): 19.

59. Libro de Actas, Sección de Escuelas 1920–1926, May–Oct. 1922, 9–11, AHUFCM; *LDC* 2 (1 Nov. 1922): 23–24. See H-LATAM for a discussion thread about kermises and the origin of the word. H-LATAM [electronic bulletin board] 14–16 November 2000, available from http:/www2.h-net.msu.edu/search/searching under "kermese."

Chapter 6. Adults in the Classroom

1. Statistics on vocational school numbers in Massieu, 27 Dec. 1922, AHSEP DE 63/5/13. The commercial schools enrolled a further 5,000 students. On the unequal gender ratio see Blum, "Public Welfare and Child Circulation," 256–57. See inspector to director of DETIC, 28 Aug. 1922, AHSEP DETIC 68/3/3–4, for the use of practical problems in a math class.

2. SEP, *Esfuerzo educativo,* 1:489–91. SEP, *Noticia estadística, 1925,* 194–95, contains more statistics on grants for study abroad.

3. Headmistress of Querétaro School to teachers, 11 Nov. 1926, AHSEP DETIC 74/16/33; SEP, *Esfuerzo educativo,* 1:474–75.

4. Federico Cervantes,"Temas de la conferencia sustentada por el suscrito," 17 Jan. no year (filed in 1927), AHSEP DETIC 74/19/31–37.

5. See Raby, "Ideología y construcción del estado," 317–18; Knight, "Popular Culture and the Revolutionary State," 393–444; and Vaughan, *Cultural Politics in Revolution,* chap. 2 for discussions of how and why education was radicalized.

6. Joseph, *Revolution from Without,* 216; see Buck, "Control de la natalidad," for a detailed study on Sanger's work in Yucatán.

7. *La Raza,* "Si es inmoral el libro de la Sanger será prohibido . . . ," 30 July 1922. For articles on Mistral's visit see *Excélsior,* 5 Aug. 1922, sec. 2; *Heraldo de México,* 23 July 1922, editorial and sec. 1; 26 July, sec. 2; 27 July; 29 July; 31 July, sec. 2; *La Raza,* 29 July 1922; *Universal,* 22 July 1922, sec. 2; 25 July; 26 July sec. 2; 27 July, editorial.

8. Meeting report, 10 Aug. 1922, AHSEP DETIC 72/7/4; Mistral teachers to unidentified addressee, 10 Aug. 1922, AHSEP DETIC 72/7/17.

9. See Bliss, "Science of Redemption," for public health reformers' work on syphilis in the capital and their rhetoric regarding sexual ignorance.

10. "Propaganda inmoral en la Escuela 'Gabriela Mistral,'" *Universal,* 19 Aug. 1922; "La Secretaría de Educación impedirá que en las escuelas se haga campaña contra la natalidad," Ibid., 24 Aug. 1922, sec. 2.

11. This account is taken from "Dolores Castillo," 5222, AHSEP Antiguo Magisterio. Quotation from document no. 12, Rodolfo Rodríguez to SIPBA, 6 March 1912.

12. Quotation in Cano and Radkau, *Ganando espacios,* 62. See also Herrera, *Frida,* 26.

13. Profesora Castillo's veteran file is in the Archivo Histórico de la Secretaría de

Defensa Nacional 55 D/112/C-1293. Martha Eva Rocha has worked extensively on this archive and kindly provided me with the information on Castillo. See Rocha, "Veteranas de guerra en el archivo militar."

14. Inspector to director of DETIC, 22 Aug. 1922, AHSEP DETIC 68/11/2–4. All quotations from León's report are from this source. In a report of just over three pages, León devoted one paragraph to Rodríguez, noting that she had good knowledge and teaching skills and that he observed nothing improper, and most of the report was devoted to Castillo.

15. Correspondence in AGN O/C 609-C-15, Sept. 1922.

16. Head of DE to director of DETIC, 24 Aug. 1922; director of DETIC to head-mistresses of women's technical schools, 25 Aug. 1922, AHSEP DETIC 72/7/26–31; "La Secretaría de Educación impedirá que en las escuelas se haga campaña contra la natalidad," *Universal*, 24 Aug. 1922, sec. 2; "En la Escuela Miguel Lerdo no se hace propaganda inmoral," Ibid., 26 Aug. 1922; "Una aclaración de la Escuela 'Miguel Lerdo,' " *Excélsior* 30 Aug. 1922.

17. Massieu, 6 Oct. 1922, AHSEP DETIC 72/7/49–50.

18. Castillo's interview in *Universal*, "La sesión de ayer en el Congreso de Mujeres . . . ," 25 May 1923.

19. Biographical information from *BPAU* 55 (July 1923): 93; Tuñón Pablos, *Women in Mexico*, 81; Galván de Terrazas, *Educación superior de la mujer*, 32; Macías, *Against All Odds*, 106; Soto, *Emergence of the Modern Mexican Women*, 105.

20. Vaughan, *State, Education, and Social Class*, 204.

21. Torres to unidentified addressee, March 1925, Acervo Histórico de la Universidad Iberoamericana, Fondo Elena Torres, folder 51; Macías, *Against All Odds*, 104–5.

22. "Crónica nacional, el Congreso Feminista," *Gaceta Oficial* 19, 6 (15 June 1923): 303.

23. Bliss, "Science of Redemption," 1–2, 7, 11, 13–14.

24. Vasconcelos to headmistresses, teachers, and students at women's technical schools, 8 April 1923, AHSEP DETIC 68/18/1.

25. Quotations in Pilcher, *¡Qué Vivan los Tamales!*, 55, 62. On Sierra's regulation see Vaughan, *State, Education, and Social Class*, 36.

26. Inspectora de cocina y repostería to director of DETIC, 22 Sept. 1923, AHSEP DETIC 68/18/9–10; head of DE to director of DETIC, 10 Oct. 1923, AHSEP DETIC 68/18/11.

27. Teachers' plans for May–July 1923 in AHSEP DETIC 68/19.

28. *BPAU* 58 (June 1925): 578–79. On style inspectors see Vasconcelos to head-mistresses, teachers, and students, 8 April 1923, AHSEP DETIC 86/18/2. Descriptions are from the photographs in SEP, *Escuelas del Departamento de Enseñanza Técnica, Industria y Comercial*.

29. See his own comments: Vasconcelos, *Mexican Ulysses*, 119–20, 131–33, 138, 162–63, 166–67, 218, 265.

30. Vaughan, *State, Education, and Social Class*, 259.

31. Inspector to director of DEPN, 31 March 1923, AHSEP DETIC 68/30/29; list of night schools, 12 April 1923, AHSEP DETIC 72/18/5; inspectora to director of DETIC, 13 May 1923, AHSEP DETIC 68/32/3.

32. See inspectors' reports: Arellanos to director of DETIC, 26 July 1923, AHSEP DETIC 68/29/3; inspector to director of DETIC, 4 Dec. 1923, AHSEP DETIC 68/29/15; inspector to director of DEPN, 8 Feb. 1923, AHSEP DETIC 68/30/3; Inspector Con-

treras to director of DEPN, 9 March 1923, AHSEP DETIC 68/30/19; inspector to director of DETIC, 7 June 1924, AHSEP DETIC 68/35/15.

33. See inspectora to director of DETIC, 22 Dec. 1923, AHSEP DETIC 68/32/19; and inspector to director of DETIC, 26 July 1923, AHSEP DETIC 68/29/5, for two inspectors' views on students.

34. Rubenstein, *Bad Language, Naked Ladies,* discusses the emergence of the *chica moderna* as a stock figure in comic books, set against the figure of the traditional woman.

35. Mancera, "Número de alumnos," 26 Feb. 1923, AHSEP DE 63/5/28; Arellanos to director of DETIC, 26 July 1923, AHSEP DETIC 68/29/5; SEP, *Esfuerzo educativo,* 2:506; Fell, *José Vasconcelos,* 202 n. 305.

36. *BSEP 5* (March 1926): 114–15.

37. Arellanos to director of DETIC, 26 July 1923, AHSEP DETIC 68/29/5; Rafols to director of DETIC, 14 May 1923, AHSEP DETIC 68/32/4.

38. Inspector to director of DETIC, 26 July 1923, AHSEP DETIC 68/29/3–5.

39. SEP, *Esfuerzo educativo,* 1:182, 506–7; Vaughan, *State, Education, and Social Class,* 149.

40. Inspector Contreras to director of DEPN, 9 March 1923, AHSEP DETIC 68/30/18; Inspectora Baños Contreras to director of DETIC, 18 June 1924 and response, 3 July 1924, AHSEP DETIC 68/31/1–2; inspectora to director of DETIC, 14 Oct. 1924, AHSEP DETIC 68/31/6; director of DEPN to director of DETIC, 2 June 1923, AHSEP DETIC 68/37/16.

41. *BSEP 1* (Sept. 1922): 208. Quotation in *BSEP* 3–4 (1923): 415.

42. Inspector to director of DETIC, 5 Sept. 1923, AHSEP DETIC 68/34/14.

43. "Las escuelas nocturnas convertidas en cabarets y centros de prostitución," *La Raza,* 13 June 1922.

44. SEP, *Esfuerzo educativo,* 2:393.

45. Arellanos to director of DETIC, 5 Sept. 1923, AHSEP DETIC 68/34/13.

46. Inspectora to director of DETIC, 13 May and 23 May 1923, AHSEP DETIC 68/32/3, 9.

47. On judicial issues and violence against women see Macías, *Against All Odds,* 109–10, 118–19; and Piccato, chap. 5. Attitudes among some religious officials and politicians have not changed. For instance, in 1991, Hernán Zambrano, chancellor to the archbishop of Monterrey, doubted that adult women could be forced to have sexual intercourse, unless they were tied up ("Del catecismo panista," *La Jornada,* 7 Oct. 1999). Members of the Partido Acción Nacional (National Action Party) doubted that martial rape existed and opposed the eight- to fourteen-year jail sentence it was given in new legislation in 1997. Del Valle, "Catorce años a los culpables de violación conyugal," Dec. 1997, and "Mexico Congress Strikes Blow against Spousal Rape," 4 Dec. 1997, both available from Chronicle News Services http:/members.aol.com/ncmdr/lower.html.

48. Piccato, " 'Chalequero,' " 643. This article offers a detailed discussion of contemporary understandings of rape. See also Piccato's *City of Suspects,* chap. 5. Rivera-Garza, " 'She Neither Respected nor Obeyed Anyone,' " 680–81, discusses marital infidelity and violence as causes of mental illness. Professionals ignored domestic abuse, believing it to be natural behavior among the poor.

49. Vaughan, "Rural Women's Literacy and Education," 113.

50. Knight, "Popular Culture and the Revolutionary State," 424.

51. Fell, *José Vasconcelos,* 203; Díaz Zermeño, "Escuela nacional primaria," 73.

52. On attendance issues see Arellanos to director of DETIC, 5 Sept. 1923, AHSEP

DETIC 68/34/13–14; inspector to director of DETIC, 17 May 1923, AHSEP DETIC 68/35/14; inspector to director of DETIC, 1 Nov. 1924, AHSEP DETIC 68/35/24; "Informe año de 1923 escuelas nocturnas para obreras," Dec 1923, AHSEP DETIC 68/37/41. The Eucharistic Congress lasted eight days in early October 1924. Catholics came from all over the republic to masses and conferences held around the capital city. On the congress see *MSCJM,* Nov. 1924, 646–64.

53. Inspector to director of DEPN, 9 March 1923, AHSEP DETIC 68/30/13; inspectora to director of DETIC, 13 May 1923, AHSEP DETIC 68/32/2; inspector to director of DEPN, 8 Feb. 1923, AHSEP DETIC 68/30/5–6; inspector to director of DEPN, 9 March 1923, AHSEP DETIC 68/30/17.

54. Inspector Contreras to director of DEPN, 9 March 1923, AHSEP DETIC 68/30/20.

55. Inspector to director of DEPN, 8 Feb. 1923, AHSEP DETIC 68/30/10; inspector to director of DETIC, 13 May 1923, AHSEP DETIC 68/18/7; inspector to director of DETIC, 27 Oct. 1923, AHSEP DETIC 68/34/19; Arellanos to director of DETIC, AHSEP DETIC 19 May 1923, 68/29/1.

56. Students at Escuela Nocturna Número 21 to SEP, 25 May 1923, and response of 9 June 1923, AHSEP DETIC 72/42/2–3.

57. *LDC* 3 (1 May 1923): 31.

58. *LDC* 4 (1 Dec. 1924): 18.

59. Libro de Actas, Sección de Escuelas, Nov. 1921, 5, AHUFCM.

60. *AyF* 1 (April 1922): 293–94.

61. This section is complied from *LDC* de Escuelas monthly reports from Oct. 1921, Nov. 1921, June 1922, Oct. 1922, Nov. 1922, and Feb. 1923, and Libro de Actas, Sección de Escuelas, Jan 1923, 13, AHUFCM.

62. *AyF* 4 (1 April 1925): 68–72.

63. See Curley, "Slouching towards Bethlehem," chap. 7, sec. 1.5 and chap. 8 sec. 1.3 for discussion of Catholic unions generally and in Jalisco. The Knights of Columbus (*Caballeros de Colón*) also planned to open a workers' house to offer training for working men and child care. See *BPAU* 52 (June 1921): 626.

64. *LDC* 2 (1 Nov. 1922): 21; and 2 (1 March 1922): 21–22.

65. Boylan, "Mexican Catholic Women's Activism," 157–63.

66. Meyer, *Cristiada,* 1:48; *AyF* 3 (1 Sept. 1924): 395–97.

67. *LDC* 3 (1 May 1923): 31; Libro de Actas, Sección de Escuelas, Sept. 1923, 17; and May 1923, 14, AHUFCM. See "Santa visita pastoral en las parroquias 1921," Sept. 1921, May–April 1922, AHAM 10/L10C/43, for information on catechism classes.

68. *AyF* 1 (1 Oct. 1922): 769; 2 (1 Jan. 1923): 63; 2 (May 1923): 320; and 2 (1 July 1923): 446.

69. *AyF* 4 (1 Feb. 1925): 52. Information on products in González Navarro, *Porfiriato,* 297, 304.

70. Quotation in *BPAU* 55 (Nov. 1922): 471; SEP, *Esfuerzo educativo,* 2:465–66.

71. Vaughan, *State, Education, and Social Class,* 69.

72. Morales to inspectors/principals, 27 May 1921, AHSEP DE 39/17/128. Quotations from *BSEP* 1 (March 1922): 112, and 4 (Dec. 1925): 206; María González et al. to Obregón, 24 Nov. 1926, and response, 8 Dec. 1926, AGN O/C 205-E-62.

73. Head of DE to Directora Desayunos Escolares, 11 July 1924, and head of DE to director of DETIC, 24 July 1924, both in AHSEP DETIC 68/31/3. Quotation in *BPAU* 58 (June 1924): 582.

74. Director of primary education to head of DE, 24 June 1924, AHSEP DE 41/13/3.

75. On population see Blum, "Public Welfare and Child Circulation," 256–57 n. 130; SEP, *Noticia estadística, 1926,* 282–83, 288–89.

76. Inspector to director of DETIC, 7 March 1923, AHSEP DETIC 68/15/1.

77. *BSEP 5–6* (1924): 111–12; Fell, *José Vasconcelos,* 203.

78. SEP, *Noticia estadística, 1925,* tables l, li, and xlv.

79. SEP, *Noticia estadística, 1926,* 101–4; SEP, *Esfuerzo educativo,* 1:480.

80. *BSEP 3–4* (1923): 236.

81. *LDC 2* (1 June 1922): 20; Méndez Medina, *Manual de formación sindical,* 63–64.

82. *LDC 2* (1 July 1922): 24.

83. *LDC 2* (1 Aug. 1922): 18, and 2 (1 Nov. 1922): 22.

84. *AyF 4* (1 March 1925): 60.

85. Fell, *José Vasconcelos,* 196.

86. *BPAU 58* (June 1924): 582.

87. Workers in Colonias Peralvillo, Vallejo etc. to director general of Educación Pública, 21 March 1918, AHCM IP 2571/292.

Chapter 7. Community Education in Public Spaces

1. *BPAU 56* (March 1923): 240; Loyo, "Lecturas para el pueblo," 311; Fell, *José Vasconcelos,* 513–19; Meneses Morales, *Tendencias educativas, 1911–1934,* 349.

2. SEP, *Noticia estadística, 1925,* 279–80; Loyo, "Lecturas para el pueblo," 319 n. 47.

3. Dewey, *Impressions of Soviet Russia,* 164–65.

4. Loyo, "Lecturas para el pueblo," 325–27; *BPAU 60* (July 1926): 660; SEP, *Noticia estadística, 1925,* 279–80; Meneses Morales, *Tendencias educativas, 1911–1934,* 349. The Department of Industry, Commerce, and Labor set the daily cost of living in the Federal District at 2.81 pesos, including food, housing, clothing, bathing, and soap, for an "average family" of mother, father, baby, nine- or ten-year-old child, and an older dependent person; from *BPAU 56* (May 1923): 521.

5. For groups asking for libraries see SEP, *Noticia estadística, 1925,* 279–80; *Noticia estadística, 1926,* 419 and report on founding libraries, 1927, AGN O/C 121-E-B-26.

6. SEP, *Esfuerzo educativo,* 1:xxv.

7. *BSEP 3–4* (1923): 323–26; *BPAU 60* (July 1926): 662. For more information on libraries see SEP, *Noticia estadística, 1925,* 280, 285; and *Noticia estadística, 1926,* 417.

8. *AyF 1* (July 1922): 558; and 2 (June 1923): 384.

9. See note 4 for cost-of-living figures. Actas 8, 10, Nov. 1922, AHUFCM 6/32; "Bibliotecas populares," prepared for 1922 UDCM National Congress, AHUFCM 6/34. Pamphlet entitled "Bibliotecas Populares de Nuestra Señora del Sagrado Corazón," April 1924; Pedro Benavides to José Covarrubias, 10 Oct. 1921; and "Estatutos y reglamento interior de las bibliotecas populares," n.d., all in ASSM, Bibliotecas Populares, "Bibliotecas Populares de Nuestra Señora del Sagrado Corazón." See also *Christus,* 16 (March 1937), 273–74.

10. On cultural politics see Vaughan, *Cultural Politics in Revolution,* chap. 2, and *State, Education, and Social Class,* chap. 8. On Porfirian cultural programs see Illades, "Organización y formas de resistencia artesanales," 332.

11. *BPAU 56* (March 1923): 242–43; Fell, *José Vasconcelos,* 414; *BSEP 1* (1 Sept. 1922): 209; SEP, *Esfuerzo educativo,* 2:386. See "Cuadro estadístico de cines," *BM 9* (9 March 1923), for figures on cinema seating capacities.

12. Fell, *José Vasconcelos*, 414–16; Meneses Morales, *Tendencias educativas, 1911–1934*, 343; *BSEP* 1 (1 Sept. 1922): 209.

13. SEP, *Esfuerzo educativo*, 2:386, 408.

14. *AyF* 3 (Oct. 1922): 721.

15. De los Reyes, "Part 2: History, The Silent Cinema," 63–77; Mora, *Mexican Cinema*, 6–8, 24; Pineda and Paranaguá, "Part I: Chronicle, Mexico and Its Cinema," 15–26; Rubenstein, "Raised Voices in the Cine Montecarlo," 316–17.

16. "Población de la Ciudad de México, según el censo de 1921," 13 Feb. 1923, AHSEP DE 63/6/88. In Monterrey a year later, for a population of 80,000 there were 21,000 cinema seats. Pineda and Paranaguá, "Part I: Chronicle, Mexico and Its Cinema," 25.

17. *BSEP* 1 (1 March 1922): 106.

18. See AHSEP DE 56/9 for 1923 cultural program flyers. On whispering audiences see Cleland, *Mexican Year Book, 1920–1921*, 372. On opposition politics at the Cine Montecarlo see Rubenstein, "Raised Voices in the Cine Montecarlo."

19. SEP, *Esfuerzo educativo*, 2:411; Vaughan, *State, Education, and Social Class*, 149.

20. Libro de Actas, Sección de Escuelas (Feb.–Aug. 1924), AHUFCM; *LDC* 2 (1 Nov. 1922): 21.

21. *LDC* 4 (1 July 1924): 7. The Second Pan American Child Congress, held in Montevideo in 1919, also passed a resolution to restrict children's entry to films. See Guy, "Pan American Child Congresses," 279.

22. "Un grupo de Damas Católicas construirá una gran escuela para 30.000 niños," *La Raza*, 20 July 1922.

23. *MSCJM*, May 1924, 314, and June 1924, 390. On carpa theater see Mora, *Mexican Cinema*, 12.

24. *LDC* 2 (1 Oct. 1922): 22.

25. *BSEP* 3–4 (1923): 259–64, and 5–6 (1924): 296–302; *BPAU* 58 (June 1924): 578–79.

26. *BPAU* 60 (March 1926): 306; SEP, *Esfuerzo educativo*, 1:470–71.

27. *BPAU* 58 (June 1924): 578–81; *BSEP* 5–6 (1924): 300. See Vaughan, *State, Education, and Social Class*, 259, on style changes.

28. *BM* 6 (14 Jan. 1921): 14; head of Educación Pública to Director of Compañía Tranvías, 9 Aug. 1917, AHCM IP 2535/4, "Circulares, acuerdos, comunicaciones, etc." On tram routes see Terry, *Terry's Mexico*, 236–38.

29. Headmistress to inspector, 10 July 1918, 19 April 1918, AHCM IP 2559 "Escuela Elemental número 246 1906–1918 Comunicaciones mandadas" describe both field trips. Quotation in *Terry's Mexico*, 393.

30. Morales to principals/inspectors, 26 Jan. 1921, AHSEP DE 39/17/31; head of DETIC to parents, 10 May 1927, AHSEP DETIC 74/19/43.

31. Section summarized from *Pulgarcito* (Jan.–Nov. 1926); quotation from *Pulgarcito*, 2 (1 Feb. 1926): 28.

32. Descriptions of camping trips are in Federico Cervantes, "Temas de la conferencia sustentada por el suscrito," 17 Jan. no year (filed in 1927), AHSEP DETIC 74/19/37–38; "Un cuerpo de exploradores de la Escuela 'Dr. Mora,' " *Universal*, 30 June 1926.

33. *LDC* 2 (1 Nov. 1922): 21; Colegio-Casa Nazaret pamphlet, Feb. 1919, 4, AHAM 155, "Censuras del Libro," "Nazaret"; *AyF* 1 (Oct. 1922): 721, and 3 (Feb. 1924), 100; *Gaceta Oficial*, 18 (15 Aug. 1922), 80; Libro de Actas, Sección de Escuelas (14 June 1926), 41, AHUFCM.

34. *BM* 19 (31 Aug. 1926): 29–31. These signs are still present in the Parque México, Colonia Condesa, Mexico City, and are labeled "H. Ayto 1927."

35. Ceballos Ramírez, "Sindicalismo católico en México," 625–26, and "Encíclica 'Rerum Novarum,' " 33; *Revista Eclesiástica,* 5 (Feb. 1923): 96.

36. Curley, "Slouching towards Bethlehem," chap. 8, sec. 1.3.

37. Statistics on the CNCT are in Ceballos Ramírez, "Sindicalismo católico en México," 625, 633–35, 639, and "Encíclica 'Rerum Novarum,' " 33. On women's participation see *LDC* 3 (1 May 1923): 33. On Catholic syndicalism see Curley, "Slouching towards Bethlehem," chap. 8, sec. 1.3.

38. Curley, "Slouching towards Bethlehem," chap. 7, sec. 1.5; Hanson, "Day of Ideals," 366, 375–79.

39. Ceballos Ramírez, "Sindicalismo católico en México," 652, 655.

40. Clark, *Organized Labor,* 94; Curley, "Slouching towards Bethlehem," 334–35.

41. This brief history of El Buen Tono is from the program for the consecration of the factory's chapel, June 1914, CESU LNDLR 2/13/909; González Navarro, *Porfiriato,* 90; Lear, "Workers, *Vecinos,* and Citizens," 47, 133, 216; Hanson, "Day of Ideals," 186, 652–55; Gruening, *Mexico and Its Heritage,* 351. For flyers calling for a boycott see 15 Aug. 1926, CESU LNDLR 47/346/270; and flyer of LNDLR Comité Regional del DF, 4 Aug. 1926, AHUFCM Impresos, 48.

42. Núñez to María Olmedo de Urquiaga, 20 June 1923; Jacinta Paredeo and Angela Parela to Núñez, 14 June 1923, both in ASSM, "Correspondencia II 1922–1924."

43. Mora y del Río to Méndez Medina, June 1922, ASSM, "Episcopado I Nov. 1919–Dec. 1924"; Darío Miranda, "Seis años de actividades del Secretariado Social Mexicano 1925–1931," 1931, ASSM, "Episcopado Informes 1924–1920"; Ceballos Ramírez, "Sindicalismo católico en México," 648–49.

44. Hanson, "Day of Ideals," 370, 381.

45. Ibid., 347.

46. *AyF* 1 (Dec. 1922): 876–77, quotation on 876; the italicized portion was bolded in the original.

47. *LDC* 1 (31 May 1921): 17; 2 (1 May 1922): 20; and 3 (1 May 1923): 29, 32.

48. *LDC* 4 (1 July 1924): 28; *BPAU* 56 (May 1923): 504.

49. Hanson, "Day of Ideals," 408; *LDC* 3 (1 May 1923): 13.

50. See Schell, "Damas del catolicismo social," for more discussion on unionization.

51. *LDC* 1 (31 Aug. 1921): 17; 2 (1 May 1922): 21; and 3 (1 May 1923): 33.

52. Ceballos Ramírez, "Encíclica 'Rerum Novarum,' " 33, and "Sindicalismo católico en México," 625; Curley, "Slouching towards Bethlehem," 280.

Chapter 8. Church-State Tensions Turn into Conflict

1. Bailey, *¡Viva Cristo Rey!,* 36–37; Gutiérrez Casillas, *Historia de la iglesia en México,* 431–32.

2. Aguilar Camín and Meyer, *In the Shadow of the Mexican Revolution,* 84; Quirk, *Mexican Revolution and the Catholic Church,* 132–33. Quotation from Obregón to Mora y del Río et al., 27 Jan. 1923, AHAM 158, "Presidencia de la República."

3. Bishops of Guadalajara, Oaxaca, Puebla, Michoacán, and México to Obregón, 5 Feb. 1923, Ibid.

4. Gutiérrez Casillas suggests that Pérez's friendship with CROM leader Morones, formed during the heyday of the anarcho-syndicalist Casa del Obrero Mundial (House of

the World Worker), prompted the 1925 schism. Gutiérrez Casillas, *Historia de la iglesia en México,* 435. José Vasconcelos, who detested Calles, claims that Calles and Morones cooked up the scheme together. Vasconcelos, *Desastre,* 310.

5. On the seizure see Gutiérrez Casillas, *Historia de la iglesia en México,* 435; Hanson, "Day of Ideals," 514–15; Quirk, *Mexican Revolution and the Catholic Church,* 140–41. The residents' letter to Calles: Suarez Escalante et al. to Calles, n.d., AGN O/C 438-M-6.

6. On harassment of Catholics in the workplace see Carr, *Movimiento obrero,* 224, and "Organized Labour and the Mexican Revolution," 28; Hanson, "Day of Ideals," 386; Quirk, *Mexican Revolution and the Catholic Church,* 176. On Catholics being forced to attend pro-government demonstrations see the flyer "La manifestación," n.d., CESU LNDLR 47/346/281.

7. De la Cerda Silva, *Movimiento obrero en México,* 141.

8. "Los trabajadores y la cuestión religiosa" [flyer], July 1926, CESU, Palomar y Vizcarra 61/469/328. On Catholics in the CROM see Carr, *Movimiento obrero,* 219.

9. Ceballos Ramírez, "Sindicalismo católico en México," 662–64; Hanson, "Day of Ideals," 420, 424, 428–29, 437, 441.

10. Hanson, "Day of Ideals," 489–91.

11. Calles to Mora y del Río, 2 June 1926, AHAM 158, "Presidencia de la República."

12. Mora y del Río to Calles, two letters, n.d. and 4 June 1926, AHAM 158, "Presidencia de la República." The two drafts of the archbishop's reply to Calles suggests that he carefully crafted his letter. It appears that he sent the more moderate letter.

On divisions in the Catholic hierarchy see Bailey, *¡Viva Cristo Rey!,* 69; Meyer, *Cristiada,* 1:19–29; Tuck, *Holy War in Los Altos,* 35–36.

13. Bailey, *¡Viva Cristo Rey!,* 79, 83; flyer calling for boycott, CESU LNDLR 47/346/270; Lynch, "Catholic Church in Latin America," 592; Quirk, *Mexican Revolution and the Catholic Church,* 175–76. According to Quirk, Archbishops Orozco y Jiménez and José María González Valencia (Durango) wanted a stronger response and had called for military action on 11 July.

14. "Memorial que dos millones de católicos mexicanos . . . ," Sept. 1926, CESU LNDLR 47/346/325.

15. Hanson, "Day of Ideals," 193. Quotation from "Segundo Congreso Nacional de la UDCM 5–7 Oct. 1925," 1, AHUFCM 6/35.

16. "De la sublime y alta misión de las madres de familia," n.d., AHUFCM 2/11/769.

17. This account is taken from the following: Call from the UDCM central committee, 25 Feb. 1926, AHUFCM Impresos, 38; "Las órdenes de clausura de la iglesia," "Un escándalo provocado por la cuestión religiosa, frente al Templo de la Sagrada Familia y ante la Sría. de Gobierno," *Universal,* 24 February 1926; "Las Damas Católicas se dirigen al primer magistrado de la nación," Ibid., 25 February 1926; "Graves desordenes ocurrieron ayer al clausurarse un templo católico," *Excélsior,* 24 February 1926; "El Sr. Tejeda informa sobre estos sucesos," *Excélsior,* 24 February 1926; Miller, "Role of Mexican Women"; Quirk, *Mexican Revolution and the Catholic Church,* 154.

18. Quotation attributed to Minister of the Interior Tejeda by L. M. Escandón Barreda, 11 March 1926, AHUFCM 2/11/636.

19. Lear, "Workers, *Vecinos,* and Citizens," 281, 356.

20. Knight, *Mexican Revolution,* 2:208.

21. Quirk, *Mexican Revolution and the Catholic Church,* 120.

22. The freedom-of-education banner that the Catholics waved meant different things

at different times. During the Porfiriato, liberals opposed obligatory schooling as an attack on parents' rights. When these liberals in Congress called for "freedom of education," Minister of Public Instruction Sierra overruled them on the grounds that the society as a whole had a right that superceded the right of individuals within the society. In the early twentieth century, Catholics appropriated the phrase *freedom of education* to mean freedom to teach Catholic doctrine in private schools. Torres Septién, "Unión Nacional de Padres de Familia," 927–28; Vaughan, *State, Education, and Social Class,* 22, 24.

23. See *AyF* 1 (Dec. 1922): 861–64, and 2 (March 1923), 185–88.

24. Subjefe director técnico to principal of Escuela Número 232 (incorporated), 6 March 1926, AHUFCM 2/11/642.

25. Torres Septién, *Educación privada,* 106. Torres does not specify who within the church promoted the organization, and hers is the only reference to it that I have found in either primary or secondary sources.

26. Torres Septién, *Educación privada,* 107–8. The correspondence between Puig and the Catholic representatives, as well as the related regulation, is reproduced in SEP, *Esfuerzo educativo,* 1:xxxix–lxxxii. See also "Todas las asociaciones religiosas que había en la ciudad de la República quedaron disueltas," *Universal,* 18 July 1926; "Los colegios católicos y la enseñanza de la religión," Ibid., 21 July 1926; "Los colegios católicos de México no serán vendidos declara el Sr. Arzobispo," *Excélsior,* 20 July; "El reglamento de educación se hará cumplir con energía," Ibid., 24 July 1926.

27. On school closures see Arce Gurza, "En busca de una educación revolucionaria," 169; Fernández-Aceves, "Political Mobilization of Women," 146; Macías, "Rural and Urban Women in Revolutionary Yucatán," 615. See also "Las restricciones a la libertad de enseñanza," n.d., AGN Gobernación 2/340 14–A 5. Withdrawal of students from public schools was not without precedent: In Yucatán the anticlerical policies of Governor Salvador Alvarado (1915–1918) prompted parents to remove their children from public schools. Macías, "Rural and Urban Women in Revolutionary Yucatán," 615.

28. Meneses Morales, *Tendencias educativas, 1911–1934,* 507; Ruís Facius, *Méjico Cristero,* 20.

29. Torres Septién, *Educación privada,* 113.

30. SEP, *Esfuerzo educativo,* 1:xxxiii.

31. "Relación en la que se manifiesta los informes rendidos a esta Secretaría por los CC Gobernadores de los Estados y Territorios Federales, con motivo de la clausura de conventos, colegios religiosos, y templos que no unan los requisitos establecidos por la ley," n.d., AGN Gobernación 2/340 14–A 5; "Lista de colegios, algunos anexos a conventos, en donde se clausuró la capilla ú oratorio que existía," 6 March 1926, AGN Gobernación 2–345 (29) 31.

32. SEP, *Esfuerzo educativo,* 1:xlvi.

33. "Consulta sobre el artículo 3 constitucional, tesis, comentario," 8–9, AHAM 73, Escuelas/Colegios (no date or signature, but probably from 1926).

34. On clandestine education see Libro de Actas, Sección de Escuelas, March–Oct. 1926, AHUFCM; Meneses Morales, *Tendencias educativas, 1911–1934,* 507. On the San Felipe de Jesús School, March–Sept. 1926, see AHUFCM 2/11.

35. The correspondence on the Colegio Franco-Mexicano is in March 1926–Jan. 1931, AHSEP DEPN 4738/6.

36. Letters to Minister of the Interior, 2 and 6 Sept. 1926, AGN Gobernación 2.347 (29) 44, on need for investigation of Catholic schools. Denunciations from teachers are in

AGN Gobernación 2.347 (29) 21, 34 and 38. Gobernación 2.347 box 29 includes denunciations of government employees who were members of the Knights of Columbus, of foreign priests who were practicing, of convents that were functioning illegally, and of a bishop who continued acting in hiding.

37. Letters from teachers to Calles, 28 Aug. and 12 Sept. 1926, AGN Gobernación 2.347 (29) 21. Folder 34 of the same box includes inspectors' reports on the UDCM-sponsored Ejercito de Defensa de la Mujer (Army of the Defense of Women), which offered prostitutes training and housing to get out of sexual commerce. The organization operated with the support of Beneficencia Pública (Public Welfare), which received regular reports on the Ejercito's activities and donated fifty-five food rations each day.

38. Teachers to Calles, 12 Sept. 1926, AGN Gobernación 2.347 (29) 21. On problems with inspection see SEP, *Esfuerzo educativo,* 1:xxi, 147, 152.

39. Sylve to Lascurain de Silva, 1 May 1926, AHUFCM 2/11/690.

40. SEP, *Esfuerzo educativo,* 1:lxxxi.

41. Torres Septién, *Educación privada,* 108.

42. Unión de Colegios Católicos Mexicanos flyer, 16 Oct. 1926, AHUFCM 2/11/756. Quotations in SEP, *Esfuerzo educativo,* 1:lxvi–ii.

43. SEP, *Esfuerzo educativo,* 1:lxxi. Catholic response in Pallares, "Cristianismo Laico," 18 Aug. 1926, CESU LNDLR 43/305, emphasis in original.

44. *Pulgarcito,* 2 (1 Feb. 1926): 15, 2 (1 May 1926), 41, and 2 (1 Dec. 1926), 24.

45. Ceballos Ramírez, "Sindicalismo católico en México," 668. On Catholic Action see Barranco, "Posiciones políticas en la historia," 57. Boylan, "Mexican Catholic Women's Activism," discusses the work of the UDCM's descendent in Jalisco in the 1930s.

46. Torres Septién, *Educación privada,* 38.

Epilogue

1. Morris, "Reforming the Nation," 383, quotation on 380. Robert Curley suggests that municipal governments lost power because of their potential to oppose the national government, in part through the Catholic political opposition that flourished on a local level. E-mail communication with the author, 8 March 2002.

2. Blancarte, *Historia de la iglesia católica,* 95–96.

3. Ibid., 126–30; and Hanson, "Mujeres Militantes," 27.

4. Rubenstein, *Bad Language, Naked Ladies,* chaps. 4–5.

5. On the miniskirt controversy see Monsiváis, "Por mi madre, bohemios"; Cano, "ABC de la intolerancia"; Ortiz Ledezma, "Protestan en minifalda contra la represión."

6. On the Wonderbra billboards see Preston, "How Brazen Can You Get?," *New York Times,* 31 July 1996; "Las diez mentiras sobre el PAN," *Revista Peninsular.* The PAN's open letter, is available online: Calderón, Felipe, "On the Subject of Politics, Morality, and Bras," *La Jornada* (México, D.F.), 20 July 1996, http://www.jornada.unam.mx/1996/jul96/960720/CALDEROQ-1907.html (last accessed 17 July 2002).

7. Torres Septién, *Educación privada,* 38–47.

8. Reich, *Mexico's Hidden Revolution,* 105. See chap. 8 for many examples of the Catholic Church hierarchy supporting the PRI.

9. Blancarte, "Católicismo social," 289–90; see pp. 308–9 for other condemnations from Mexican prelates. Quotation from "Pope Condemns Dogmatic Communism and Capitalism," 25 Jan. 1998, BBC News.

10. Cockcroft, *Mexico's Hope,* 346–47.

11. "John Paul II Comments on Chiapas, Cuba," *Miami Herald,* 23 Jan. 1999.

12. Craske, "Another Mexican Earthquake?," particularly the section entitled "The Campaign."

13. Blancarte, *Historia de la iglesia católica,* 85, 94.

14. Hernández López, "Lo foxifiesta"; "Fox empezó la jornada en la Basílica," *Diario de Yucatán,* 2 Dec. 2000.

15. Ballinas and Garduño, "El nuevo Presidente"; Craske, "Another Mexican Earthquake?," 33, 35.

16. Gallegos, "La bancada príista."

17. Craske, "Another Mexican Earthquake?," 33, 44.

18. Jo Tuckman, "Abortion Issue Stirs up Mexican Emotions," *Guardian* (London), 6 Sept. 2000.

19. Pantin, "Mexico High Court Opens Door to Abortion Rights Run Date."

Selected Bibliography

Archival Sources

Archivo General de la Nación, México, D.F.
  Gobernación
  Departamento de Trabajo
  Secretaría de Instrucción Pública y Bellas Artes
  Presidentes Alvaro Obregón y Plutarco Elías Calles
Archivo Histórico de la Ciudad de México, México, D.F.
  Instrucción Pública
Archivo Histórico Elena Torres (at the Universidad Iberoamericana, México, D.F.)
Archivo Histórico de la Secretaría de Educación Pública, México, D.F.
  Antiguo Magisterio
  Departamento de Enseñanza Primaria y Normal
  Departamento de Enseñanza Técnica, Industria y Comercial
  Departamento Escolar
  Dirección General de Educación Pública en el Distrito Federal
Archivo Histórico de la Secretaría de Salud Pública, México, D.F.
  Salubridad Pública, Higiene Escolar
Archivo Histórico del Arzobispado de México, México, D.F.
Archivo Histórico del Secretariado Social Mexicano, México, D.F.
Archivo Histórico Plutarco E. Calles y Fernando Torreblanca
The Bancroft Library (at the University of California, Berkeley)
Biblioteca Privada del Seminario Conciliar Mexicano, México, D.F.
The British Library, London, England
Centro de Estudios Históricos Condumex, México, D.F.
  Cristeros
Centro de Estudios Sobre la Universidad (at the Universidad Nacional Autónoma de
  México, México, D.F.)
  Liga Nacional Defensora de la Libertad Religiosa
  Miguel Palomar y Vizcarra
Hemeroteca Nacional, México, D.F.
Instituto de Investigaciones Dr. José María Luis Mora
Instituto Nacional de Antropología e Historia, México, D.F.
  Conflicto Religioso

Periodicals

Acción Femenina, 1937
Acción y Fe (AyF), 1922–1926

Boletín de la Secretaría de Educación Pública (BSEP), 1922–1926
Boletín Municipal (BM), 1918–1926
Bulletin of the Pan American Union (BPAU), 1917–1926
Christus, 1937
La Dama Católica: La Revista del Hogar Mexicano (LDC), 1921–1926
El Excélsior, 1922, 1926
Gaceta Oficial del Arzobispado de México, 1913, 1921–1926
The Guardian (London), Sept. 2000
El Heraldo de México, 1922
El Maestro, 1922
El Mensajero del Sagrado Corazón de Jesús de México (MSCJM), 1920–1926
New York Times, July 1996
Pulgarcito: Periódico Infantil, 1926
La Raza, 1922
Revista Eclesiástica, 1919–1923
El Tepeyac, 1926
El Universal, 1922, 1926

Works Consulted

Adame Goddard, Jorge. *El pensamiento político y social de los católicos mexicanos, 1867–1914*. México, D.F.: Instituto Mexicano de Doctrina Social Cristiana, 1981.

Adler Lomnitz, Larisa, and Marisol Pérez Lizaur. *Una familia de la élite mexicana, 1820–1980. Parentesco, clase y cultura*. Trans. Pastora Rodríguez Aviñoá. México, D.F.: Alianza Editorial, 1993.

Aguilar Camín, Héctor, and Lorenzo Meyer. *In the Shadow of the Mexican Revolution: Contemporary Mexican History, 1910–1989*. Trans. Luis Alberto Fierro. Austin: University of Texas Press, 1993.

Aguirre, Carlos. "La promoción de un fraccionamiento: Santo Tomás." In *Ciudad de México: Ensayo de construcción de una historia*, ed. Alejandra Moreno Toscano. México, D.F.: Secretaría de Educación Pública, Instituto Nacional de Antropología e Historia, Departamento de Investigaciones Históricas, 1978.

Anderson, Benedict. *Imagined Communities: Reflections on the Origins and Spread of Nationalism*. Rev. ed. London and New York: Verso, 1991.

Anderson, Rodney D. *Outcasts in Their Own Land: Mexican Industrial Workers, 1906–1911*. DeKalb: Northern Illinois University Press, 1976.

Araiza, José Luis. *Historia del movimiento obrero mexicano*. México, D.F.: n.p., 1964.

Arce Gurza, Francisco. "En busca de una educación revolucionaria: 1924–1934." In *Ensayos sobre historia de la educación en México*, ed. Josefina Zoraida Vázquez, Dorothy Tanck de Estrada, Ann Staples, and Francisco Arce Gurza. 2d ed. México, D.F.: Colegio de México, 1985.

Arnaut, Alberto. *Historia de una profesión: los maestros de educación primaria en México 1887–1994*. México, D.F.: Centro de Investigación y Docencia Económicas, 1996.

Arrom, Silvia Marina. *The Women of Mexico City, 1790–1857*. Stanford: Stanford University Press, 1985.

Bailey, David C. *¡Viva Cristo Rey! The Cristero Rebellion and the Church-State Conflict in Mexico*. Austin: University of Texas Press, 1974.

————. "Revisionism and the Recent Historiography of the Mexican Revolution." *Hispanic American Historical Review* 58 (Feb. 1978): 62–79.

Baldwin, Deborah. "Diplomacia cultural: escuelas misionales protestantes en México." *Historia Mexicana* 36 (Oct.–Dec. 1986): 287–322.

————. *Protestants and the Mexican Revolution: Missionaries, Ministers, and Social Change.* Urbana and Chicago: University of Illinois Press, 1990.

Ballinas, Victor, and Roberto Garduño. "El nuevo Presidente se adueñó del escenario del Auditorio Nacional." *La Jornada* (México, D.F.), 2 Dec. 2000, http:/www.jornada.unam.mx/2000/dic00/001202/009n1pol.html (last accessed 30 Jan. 2003).

Banegas Galván, Francisco. *El porqué del Partido Católico Nacional.* México, D.F.: Editorial Jus, 1960.

Barranco V., Bernardo. "Posiciones políticas en la historia de la acción católica mexicana." In *El pensamiento social de los católicos mexicanos,* ed. Roberto J. Blancarte. México, D.F.: Fondo de Cultura Económica, 1996.

Bastian, Jean-Pierre. "Modelos de mujer protestante: ideología religiosa y educación femenina, 1880–1910." In *Presencia y transparencia: la mujer en la historia de México,* ed. Carmen Ramos Escandón. México, D.F.: Colegio de México, Programa Interdisciplinario de Estudios de la Mujer, 1987.

————. *Los disidentes: sociedades protestantes y revolución en México, 1872–1911.* México, D.F.: Fondo de Cultura Económica, 1989.

Bazant, Jan. "La escuela primaria de la hacienda de San Bartolomé Tepetates: alumnos, maestros, equipo." *Historia Mexicana* 29 (July–Sept. 1979): 163–79.

Bazant, Mílada. *Historia de la educación durante el Porfiriato.* México, D.F.: Colegio de México, 1996.

BBC News. "Pope Condemns Dogmatic Communism and Capitalism." January 25, 1998, http:/news.bbc.co.uk/1/hi/world/50480.stm (last accessed 31 Jan. 2003).

Becker, Marjorie. *Setting the Virgin on Fire: Lázaro Cárdenas, Michoacán Peasants, and the Redemption of the Mexican Revolution.* Berkeley and Los Angeles: University of California Press, 1995.

Beddoe, Deirdre. *Back to Home and Duty: Women Between the Wars, 1918–1939.* London: Pandora, 1989.

Beezley, William H. *Judas at the Jockey Club and Other Episodes of Porfirian Mexico.* Lincoln and London: University of Nebraska Press, 1987.

Beezley, William H., Cheryl E. Martin, and William E. French, eds. *Rituals of Rule, Rituals of Resistance: Public Celebrations and Popular Culture in Mexico.* Wilmington, Del.: Scholarly Resources, 1994.

Benjamin, Thomas, and William McNellie, eds. *Other Mexicos: Essays on Regional Mexican History, 1876–1911.* Albuquerque: University of New Mexico Press, 1984.

Benjamin, Thomas, and Mark Wasserman, eds. *Provinces of the Revolution: Essays on Regional Mexican History, 1910–1929.* Albuquerque: University of New Mexico Press, 1990.

Bethell, Leslie. "A Note on the Church and the Independence of Latin America." In *Cambridge History of Latin America.* Vol. 3, *From Independence to c. 1870,* ed. Leslie Bethell. Cambridge: Cambridge University Press, 1985.

————, ed. *Mexico since Independence.* Cambridge: Cambridge University Press, 1991.

Birn, Anne-Emanuelle. "Local Health and Foreign Wealth: The Rockefeller Foundation's Public Health Programs in Mexico, 1924–1951." Sc.D. diss., Johns Hopkins University, 1993.

Blancarte, Roberto J. *Historia de la iglesia católica en México*. México, D.F.and Zinacan-tepec, Edo. de México: Fondo de Cultura Económica and Colegio Mexiquense, 1992.

——. "El catolicismo social en el desarrollo del conflicto entre la iglesia y el estado en el siglo XX: neoliberalismo y neointransigencia católica." In *Catolicismo social en México*. Vol. 1, *Teoría, fuentes e historiografía*, coord. Manuel Ceballos Ramírez and Alejandro Garza Rangel. Monterrey: Academia de Investigación Humanística, 2000.

——, comp. *El pensamiento social de los católicos mexicanos*. México, D.F.: Fondo de Cultura Económica, 1996.

Bliss, Katherine Elaine. "Feminist and Catholic Social Action in the Mexico City Sifili-comio." Paper presented at the Latin American Studies Association International Congress, Guadalajara, México, 16–18 April 1997.

——. "The Science of Redemption: Syphilis, Sexual Promiscuity, and Reformism in Revolutionary Mexico." *Hispanic American Historical Review* 79 (Aug.–Nov. 1999): 1–40.

——. "Guided by an Imperious Moral Need: Prostitutes, Mothers, and Nationalists in Revolutionary Mexico City." In *Reconstructing Criminality in Latin America*, ed. Carlos Aguirre and Robert Buffington. Wilmington, Del.: Scholarly Resources, 2000.

——. *Compromised Positions: Prostitution, Public Health, and Gender Politics in Revolutionary Mexico City*. University Park, Pa.: Pennsylvania State University Press, 2001.

Blum, Ann S. "Public Welfare and Child Circulation, Mexico City, 1877 to 1925." *Journal of Family History* 23, no. 3 (1998): 240–71.

——. "Conspicuous Benevolence: Liberalism, Public Welfare, and Private Charity in Porfirian Mexico City, 1877–1910." *The Americas* 58, no. 1 (2001): 7–38.

Booth, George C. *Mexico's School-Made Society*. Stanford: Stanford University Press, 1941.

Boylan, Kristina A. "Mexican Catholic Women's Activism, 1929–1940." D. Phil. diss., University of Oxford, 2000.

Brading, D. A., ed. *Caudillo and Peasant in the Mexican Revolution*. Cambridge: Cambridge University Press, 1980.

Bravo Ugarte, José. *La educación en México (. . . '1965)*. México, D.F.: Editorial Jus, 1966.

Britton, John A. "Teacher Unionization and the Corporate State in Mexico, 1931–1945." *Hispanic American Historical Review* 59 (Nov. 1979): 674–90.

Britton, John A., ed. *Molding the Hearts and Minds: Education, Communications, and Social Change in Latin America*. Wilmington, Del.: Scholarly Resources, 1994.

Buck, Sarah A. "El Control de la natalidad y el día de la madre: política feminista y reaccionaria en México, 1922–1923." *Signos históricos* 5 (Jan.–June 2001): 9–53.

Buffington, Robert M. *Criminal and Citizen in Modern Mexico*. Lincoln and London: University of Nebraska Press, 2000.

Butler, Matthew. "The 'Liberal' *Cristero*: Ladislao Molina and the *Cristero* Rebellion in Michoacán, 1927–29." *Journal of Latin American Studies* 31, no. 3 (1999): 645–71.

Cadena, Longinos. *El lector católico mexicano*. México, D.F.: Herrero Hermanos Sucesores, 1921.

Calderón Ita, Concepción, and Luz María Deloya Domínguez. *Maestros de primeras letras: cien años de su formación (Estudio histórico-pedagógico)*. México, D.F.: Costa-Amic Editores, 1987.

Camarena Ocampo, Mario, and Lourdes Villafuerte García, coords. *Los andamios del historiador: construcción y tratamiento de fuentes*. México, D.F.: Archivo General de la Nación and Instituto Nacional de Antropología e Historia, 2001.

Camp, Roderic Ai. "The Cross in the Polling Booth: Religion, Politics, and the Laity in Mexico." *Latin American Research Review* 29, no. 3 (1994): 69–100.

Cano, Arturo. "El ABC de la intolerancia." *La Jornada* (México, D.F.), 11 July 1999, http:/www.geocities.com/guds'unam/recursos/intole.html (last accessed 31 Jan. 2003).

Cano, Gabriela, and Verena Radkau. *Ganando espacios, historias de vida: Guadalupe Zúñiga, Alura Flores y Josefina Vicens, 1920–1940*. México: Universidad Autónoma Metropolitana, 1989.

Carr, Barry. "Organized Labour and the Mexican Revolution 1915–1928." Occasional Papers 2, Latin American Centre, St. Antony's College, Oxford, 1972.

———. "The Casa del Obrero Mundial, Constitutionalism, and the Pact of February 1915." In *El trabajo y los trabajadores en la historia de México*, ed. Elsa Cecilia Frost, Michael C. Meyer, and Josefina Zoraida Vázquez. México, D.F.: Colegio de México; Tucson: University of Arizona Press, 1979.

———. *El movimiento obrero y la política en México 1910–1929*. 2d ed. México, D.F.: Era, 1981.

———. *Marxism and Communism in Twentieth-Century Mexico*. Lincoln: University of Nebraska Press, 1992.

Carreño, Manuel Antonio. *Compendio del manual de urbanidad y buenas maneras*. México, D.F.: Herrero Hermanos Sucesores, 1906.

Casasola, Gustavo. *Historia gráfica de la revolución mexicana, 1900–1960*. México, D.F.: Editorial Trillas, 1970.

Castillo y Piña, José. *Cuestiones sociales*. México, D.F.: Impresores, S.A., 1934.

Ceballos Ramírez, Manuel. "La encíclica 'Rerum Novarum' y los trabajadores católicos en la ciudad de México (1891–1913)." *Historia Mexicana* 33 (July–Sept. 1983): 3–38.

———. "El sindicalismo católico en México, 1919–1930." *Historia Mexicana* 35 (April–June 1986): 621–73.

———. *El catolicismo social: un tercero en discordia: Rerum Novarum, la "cuestión social" y la movilización de los católicos mexicanos (1891–1911)*. México, D.F.: Colegio de México, 1991.

———. "La vida de los vencidos: los orígenes del catolicismo social mexicano." In *Cincuenta años de historia en México: en el cincuentenario del Centro de Estudios Históricos*. Vol. 2, coord. Alicia Hernández Chávez and Manuel Miño Grijalva. México, D.F.: Colegio de México, 1991.

———. "La democracia cristiana en el México liberal: un proyecto alternativo (1867–1929)." In *El nacionalismo en México. VIII coloquio de antropología e historia regionales*. Coloquio de Antropología e História Regionales 1986: Zamora, Michoacán de Ocampo, México. Colegio de Michoacán, 1992.

Ceballos Ramírez, Manuel, and Alejandro Garza Rangel, coords. *Catolicismo social en México*. Vol. 1., *Teoría, fuentes e historiografía*. Monterrey: Academia de Investigación Humanística, 2000.

Centro de Estudios Históricos del Movimiento Obrero Mexicano. *La mujer y el movimiento obrero mexicano en el siglo XIX. Antología de la prensa obrera*. : Centro de Estudios Históricos del Movimiento Obrero Mexicano, 1975.

Chesler, Ellen. *Woman of Valor: Margaret Sanger and the Birth Control Movement in America.* New York and London: Simon and Schuster, 1992.

Chronicle News Services. "Mexico Congress Strikes Blow against Spousal Rape." National Clearinghouse on Marital and Date Rape, 4 Dec. 1997, http:/members.aol .com/ncmdr/lower.html (last accessed 31 Jan. 2003).

Clark, Marjorie Ruth. *Organized Labor in Mexico.* Chapel Hill: University of North Carolina Press, 1934.

Cleland, Robert Glass, ed. *The Mexican Year Book: The Standard Authority on Mexico 1920–1921.* Los Angeles: Mexican Year Book Publishing Co., 1922.

———. *The Mexican Year Book 1922–1924.* Los Angeles: Mexican Year Book Publishing Co., 1924.

Cockcroft, James D. "El maestro de primaria en la revolución mexicana." *Historia Mexicana* 16 (April–June 1967): 565–87.

———. *Mexico's Hope: An Encounter with Politics and History.* New York: Monthly Review Press, 1998.

Coloquio de Antropología e História Regionales 1986: Zamora, Michoacán de Ocampo, México. *El nacionalismo en México. VIII coloquio de antropología e historia regionales.* Zamora: Colegio de Michoacán, 1992.

"¡Comencemos hoy! — Convoca Vicente Fox: Texto íntegro del mensaje de Vicente Fox Quesada en su toma de posesión como Presidente de la República." *Diario de Yucatán,* 2 Dec. 2000, http:/www.yucatan.com.mx/especiales/tomadeposesion/ 02120003.asp (last accessed 31 Jan. 2003).

Correa, Eduardo J. *El Partido Católico Nacional y sus directores: explicación de su fracaso y deslinde de responsabilidades.* México, D.F.: Fondo de Cultura Económica, 1991.

Corrigan, Philip, and Derek Sayer. *The Great Arch: English State Formation as Cultural Revolution.* Oxford: Basil Blackwell, 1985.

Cortina, Regina. "Poder y cultura sindical: la mujer en el sindicato de trabajadores de la educación en el Distrito Federal." In *Trabajo, poder y sexualidad,* ed. Orlandina de Oliveira. México, D.F.: Colegio de México, 1991.

Craig, Ann L. *The First Agraristas: An Oral History of a Mexican Agrarian Reform Movement.* Berkeley and Los Angeles: University of California Press, 1983.

Craske, Nikki. "Another Mexican Earthquake? An Assessment of the 2 July 2000 Elections." *Government and Opposition* 36 (Winter 2001): 27–47.

Cuevas, Mariano. *Historia de la iglesia en México.* Vol. 5, *1800–1910.* 5th ed. México, D.F.: Editorial Patria, 1947.

Curley, Robert. "Los laicos, la democracia cristiana y la revolución mexicana (1911– 1926)." *Signos Históricos* 5 (July–Dec. 2001): 149–70.

———. "Slouching towards Bethlehem: Catholics and the Political Sphere in Revolutionary Mexico." Ph.D. diss., University of Chicago, 2001.

Davies, Keith A. "Tendencias demográficas urbanas durante el siglo XIX en México." *Historia Mexicana* 21 (Jan.–March 1972): 481–524.

Davis, Diane E. *Urban Leviathan: Mexico City in the Twentieth Century.* Philadelphia: Temple University Press, 1994.

Dawson, Alexander S. "From Models for the Nation to Model Citizens: Indigenismo and the 'Revindication' of the Mexican Indian, 1920–1940." *Journal of Latin American Studies* 30, no. 2 (1998): 279–308.

De Amicis, Edmundo. *Corazón, diario de un niño*. Trans. H. Giner de los Ríos. Rev. ed. México, D.F.: C. Bouret, 1911.

De Gortari, Hira, and Regina Hernández Franyuti. *Memoria y encuentros: la ciudad de México y el Distrito Federal (1824–1928)*, vol. 1. México, D.F.: Departamento del Distrito Federal, Instituto de Investigaciones Dr. José María Luis Mora, 1988.

De la Cerda Silva, Roberto. *El movimiento obrero en México*. México, D.F.: Universidad Nacional Autónoma de México, Instituto de Investigaciones Sociales, 1961.

De la Luz Parcero, María. *Condiciones de la mujer en México durante el siglo XIX.* México, D.F.: Instituto Nacional de Antropología e Historia, 1992.

De los Reyes, Aurelio. "Part 2: History, The Silent Cinema." In *Mexican Cinema*, ed. Paulo Antonio Paranaguá. Trans. Ana M. López. London: British Film Institute; México, D.F.: IMCINE, 1995.

"Del catecismo panista." *La Jornada* (México, D.F.), 7 Oct. 1999, http:/www.jornada .unam.mx/1999/oct99/991008/ls-catecismo.html (last accessed 31 Jan. 2003).

Del Valle, Sonia. "Catorce años a los culpables de violación conyugal." Dec. 1997, http:/ nodo50.org/mujeresred/mexico-violencia.htm (last accessed 31 Jan. 2003).

Dewey, John. *Impressions of Soviet Russia and the Revolutionary World: Mexico — China — Turkey.* New York: New Republic, 1929.

———. *Experience and Education*. New York: Macmillan, 1938.

Díaz, María Elena. "The Satiric Penny Press for Workers in Mexico, 1900–1910: A Case Study in the Politicization of Popular Culture." *Journal of Latin American Studies* 22 (Nov. 1990): 497–526.

Díaz Zermeño, Héctor. "La escuela nacional primaria en la ciudad de México, 1876–1910." *Historia Mexicana* 29 (July–Sept. 1979): 59–90.

Diccionario Porrúa de historia, biografía y geografía de México. México, D.F.: Editorial Porrúa, 1964.

Dirección General de Estadística. *Estadísticas sociales del Porfiriato 1877–1910.* México, D.F.: Talleres Gráficos de la Nación, 1956.

Dore, Elizabeth, and Maxine Molyneux, eds. *Hidden Histories of Gender and the State in Latin America.* Durham and London: Duke University Press, 2000.

Douglas, Emily Taft. *Margaret Sanger: Pioneer of the Future.* New York: Holt, Rinehart and Winston, 1970.

Dworkin, Martin S. *Dewey on Education: Selections with an Introduction and Notes by Martin S. Dworkin.* New York: Teachers College, Columbia University, 1959.

Ezpeleta, Justa, and Elsie Rockwell. "Escuelas y clases subalternas." *Cuadernos Políticos* 37 (1983): 70–80.

Fallaw, Ben. "Dry Law, Wet Politics: Drinking and Prohibition in Post-Revolutionary Yucatán, 1915–1935." *Latin American Research Review* 37, no. 2 (2002): 37–64.

Fell, Claude. *José Vasconcelos, los años del águila (1920–1925): educación, cultura e iberoamericanismo en el México posrevolucionario.* México, D.F.: Universidad Nacional Autónoma de México, Instituto de Investigaciones Históricas, 1989.

Fernández-Aceves, María Teresa. "The Political Mobilization of Women in Revolutionary Guadalajara, 1910–1940." Ph.D. diss., University of Illinois at Chicago, 2000.

Fisher, Lillian Estelle. "The Influence of the Present Mexican Revolution upon the Status of Mexican Women." *Hispanic American Historical Review* 22 (Feb. 1942): 211–28.

Foweraker, Joe, and Ann L. Craig, eds. *Popular Movements and Political Change in Mexico.* Boulder: Lynne Rienner, 1990.

Fowler-Salamini, Heather. "The Boom in Regional Studies of the Mexican Revolution: Where Is It Leading?" *Latin American Research Review* 28, no. 2 (1993): 175–90.

Fowler-Salamini, Heather, and Mary Kay Vaughan, eds. *Women of the Mexican Countryside, 1850–1990: Creating Spaces, Shaping Transitions.* Tucson and London: University of Arizona Press, 1994.

"Fox empezó la jornada en la Basílica." *Diario de Yucatán,* 2 Dec. 2000, http:/www .yucatan.com.mx/especiales/tomadeposesion/02120008.asp (last accessed 31 Jan. 2003).

Franco, Jean. *Plotting Women: Gender and Representation in Mexico.* London: Verso, 1989.

French, John D., and Daniel James, eds. *The Gendered Worlds of Latin American Women Workers: From Household and Factory to the Union Hall and Ballot Box.* Durham and London: Duke University Press, 1997.

Gallegos, Elena. "La bancada príista, *como agua para chocolate." La Jornada* (México, D.F.), 2 Dec. 2000, http:/www.jornada.unam.mx/2000/dic00/001202/006n1pol .html (last accessed 31 Jan. 2003).

Galván de Terrazas, Luz Elena. *La educación superior de la mujer en México, 1876– 1940.* México, D.F.: Centro de Investigaciones y Estudios Superiores en Antropología Social, 1985.

———. *Los maestros y la educación pública en México: un estudio histórico.* México, D.F.: Centro de Investigaciones y Estudios Superiores en Antropología Social, 1985.

———. *Soledad compartida: una historia de maestros 1908–1910.* México, D.F.: Centro de Investigaciones y Estudios Superiores en Antropología Social, 1991.

Gamboa, Ignacio. *Santa.* México, D.F.: Editorial Grijalbo, 1992.

George, Henry. *The Condition of Labour: An Open Letter to Pope Leo XIII.* London: Henry George Foundation of Great Britain, 1934.

Gilly, Adolfo. *La revolución interrumpida. México, 1910–1920, una guerra campesina por la tierra y el poder.* México, D.F.: Ediciones "El Caballito," 1971.

González y González, Luis. *San José de Gracia: Mexican Village in Transition.* Trans. John Upton. Austin: University of Texas Press, 1974.

González y González, Luis, Emma Cosío Villegas, and Guadalupe Monroy. *La república restaurada, la vida social.* Vol. 3 of *Historia moderna de México,* ed. Daniel Cosío Villegas. México, D.F. and Buenos Aires: Editorial Hermes, 1956.

González Navarro, Moisés. *El Porfiriato, la vida social.* Vol. 4 of *Historia moderna de México,* ed. Daniel Cosío Villegas. México, D.F.: Editorial Hermes, 1957.

———. *Sociedad y cultura en el Porfiriato.* México, D.F.: Consejo Nacional para la Cultura y las Artes, Dirección General de Publicaciones, 1994.

Gruening, Ernest. *Mexico and Its Heritage.* New York and London: Century Co., 1928.

Guardino, Peter F. *Peasants, Politics, and the Formation of Mexico's National State: Guerrero, 1800–1857.* Stanford: Stanford University Press, 1996.

Guerra, François-Xavier. "Teoría y método en el análisis de la revolución mexicana." *Revista Mexicana de Sociología* 51 (1989): 3–24.

Guerrero, Julio. *La génesis del crimen en México.* México, D.F. and Paris: Librería de la Vda. de C. Bouret, 1901.

Gutiérrez Casillas, José. *Jesuitas en México durante el siglo XX.* México, D.F.: Editorial Porrúa, 1981.

———. *Historia de la iglesia en México.* México, D.F.: Editorial Porrúa, 1984.

Guy, Donna J. "The Pan American Child Congresses, 1916 to 1924: Pan Americanism,

Child Reform, and the Welfare State in Latin America." *Journal of Family History* 23 (July 1998): 272–92.

Hamilton, Nora. *The Limits of State Autonomy: Post-Revolutionary Mexico.* Princeton: Princeton University Press, 1982.

Hanson, Randall D. "The Day of Ideals: Catholic Social Action in the Age of the Mexican Revolution." Ph.D. diss., Indiana University, Bloomington, 1994.

———. "Mujeres Militantes: Las Damas Católicas and the Mobilization of Women in Revolutionary Mexico, 1912–1929." Paper presented at the Conference on Latin American History, New York, January 1997.

Hart, John Mason. *Anarchism and the Mexican Working Class, 1860–1931.* Austin: University of Texas Press, 1978.

———. *Revolutionary Mexico: The Coming and Process of the Mexican Revolution.* Berkeley and Los Angeles: University of California Press, 1987.

Hernández Chávez, Alicia, and Manuel Miño Grijalva, coords. *Cincuenta años de historia en México: en el cincuentenario del Centro de Estudios Históricos.* Vol. 2. México, D.F.: Colegio de México, 1991.

Hernández López, Julio. "La foxifiesta, un enorme *Siempre en Domingo.*" *La Jornada* (México, D.F.), 2 Dec. 2000, http:/www.jornada.unam.mx/2000/dic00/001202/007n1pol.html (last accessed 31 Jan. 2003).

Herrera, Hayden. *Frida: A Biography of Frida Kahlo.* New York: Harper and Row, 1983.

Hobsbawm, Eric J. *Nations and Nationalism since 1780: Programme, Myth, Reality.* 2d ed. Cambridge: Cambridge University Press, 1992.

Huitrón, Jacinto. *Orígenes e historia del movimiento obrero en México.* México, D.F.: Editores Mexicanos Unidos, 1974.

Illades, Carlos. "Organización y formas de resistencia artesanales: los sastres de le ciudad de México, 1864–1873." In *Cincuenta años de historia en México: en el cincuentenario del Centro de Estudios Históricos.* Vol. 2., coord. Alicia Hernández Chávez and Manuel Miño Grijalva. México, D.F.: Colegio de México, 1991.

"John Paul II Comments on Chiapas, Cuba." *Miami Herald,* 23 Jan. 1999, available through Global Exchange, http:/www.globalexchange.org/campaigns/mexico/news/012399.html (last accessed 31 Jan. 2003).

Joseph, Gilbert M. *Revolution from Without: Yucatán, Mexico, and the United States, 1880–1924.* Cambridge: Cambridge University Press, 1982.

Joseph, Gilbert M., and Daniel Nugent, eds. *Everyday Forms of State Formation: Revolution and the Negotiation of Rule in Modern Mexico.* Durham: Duke University Press, 1994.

Kaplan, Temma. "Female Consciousness and Collective Action: The Case of Barcelona, 1910–1918." *Signs* 7, no. 3 (1982): 545–66.

———. *Red City, Blue Period: Social Movements in Picasso's Barcelona.* Berkeley and London: University of California Press, 1992.

Knight, Alan. "The Working Class and the Mexican Revolution, c. 1900–1920." *Journal of Latin American Studies* 16 (May 1984): 51–79.

———. "The Mexican Revolution: Bourgeois? Nationalist? Or Just a 'Great Rebellion'?" *Bulletin of Latin American Research* 4, no. 2 (1985): 1–37.

———. *The Mexican Revolution.* 2 vols. Lincoln and London: University of Nebraska Press, 1990.

———. "Revolutionary Project, Recalcitrant People: Mexico, 1910–1940." In *The Revo-*

lutionary Process in Mexico: Essays on Political and Social Change, 1880–1940, ed. Jaime E. Rodríguez O. Los Angeles and Irvine: UCLA Latin American Center Publications and Mexico/Chicano Program of the University of California, 1990.

——. "Social Revolution: A Latin American Perspective." *Bulletin of Latin American Research* 9, no. 2 (1990): 175–202.

——. "Cardenismo: Juggernaut or Jalopy?" *Journal of Latin American Studies* 26 (Feb. 1994): 73–107.

——. "Popular Culture and the Revolutionary State in Mexico, 1910–1940." *Hispanic American Historical Review* 73 (Aug. 1994): 393–444.

Knowlton, Robert J. *Church Property and the Mexican Reform, 1856–1910.* DeKalb: Northern Illinois University Press, 1976.

"Las diez mentiras sobre el PAN," *La Revista Peninsular* (Mérida), 9 Jan. 1998, http://www.larevista.com.mx/ed429/nota4.htm (last accessed 31 Jan. 2003).

Lavrin, Asuncion. *Women, Feminism, and Social Change in Argentina, Chile, and Uruguay, 1890–1940.* Lincoln: University of Nebraska Press, 1995.

Lear, John Robert. "Workers, *Vecinos,* and Citizens: The Revolution in Mexico City, 1909–1917." Ph.D. diss., University of California, Berkeley, 1993.

——. "Mexico City: Space and Class in the Porfirian Capital, 1884–1910." *Journal of Urban History,* 22 (May 1996): 454–92.

Lerner, Victoria. *La educación socialista.* Vol. 17 of *Historia de la revolución mexicana, 1934–1940.* México, D.F.: Colegio de México, 1979.

Loyo, Engracia. "Lecturas para el pueblo, 1921–1940." *Historia Mexicana* 33 (Jan.–March 1984): 298–345.

——. "La difusión del Marxismo y la educación socialista en México, 1930–1940." In *Cincuenta años de historia en México: en el cincuentenario del Centro de Estudios Históricos.* Vol. 2, coord. Alicia Hernández Chávez and Manuel Miño Grijalva. México, D.F.: Colegio de México, 1991.

——. "Los medios extraescolares de educación en el campo (1920–1940)." In *La ciudad y el campo en la historia de México.* Vol. 2, *Memoria de la VII Reunión de Historiadores Mexicanos y Norteamericanos.* Conference of Mexican and United States Historians 1985: Oaxaca de Juárez, México. México, D.F.: Universidad Nacional Autónoma de México, Instituto de Investigaciones Históricas, 1992.

Luque Alcaide, Elisa. *La educación en Nueva España en el siglo XVIII.* Sevilla: Escuela de Estudios Hispano-Americanos, 1970.

Lynch, John. "The Catholic Church in Latin America, 1830–1930." In *Cambridge History of Latin America.* Vol. 4, *c. 1870–1930,* ed. Leslie Bethell. Cambridge: Cambridge University Press, 1986.

Macías, Anna. *Against All Odds: The Feminist Movement in Mexico to 1940.* Westport, Conn.: Greenwood Press, 1982.

——. "Rural and Urban Women in Revolutionary Yucatán." In *La ciudad y el campo en la historia de México.* Vol. 2, *Memoria de la VII Reunión de Historiadores Mexicanos y Norteamericanos.* Conference of Mexican and United States Historians 1985: Oaxaca de Juárez, México. México, D.F.: Universidad Nacional Autónoma de México, 1992.

Martínez Assad, Carlos R. *El laboratorio de la revolución: el Tabasco garridista.* México: Siglo Veintiuno Editores, 1979.

Martínez Jiménez, Alejandro. "La educación elemental en el Porfiriato." *Historia Mexicana* 22 (April–June 1973): 514–52.

Mayer, Leticia. "El proceso de recuperación simbólica de cuatro héroes de la revolución mexicana de 1910 a través de la prensa nacional." *Historia Mexicana* 45, no. 2 (1995): 353–81.

McManners, John. *Church and State in France, 1870–1914*. London: S.P.C.K. for the Church Historical Society, 1972.

Méndez Medina, Alfredo. *La cuestión social en México: orientaciones. Estudio presentado en la dieta de la Confederación Nacional de Círculos Católicos de Obreros celebrada en Zamora en los días 19–22 de enero de 1913*. México, D.F.: El Cruzado, 1913.

———. *Manual de formación sindical*. México, D.F.: Impreso del Asilo "Patricio Sanz," 1923.

Mendieta Alatorre, Angeles. *La mujer en la revolución mexicana*. México, D.F.: Talleres Gráficos de la Nación, 1961.

Meneses Morales, Ernesto. *Tendencias educativas oficiales en México 1911–1934. La problemática de la educación mexicana durante la revolución y los primeros lustros de la época posrevolucionaria*. México, D.F.: Centro de Estudios Educativos, 1983.

———. *Tendencias educativas oficiales en México, 1821–1911. La problemática de la educación mexicana en el siglo XIX y principios del siglo XX*. México, D.F.: Centro de Estudios Educativos, 1983.

Meyer, Jean. "Los obreros en la revolución mexicana: los Batallones Rojos." *Historia Mexicana* 21 (July–Sept. 1971): 1–37.

———. *La Cristiada*. 3 vols. México, D.F.: Siglo Veintiuno Editores, 1973.

———. Prologue to *El Partido Católico Nacional y sus directores: explicación de su fracaso y deslinde de responsabilidades,* by Eduardo J. Correa. México, D.F.: Fondo de Cultura Económica, 1991.

Miller, Barbara. "The Role of Mexican Women in the Mexican Cristero Rebellion: Las Señoras y Las Religiosas." *The Americas* 40 (Jan. 1984): 303–23.

Miller, Beth. "Concha Michel, revolucionaria mexicana." *La Palabra y el Hombre* 50 (1984): 21–25.

Miller, Simon. "Revisionism in Recent Mexican Historiography." *Bulletin of Latin American Research* 4, no. 1 (1985): 77–88.

Mistral, Gabriela. *Lecturas para mujeres*. Introduction by Palma Guillén de Nicolau. México, D.F.: Editorial Porrúa.

Monroy Huitrón, Guadalupe. *Política educativa de la revolución (1910–1940)*. México, D.F.: Secretaría de Educación Pública, 1975.

Monsiváis, Carlos. "Por mi madre, bohemios." *La Jornada* (México, D.F.), 14 April 1997, http:/www.jornada.unam.mx/1997/abr97/970414/monsi.html (last accessed 31 July 2002).

Mora, Carl J. *Mexican Cinema: Reflections on a Society*. Rev. ed. Berkeley and London: University of California Press, 1989.

Morales, María Dolores. "La expansión de la ciudad de México en el siglo XIX: el caso de los fraccionamientos." In *Ciudad de México: ensayo de construcción de una historia*. Seminario de Historia Urbana, coord. Alejandra Moreno Toscano. México, D.F.: Secretaría de Educación Pública, Instituto Nacional de Antropología e Historia, Departamento de Investigaciones Históricas, 1978.

Moreno Toscano, Alejandra. "Un ensayo de historia urbana." In *Ciudad de México: Ensayo de construcción de una historia. Seminario de Historia Urbana,* coord. Alejandra Moreno Toscano. México, D.F.: Secretaría de Educación Pública, Instituto

Nacional de Antropología e Historia, Departamento de Investigaciones Históricas, 1978.

Morgan, Anthony. "Industry and Society in the Mexico City Area, 1875–1920." Ph.D. diss., Cambridgeshire College of Arts and Technology, 1984.

Morris, Stephen D. "Reforming the Nation: Mexican Nationalism in Context." *Journal of Latin American Studies* 31, no. 7 (1999): 363–97.

Navarrete, Heriberto. *"Por Dios y por la patria": memorias de mi participación en la defensa de la libertad de conciencia y culto, durante la persecución religiosa en México de 1926 a 1929.* México, D.F.: Editorial Jus, 1961.

———. *Los cristeros eran así. . . .* México, D.F.: Editorial Jus, 1968.

Newland, Carlos. "The Estado Docente and Its Expansion: Spanish American Elementary Education, 1900–1950." *Journal of Latin American Studies* 26 (May 1994): 449–67.

O'Dogherty, Laura. "Restaurarlo todo en Cristo: Unión de Damas Católicas Mejicanas, 1920–1926." *Estudios de Historia Moderna y Contemporánea de México* 14 (1991): 129–58.

Olivera de Bonfil, Alicia. *Aspectos del conflicto religioso de 1926 a 1929.* México, D.F.: Instituto Nacional de Antropología e Historia, 1966.

O'Malley, Ilene. *The Myth of Revolution: Hero Cults and the Institutionalization of the Mexican State, 1920–1940.* Westport, Conn.: Greenwood Press, 1986.

Ortiz Ledezma, Angélica. "Protestan en minifalda contra la represión." Milenio.com, 10 March 2002, http:/www.milenio.com/guadalajara/nota.asp?idc=17070 (last accessed 31 Jan. 2003).

Palacios, Guillermo. "Postrevolutionary Intellectuals, Rural Readings, and the Shaping of the 'Peasant Problem' in Mexico: *El Maestro Rural, 1932–34.*" *Journal of Latin American Studies* 30, no. 2 (1998): 309–39.

Palavicini, Félix F. *Problemas de la educación.* Valencia: F. Sempere y Compañía, 1910.

Pani, Alberto J. *La higiene en México.* México, D.F.: Imprenta de J. Ballesca, 1916.

———. *The Constitutionalist Government Confronted with the Sanitary and Educational Problems of Mexico: Address delivered by Alberto J. Pani.* México: Imprenta "Victoria," 1917.

———. *Una encuesta sobre educación popular, por Alberto J. Pani, con la colaboración de numerosos especialistas nacionales y extranjeros y con conclusiones finales, formuladas por Ezequiel A. Chávez, Paulino Machorro Narváez y Alfonso Pruneda.* México, D.F.: Departamento de Aprovisionamientos Generales, 1918.

Pantin, Laurence. "Mexico High Court Opens Door to Abortion Rights Run Date." *Women's Enews,* 7 Feb. 2002, http:/www.womensenews.org/article.cfm/dyn/aid/808/context/archive (last accessed 31 Jan. 2003).

Paranaguá, Paulo Antonio. *Mexican Cinema.* Trans. Ana M. López. London: British Film Institute; México, D.F.: IMCINE, 1995.

Piccato, Pablo Atilio. "The Discourse about Alcoholism and Criminality in Mexico City, 1890–1917." Master's thesis, University of Texas, Austin, 1993.

———. " 'El Chalequero' or the Mexican Jack the Ripper: The Meanings of Sexual Violence in Turn-of-the-Century Mexico City." *Hispanic American Historical Review* 8 (Aug.–Nov. 2001): 623–51.

———. *City of Suspects: Crime in Mexico City, 1900–1931.* Durham and London: Duke University Press, 2001.

Pilcher, Jeffrey M. *¡Qué Vivan los Tamales! Food and the Making of Mexican Identity.* Albuquerque: University of New Mexico Press, 1998.

———. *Cantinflas and the Chaos of Mexican Identity.* Wilmington, Del.: Scholarly Resources, 2001.

Pineda, Alexander, and Paulo Antonio Paranaguá. "Part I: Chronicle, Mexico and Its Cinema." In *Mexican Cinema,* ed. Paulo Antonio Paranaguá. Trans. Ana M. López. London: British Film Institute; México, D.F.: IMCINE, 1995.

Portes Gil, Emilio. *La lucha entre el poder civil y el clero.* México: n.p., 1934.

———. *La labor sediciosa del clero mexicano.* Madrid: Editorial Cenit, 1935.

Powell, T. G. "Priests and Peasants in Central Mexico: Social Conflicts during 'La Reforma.' " *Hispanic American Historical Review* 57 (May 1977): 296–313.

Puig Casauranc, José Manuel. *Discurso pronunciado por el Secretario de Educación Pública con motivo del día del maestro.* México, D.F.: Secretaría de Educación Pública, Dirección Editorial, 1925.

———. *Para las madres.* México, D.F.: Talleres Gráficos de la Nación "Editorial," Junta Federal de la Protección de la Infancia, 1925.

———. *Public Education in Mexico.* New York: n.p., 1926.

———. *La obra integral de la revolución mexicana; discurso pronunciado por el Dr. J. M. Puig Casauranc, el 20 de noviembre de 1929.* México, D.F.: Talleres Gráficos de la Nación, 1929.

Purnell, Jennie. *Popular Movements and State Formation in Revolutionary Mexico: The Agraristas and Cristeros of Michoacán.* Durham and London: Duke University Press, 1999.

Quirk, Robert. *The Mexican Revolution and the Catholic Church, 1910–1929.* Bloomington: Indiana University Press, 1973.

Raby, David L. *Educación y revolución social en México (1921–1940).* Trans. Roberto Gómez Ciriza. México, D.F.: Secretaría de Educación Pública, 1974.

———. "Ideología y construcción del estado: la fundación de la educación rural en México, 1921–1935." *Revista Mexicana de Sociología* 51 (1989): 305–20.

Ramos Escandón, Carmen. "Señoritas porfirianas: mujer e ideología en el México progresista, 1880–1910." In *Presencia y transparencia: la mujer en la historia de México,* ed. Carmen Ramos Escandón. México, D.F.: Colegio de México, 1987.

———, ed. *Presencia y transparencia: la mujer en la historia de México.* México, D.F.: Colegio de México, 1987.

Reich, Peter Lester. *Mexico's Hidden Revolution: The Catholic Church in Law and Politics since 1929.* Notre Dame and London: University of Notre Dame Press, 1995.

Reyes, J. A. *Catecismo de historia patria.* México, D.F.: Herrerno Hermanos Editores, 1904.

Rivera-Garza, Cristina. "The Masters of the Streets: Bodies, Power, and Modernity in Mexico, 1867–1930." Ph.D. diss., University of Houston, 1995.

———. " 'She Neither Respected nor Obeyed Anyone': Inmates and Psychiatrists Debate Gender and Class at the General Insame Asylum La Castañeda, Mexico, 1910–1930." *Hispanic American Historical Review* 81 (Aug.–Nov. 2001), 653–88.

Rivero del Val, Luis. *Entre las patas de los caballos. (Diario de un Cristero).* 2d ed. México, D.F.: Editorial Jus, 1954.

Rocha, Martha Eva. *El Porfiriato y la revolución.* Vol 4. of *El álbum de la mujer: antología ilustrada de las mexicanas.* México, D.F.: Instituto Nacional de Antropología e Historia, 1991.

———. "Veteranas de guerra en el archivo militar." In *Los andamios del historiador: Construcción y tratamiento de fuentes,* coord. Mario Camarena Ocampo and Lourdes Villafuerte García. México, D.F.: Archivo General de la Nación and Instituto Nacional de Antropología e Historia, 2001.

Rockwell, Elsie. "Schools of the Revolution: Enacting and Contesting State Forms in Tlaxcala, 1910–1930." In *Everyday Forms of State Formation: Revolution and the Negotiation of Rule in Modern Mexico,* ed. Gilbert M. Joseph and Daniel Nugent. Durham and London: Duke University Press, 1994.

Rodríguez, Delfina C. *La perla de la casa.* México, D.F.: Bouret Editor, 1911.

Rodríguez Kuri, Ariel. *La experiencia olvidada: el ayuntamiento de México política y gobierno, 1876–1912.* México, D.F.: Universidad Autónoma Metropolitana, Azcapotzalco, and Colegio de México, 1996.

Rodríguez O., Jaime E., ed. *The Revolutionary Process in Mexico: Essays on Political and Social Change, 1880–1940.* Los Angeles and Irvine: UCLA Latin American Center Publications and Mexico/Chicano Program at the University of California, 1990.

Rodríguez y Cos, José Miguel. "Iniciativas presentadas por el C. José Miguel Rodríguez y Cos ante la Comisión Nacional del Centenario de la Independencia, á fin de consolidar, por medio de la educación pública, el espíritu de la nacionalidad mexicana, é incorporar á esta á la raza indígena, y celebrar dignamente el 80° aniversario del nacimiento del C. General Porfirio Díaz, Presidente de la República Mexicana." México, D.F.: Tipografía Económica, 1907.

Rubenstein, Anne. *Bad Language, Naked Ladies, and Other Threats to the Nation.* Durham and London: Duke University Press, 1998.

———. "Raised Voices in the Cine Montecarlo: Sex Education, Mass Media, and Oppositional Politics in Mexico." *Journal of Family History* 23 (July 1998): 312–24.

Rubio Goldsmith, Raquel. "Seasons, Seeds, and Souls: Mexican Women Gardening in the American Mesilla, 1900–1940." In *Women of the Mexican Countryside, 1850–1990: Creating Spaces, Shaping Transitions,* ed. Heather Fowler-Salamini and Mary Kay Vaughan. Tucson: University of Arizona Press, 1994.

Ruís Facius, Antonio. *La juventud católica y la revolución mexicana, 1910–1925.* México: Editorial Jus, 1963.

———. *Méjico cristero: historia de la ACJM, 1925 a 1931.* 2d ed. México, D.F.: Editorial Patria, 1966.

Ruiz, Luis E. *Cartilla de higiene (profilaxis de las enfermedades transmisibles) escrita para la enseñanza primaria.* México, D.F.: Librería de la Vda. de C. Bouret, 1912.

———. *Tratado elemental de pedagogía.* México, D.F.: Universidad Nacional Autónoma de México, 1986.

Ruiz, Ramón Eduardo. *Labor and the Ambivalent Revolutionaries: Mexico 1911–1923.* Baltimore: Johns Hopkins University Press, 1976.

———. *The Great Rebellion: Mexico 1905–1924.* New York: W. W. Norton, 1980.

Ruiz Gaytán, Beatriz. "Un grupo trabajador importante no incluido en la historia laboral mexicana (trabajadoras domésticas)." In *El trabajo y los trabajadores en la historia de México,* ed. Elsa Cecilia Frost, Michael C. Meyer, and Josefina Zoraida Vázquez. México, D.F.: Colegio de México; Tucson: University of Arizona Press, 1979.

Salas, Elizabeth. *Soldaderas in the Mexican Revolution: Myth and History.* Austin: University of Texas Press, 1990.

Salazar, Flora. "Los sirvientes domésticos." In *Ciudad de México: Ensayo de construcción de una historia,* ed. Alejandra Moreno Toscano. México, D.F.: Secretaría de

Educación Pública, Instituto Nacional de Antropología e Historia, Departamento de Investigaciones Históricas, 1978.

Salazar, Rosendo. *Las pugnas de la gleba*. México, D.F.: Editorial Avante, 1923.

———. *Antecedentes del movimiento obrero revolucionario en México (los años convulsos)*. México, D.F.: n.p., 1973.

Sanger, Margaret. *Margaret Sanger: An Autobiography*. New York: W. W. Norton, 1938.

Schell, Patience A. "Challenging Revolutionary Morality: Las Damas Católicas in post-1917 Mexico City." In *Current Research on Latin American Education. Occasional Paper*, ed. Ruth Aedo-Richmond. Hull: The British Association for International and Comparative Education in association with the UK Seminar on Latin American Education, 1998.

———. "Training Loving Hands: Women's Vocational Education in 1920s Mexico City." *Anuario de espacios urbanos. Historia, cultura, diseño 1998*, (1998): 249–71.

———. "An Honorable Avocation for Ladies: The Work of the Mexico City Unión de Damas Católicas Mexicanas, 1912–1926." *Journal of Women's History* 10 (Spring 1999): 78–103.

———. "Las damas del catolicismo social, 1912–1926." In *Catolicismo social en México*. Vol. 2, *Las instituciones del catolicismo social*, coord. Manuel Ceballos Ramírez and Alejandro Garza Rangel. Monterrey, México: La Academia de Investigación Humanística, forthcoming.

Schmitt, Karl M. "The Díaz Conciliation Policy on State and Local Levels 1876–1911." *Hispanic American Historical Review* 40 (Nov. 1960): 513–32.

SEP. [Secretaría de Educación Pública.] *Escuelas del Departamento de Enseñanza Técnica, Industria y Comercial*. México, D.F.: Secretaría de Educación Pública, 1924.

———. *La educación pública en México a través de los mensajes presidenciales desde la consumación de la independencia hasta nuestros días*. México, D.F.: Talleres Gráficos de la Nación, Secretaría de Educación Pública, 1926.

———. *Noticia estadística sobre la educación pública de México para el año de 1925*. México, D.F.: n.p., 1927.

———. *El esfuerzo educativo en México. La obra del gobierno federal en el ramo de educación pública durante la administración del presidente Plutarco Elías Calles (1924–1928). Memoria analítico-crítica de la organización actual de la Secretaria de Educación Pública, sus éxitos, sus fracasos, los derroteros que la experiencia señala. Presentada al h. Congreso de la unión por el dr. J. M. Puig Casauranc, secretario del ramo en obediencia al artículo 93 constitucional*. 2 vols. México, D.F.: n.p., 1928.

———. *Noticia estadística sobre la educación pública de México para el año de 1926*. México, D.F.; n.p., 1928.

Seminario de Movimiento Obrero y Revolución Mexicana. *Comunidad, cultura y vida social: ensayos sobre la formación de la clase obrera*. México, D.F.: Instituto Nacional de Antropología y Historia, 1991.

Sierra, Justo. *La educación nacional*. Vol. 8 of *Obras completas*. México, D.F.: Universidad Nacional Autónoma de México, 1977.

———. *Ensayos y textos elementales de historia*. Vol. 9 of *Obras completas*. México, D.F.: Universidad Nacional Autónoma de México, 1977.

Simpson, Lesley Byrd. *Many Mexicos*. Berkeley and Los Angeles: University of California Press, 1963.

Soto, Shirlene Ann. *The Mexican Woman: A Study of Her Participation in the Revolution, 1910–1940*. Palo Alto: R&E Research Associates, 1979.

———. *Emergence of the Modern Mexican Woman: Her Participation in Revolution and Struggle for Equality, 1910–1940*. Denver: Arden Press, 1990.

Staples, Anne. "Panorama educativo al comienzo de la vida independiente." In *Ensayos sobre historia de la educación en México,* ed. Josefina Zoraida Vázquez, Dorothy Tanck de Estrada, Ann Staples, and Francisco Arce Gurza. 2d ed. México, D.F.: Colegio de México, 1985.

Stepan, Nancy Leys. *"The Hour of Eugenics": Race, Gender, and Nation in Latin America*. Ithaca and London: Cornell University Press, 1991.

Stern, Steve J. *The Secret History of Gender: Women, Men, and Power in Late Colonial Mexico*. Chapel Hill: University of North Carolina Press, 1995.

Tanck de Estrada, Dorothy. "Tensión en la torre de marfil. La educación en la segunda mitad del siglo XVIII mexicano." In *Ensayos sobre historia de la educación en México,* ed. Josefina Zoraida Vázquez, Dorothy Tanck de Estrada, Ann Staples, and Francisco. 2d ed. Gurza. México, D.F.: Colegio de México, 1981.

Tannenbaum, Frank. "The Miracle School." *Century Magazine* 106 (Aug. 1923): 499–506.

———. *Mexico: The Struggle for Peace and Bread*. New York: Alfred A. Knopf, 1950.

Tenorio-Trillo, Mauricio. "1910 Mexico City: Space and Nation in the City of the Centenario." *Journal of Latin American Studies* 28 (Feb. 1996): 75–104.

Terry, T. Philip. *Terry's Mexico: Handbook for Travellers with Two Maps and Twenty-Five Plans*. 2nd ed. rev. London: Gay and Hancock, 1911.

Thompson, Angela T. "Children and Schooling in Guanajuato, Mexico, 1790–1840." In *Molding the Hearts and Minds: Education, Communications, and Social Change in Latin America,* ed. John A. Britton. Wilmington, Del.: Scholarly Resources, 1994.

Thompson, E. P. *The Making of the English Working Class*. New York: Vintage, 1963.

Torres Septién, Valentina. "Algunos aspectos de las escuelas particulares en el siglo XX." *Historia Mexicana* 33 (Jan.–March 1984): 346–77.

———. "La Unión Nacional de Padres de Familia." In *La ciudad y el campo en la historia de México*. Vol. 2, *Memoria de la VII Reunión de Historiadores Mexicanos y Norteamericanos*. Conference of Mexican and United States Historians 1985: Oaxaca de Juárez, México. México, D.F.: Universidad Nacional Autónoma de México, Instituto de Investigaciones Históricas, 1992.

———. *La educación privada en México (1903–1976)*. México, D.F.: Colegio de México and Universidad Iberoamericana, 1997.

Tuck, Jim. *The Holy War in Los Altos: A Regional Analysis of Mexico's Cristero Rebellion*. Tucson: University of Arizona Press, 1982.

Tuñón Pablos, Julia. *Women in Mexico: A Past Unveiled*. Trans. Alan Hynds. Austin: University of Texas Press, 1999.

Tutino, John. *From Insurrection to Revolution in Mexico: Social Bases of Agrarian Violence 1750–1940*. Princeton: Princeton University Press, 1986.

Valverde Téllez, Emeterio. *Bio-bibliografía eclesiástica mexicana (1821–1943)*. 3 vols. México, D.F.:n.p., 1949.

Vanderwood, Paul. *The Power of God against the Guns of Government: Religious Upheaval in Mexico at the Turn of the Century*. Stanford: Stanford University Press, 1998.

Vasconcelos, José. *A Mexican Ulysses: An Autobiography*. Trans. and abridged by W. Rex Crawford. Westport, Conn.: Greenwood Press, 1963.

———. *El desastre: el proconsulado*. Vol. 2 of *Memorias*. México, D.F.: Fondo de Cultura Económica, 1982.

———. *Ulises Crillo: la tormenta.* Vol. 1 of *Memorias.* México, D.F.: Fondo de Cultura Económica, 1982.

Vaughan, Mary Kay. *History Textbooks in Mexico in the 1920's.* Buffalo: Council on International Studies, State University of New York at Buffalo. 1974.

———. "Women, Class, and Education in Mexico, 1880–1928." *Latin American Perspectives* 12–13 (1977): 135–52.

———. *The State, Education, and Social Class in Mexico, 1880–1928.* DeKalb: Northern Illinois University Press, 1982.

———. "Primary Education and Literacy in Mexico in the Nineteenth Century, Research Trends, 1968–1988." *Latin American Research Review* 25, no. 1 (1990): 31–66.

———. "Women Schoolteachers in the Mexican Revolution: The Story of Reyna's Braids." *Journal of Women's History* 2, no. 1 (1990): 143–68.

———. "Rural Women's Literacy and Education during the Mexican Revolution: Subverting a Patriarchal Event?" In *Women of the Mexican Countryside: 1850–1990: Creating Spaces, Shaping Transitions,* ed. Heather Fowler-Salamini and Mary Kay Vaughan. Tucson and London: University of Arizona Press, 1994.

———. *Cultural Politics in Revolution: Teachers, Peasants, and Schools in Mexico, 1930–1940.* Tucson: University of Arizona Press, 1997.

———. "Modernizing Patriarchy: State Policies, Rural Households, and Women in Mexico, 1930–1940." In *Hidden Histories of Gender and the State in Latin America,* ed. Elizabeth Dore and Maxine Molyneux. Durham and London: Duke University Press, 2000.

Vázquez, Josefina Zoraida, Dorothy Tanck de Estrada, Ann Staples, and Francisco Gurza. *Ensayos sobre historia de la educación en México.* 2d ed. México, D.F.: Colegio de México, 1981.

Vázquez de Knauth, Josefina. *Nacionalismo y educación en México.* México, D.F.: Colegio de México, 1970.

Vidrio C., Manuel. "Sistemas de transporte y expansión urbana: los tranvías." In *Ciudad de México: ensayo de construcción de una historia,* ed. Alejandra Moreno Toscano. México, D.F.: Secretaría de Educación Pública, Instituto Nacional de Antropología e Historia, Departamento de Investigaciones Históricas, 1978.

Weber, Eugene. *Peasants into Frenchmen: The Modernization of Rural France, 1870–1914.* Stanford: Stanford University Press, 1976.

Wilkie, James W., and Edna Monzón de Wilkie. *México visto en el siglo XX.* México, D.F.: Instituto Mexicano de Investigaciones Económicas, 1969.

Wolf, Eric R. *Las luchas campesinas del siglo XX.* México, D.F.: Siglo XXI Editores, 1972.

Womack, John, Jr. *Zapata and the Mexican Revolution.* New York: Vintage Books, 1968.

———. "The Mexican Revolution, 1910–1920." In *Mexico since Independence,* ed. Leslie Bethell. Cambridge: Cambridge University Press, 1991.

Wood, Andrew Grant. *Revolution in the Streets: Women, Workers, and Urban Protest in Veracruz, 1870–1927.* Wilmington, Del.: Scholarly Resources, 2001.

Figure Credits

Archivo Histórico de la Secretaría de Educación Pública
5.1 The SEP's image of primary education. "Gráfica no. 34. Escuelas Oficiales en el Distrito Federal, dependientes de la Secretaría de Educación Pública, maestros que las atienden, e inscripción. Año de 1927." *Noticia estadistica sobre la educación pública de México correspondiente al año de 1927* (México, D.F.: Talleres Gráficos de la Nación, 1929).

Archivo Histórico de la Unión Femenina Católica Mexicana at the Universidad Ibero-americana
4.1 The UDCM general council. AHUFCM 15/78 "Fotografias."

Bancroft Library, University of California, Berkeley
8.1 Los deberes de una niña. *Pulgarcito: periódico infantil* 2 (May 1926): 41. Reference number F1225.P8.
8.2 El bautizo de mi hermanito. *Pulgarcito: periódico infantil* 2 (Feb. 1926): 15. Reference number F1225.P8.

Hemeroteca Nacional
2.1 Hernán Cortés as a Catholic hero. *La Dama Católica,* July 1921, cover.
5.3 La moda en París. *La Dama Católica,* Dec. 1922, 15.

Instituto de Investigaciones Dr. José María Luis Mora
All the figures below are from SEP, *Escuelas del Departamento de Enseñanza Técnica, Industria y Comercial* (México, D.F.: Secretaría de Educación Pública, 1924).
3.1 Physics laboratory.
3.2 Auto shop.
3.3 Physical education for young women.
3.4 Puericulture class.
6.1 Class of domestic economy.
6.2 Batik class.
7.1 Library.
7.2 Physical education for young men.

Index

adult education, Catholic: 11, 58–63, 137–142, 163
adult education, municipal, 43–44
adult education, SEP: 45–47, 56, 115–117, 122, 132–133, 143–146, 158, 162
adult night schools, SEP workers': 46, 56–58, 128–137, 144
adult vocational education: SEP men's, 9, 45, 47–51; SEP women's, 9, 47–48, 51–56, 119–128, 143
anticlericalism, xx, 13–14, 39, 175–176, 178, 182–183
Arreglos, 194
Article 3, 38, 180–181, 186–194

Baranda, Joaquín, 5–6
bra. See Wonderbra
breakfast program, 98–99, 144. See also comedores escolares
budget, reduction of education, 131
buildings: consecrations to Sacred Heart of, 170–171; revolutionary occupations of 16; symbolism of, 94

Calles, Plutarco Elías, 176, 178–180
capitalism, condemnation of, 199
Cardoso, Joaquín, 157
carpa theater. See entertainment
Carranza, Venustiano, 174
Castillo Lara, Dolores Angela, 119–123
Castillo y Piña, José (S.J.), 40, 62–63, 82, 110, 163
catechism centers. See Catholic organizations
Catholic Church: activism and social work of, xx–xix, 12, 14, 138, 196–197; attitudes toward sexuality of, 124; nineteenth century role of, 3; Obregón and hierarchy of, 175–176,

180; restrictions on, 13; social justice and, 199–200
Catholicism, as cultural or political identity, 15
Catholic organizations: Asociación de Damas Católicas, 77–78; Casa Familia, 112; catechism centers, 141–142; Centro de Madres de Familia, 61; Knights of Columbus, 122; Liga Nacional de la Clase Media, 169; Liga Nacional para la Defensa de la Libertad Religiosa, 180; Sociedad Católica de la Nación Mexicana (SCNM), 76–77; Unión de Colegios Católicos Mexicanos, 184–185; Unión Nacional de Padres de Familia, 184. See also Unión de Damas Católicas Mexicanas (UDCM)
Catholic social movements: Acción Católica Mexicana, 194; Catholic social action, xxi, 164–172
Catholic worker initiatives, 10, 61–62, 139. See also unions, Catholic
centralization, federal, 6–7, 17–18, 94, 196
children: behavior of, 88, 100; discipline of, 89; health of, 98; manners of, 99, 103; poverty of, 41, 97; rights of, 34–35
chinampas. See gardens
church-state relations, 3–4, 12–14, 174–177, 179–183
city, ideas of, 162
class, social: in SEP men's vocational schools, 51, 63–64; ruling classes, 169; student diversity of 143–145; UDCM and, 78–81
coeducation, 90
Colonias: De la Bolsa, 101, 105; Roma, 182; Santa Julia, 11; Vallejo, 38, 112–113. See also Guadalupe Hidalgo

comedores escolares, 15. *See also* breakfast program
Constitution (1917), 13, 174, 199
Constitutionalist faction, 12
Cordero, Joaquín (S.J.), 184
corporatism, 10, 166
crime, 88–89
crucifix, 188, 190–191
cuisine, 125–128
culture: consumer, 55–56, 158–159; folkloric, 126(fig.); moralizing value of, 152; nationalism in, 127–128; SEP Cultural Festivals, 155–156

De la Huerta, Adolfo, 17, 33
Del Valle, Sofía, 140–141
Dewey, John, 31
Díaz, Pascual (Bishop of Tabasco), 184
Díaz, Porfirio, 3–5, 30
diseases, 17, 86, 124. *See also* health
domestic service, 60, 61–62

education: congresses, 6; in Porfiriato 8–9
encyclicals: *Divini illius magistri*, 194–195, 198; *Rerum Novarum*, 4–5
entertainment: cinema, 86, 222n. 16; dance halls and cabarets, 124; films, 107, 154–157; open-air festivals, 153–154; orfeones populares, 132–133; SEP-sponsored, 152–156
exhibitions, SEP, 157–158

factories: Britania, 107, 138–139, 142, 171–172; Buen Tono, 154, 167–169; catechism at, 142; Larín, 161, 170; Tabacalera, 142; views on women working in, 60, 72
family: cost of living for, 211n. 4; ideal images of, 52, 129
Federal District, educational administration of, 17–19, 21–22
federal education. *See Secretaría de Educación Pública*
festivals, open-air. *See* entertainment
field trips, 159–164
Filippi, Ernesto, 174–175
Fox, Vicente, 200

gardens, 23–27, 32, 102
gender: Catholic education and, 58–59, 109–110; changing roles of, 110–112, 121–122, 124, 129–131; church-state conflict and, 181–182; municipal adult education and, 43–44; municipal primary education and, 92; night schools and, 134; physical education and, 28, 53(fig.), 163(fig.); in SEP primary schools, 32, 96, 100; sexual double standard, 60; students and, 144–145; teachers and, 86; vocational education and, 45–48, 51–52, 56
geography, 29–30
González, Abraham, 93
graduation rates, 8, 145
grants. *See* tuition
Guadalupe, Virgin of, 200
Guadalupe Hidalgo, 160

health, 27, 87, 98, 119. *See also* diseases
history, 28–29, 186–187
Huerta, Victoriano, 12, 16; education under, 15
hygiene. *See* health

Icaza, Leopoldo, 38, 78, 82–83, 138
illiteracy, 141
inspectors, 68–69, 83–84, 189
internships, 116, 212n. 22

Joaquín Pérez, José, 176
John Paul II, 199
Juárez, Benito, 29, 200

Lascurain de Silva, Elena, 79(fig.), 187, 190
laws: Calles Law, 180; chair law, 171; 1888 federal law of primary instruction, 6–7; 1908 education law, 8; Reform Laws, 3–4. *See also* Article 3
lay education, nineteenth century, 5–6, 224–225n. 22
León, Juan, 121–122, 218n. 14
liberalism, 199
libraries, 148–152
literacy. *See* illiteracy
López Banealaria, Dolores, 93

Madero, Francisco, 11, 12; education under, 15
Mancera, Juan, 122
Massieu, Luis, 121, 122
mathematics, 22–23
Medellín, Roberto, 45, 97
médicos escolares, 73
Méndez Medina, Alfredo (S.J.): political and social views of, 63, 69–70, 146, 166–167, 178; resignation of, 177–179; training of, 81–82; UDCM involvement with, 83, 170; work at SSM of, 165
miniskirts, 197
Ministry of Justice and Public Instruction, 7
Miranda, Miguel Darío, 178
Mistral, Gabriela, 118, 209n. 19
Morales, Francisco, 94, 96, 100, 133
morality: Catholic campaigns for, 196–197; in Catholic primary schools, 111–112; code, xix, 34, 191; in municipal primary education, 22–28, 86–87; in SEP adult education, 117; in SEP primary schools, 34, 191
Mora y del Río, José (archbishop of Mexico): correspondence from Calles to, 179–180, 224n. 12; Nazaret School and, 109; response to Huerta of, 12; UDCM and, 77, 170
Morones, Luis, 167
municipality, and educational jurisdiction, 22. *See also* adult education, municipal; primary schools, municipal
music, SEP promotion of, 152–153

nationalism, 22, 29, 35–36, 91–92

Obregón, Alvaro, 16, 47, 157, 174–176
one-teach-one campaign, 17
orfeones populares. See adult education, SEP
Oropeza, Arturo, 101, 104

Pacheco, Rosario, 118, 121, 123
Palavicini, Félix, 17
parents, economic burdens on, 99–100, 160–161

Parque México, 164
Partido Acción Nacional (PAN), 198, 200–201
Partido Católico Nacional (PCN), 11–12
Partido Revolucionario Institucional (PRI), 199
pedagogy, 6, 22, 31–34, 62
physical education, 28, 162, 53(fig.), 163(fig.)
piecework. *See* skills training
pilgrimages, 163–164
policía escolar, 86
Preparatoria Nacional, 120
primary education: organization of 21–23; reforms of, 7–8, 31–33
primary schools, Catholic: Article 3 and, 35, 94, 179–180, 183–194; changing role of, 198–199; Colegio-Casa Nazaret, 108–110, 163; Colegio Italiano, 108, 112, 141–142; curriculum of, 10, 36–40, 106–109; during revolution, 16; Escuela del Sagrado Corazón, 106, 138; Escuela Granja, 39–40, 112–113; evangelization through, 111–112; numbers, 35, 94, 108, 205n. 21; Porfirian, 10; revolutionary disruption to, 15–16. *See also* morality; nationalism
primary schools, municipal: conditions of, 85–89; curriculum of, 23–30, 91–92; during Porfiriato, 5; federal education and, 7, 93–94; field trips in, 159–160; schedules for, 24(fig.), 26(fig.). *See also* morality; nationalism; physical education
primary schools, SEP, 30, 32–33, 94–97, 100–106, 118
prostitutes, 87–88, 226n. 37
public behavior, 88, 124, 164
puericulture. *See* reproduction
Puig Casauranc, José Manuel, 19, 33–34, 171
pulque, 27, 87, 206n. 7

rape, 60, 133–134, 219n. 47
religion, teaching of, 6
religious orders, 10–11, 36, 58, 60–61, 106, 108, 112, 139, 142

reproduction: birth control, 118, 122, 123; eugenics, 124; maternity, 69–70, 71–73, 124, 182; puericulture, 54
revolution: Catholic cultural, 14; education during, 15; normal school students in, 66; occupation of Mexico City during, 16–17; population mobility and, 88; social impact of, xxii, 14, 87–88, 100, 110–111
Rodríguez, René, 119, 122
Román, Alberto, 72
Ruiz y Flores, Leopoldo (archbishop of Morelia), 12

Sanger, Margaret, 118, 124
Santa. See prostitutes
Santamarina, Rafael, 72
school assemblies, municipal, 90–91
school attendance, 95–97, 128–129, 133, 134–135, 137–138
schools, night (1910), 8–9
schools, normal, 5–6, 74–75, 76–77
schools, private, 10, 205n. 22
Schools Section, UDCM, 36, 82–83, 107, 141
schoolwork, 191–194, 192(fig.), 193(fig.)
Second Empire, 3
Secretaría de Educación Pública (SEP): Article 3 and, 35, 185, 187, 189–190; organization of, 18–19, 47, 117, 132, 161; parental rights in relation to, 34; Servicio Médico Escolar, 71–72
Secretaría de Instrucción Pública y Bellas Artes (SIPBA), 7, 15, 17, 21
Secretariado Social Mexicano (SSM): 39, 82, 165, 169, 177–179
secularization, 196
sexuality, 88, 119, 124. See also reproduction
Sierra, Justo, 6, 65–66
skills training: action pedagogy and, 31–32; agriculture, 23–27; dressmaking, 128; housewifery, 54–55; piecework, 56; in Porfirian education, 8; SEP cooking courses, 125–128; trabajos manuales, 52; UDCM academy, 59; UDCM primary schools, 38
social question, 9–10, 78

Spanish, teaching of, 22–23
standardized tests, 34
state: Catholic views on education of, 183–184, 198–199; intervention in poor homes of, 61; municipal challenges to, 94. See also anticlericalism; church-state relations
students, 116, 131–139, 142–145, 147, 185–186, 225n. 27
Sylve, Raúl, 187, 190

teachers: behavior of, 74, 100; Catholic primary, 40, 75–77; complaints about Catholic schools from, 188–189; difficulties for, 68, 73, 117; during the Porfiriato and revolution, 15, 65–66, 123; feminism of, 121, 123–124; gender and, 6, 48–49, 210n. 3; marriage and, 69–73; municipal government and, 66–68; perceptions of, 70; salaries and training of, 6, 73, 144; statistics on, 70–71, 211n. 15; unionization of, 67–68
Tejeda, Adalberto, 182–183
Ten Commandments, 91–92
textbooks, 44
Torres, Elena, 98
truants, 86
tuition, 10, 47, 106–109, 130

Union de Damas Católicas Mexicanas (UDCM), 39–40, 59–60, 78–82, 107, 138–140, 146, 157, 170–172, 181–182
unions, Catholic, 60–61, 140, 165–169, 172, 177
unions, secular, 50–51, 124, 175–177

Vasconcelos, José, 17–19, 30–31, 45, 51, 93, 157
Vatican II, 198
Vera, Luz, 123
violence, 89, 134, 219n. 48

women: activism of, 56, 78, 182–183; chica moderna, 129–130; commercial education for, 48; domestic role of, 48, 51–52, 55; fashion for, 111(fig.); gardens of, 102; independence of, 129–130; new behavior of, 110–111; public space and, 133–134; SEP ideals of, 56; sexual ignorance among, 119, 124; skills training of, 60, 130–131; teachers, 84; Vasconcelos and, 128; violence against, 134; voting rights for, 197

Wonderbra, 197–198

zonas de tolerancia, 87

About the Author

Patience A. Schell has been Lecturer of Latin American Cultural Studies at the University of Manchester since 2001. After receiving her doctorate in history from St. Antony's College, Oxford University, in 1998, she worked for two years at Birkbeck College, London, as a researcher. Articles from her research on education and Catholicism have appeared in various journals, including *Journal of Women's History* and *Anuario de Espacios Urbanos*. Her current research addresses the social history and cultural politics of consumers and consumption in modern Mexico. She is also coediting a volume on women's history in postrevolutionary Mexico.